# Computers at Risk

*Safe
Computing
In the
Information
Age*

4w

D1508502

19⁹⁵

System Security Study Committee
Computer Science and
   Telecommunications Board
Commission on Physical Sciences,
   Mathematics, and Applications
National Research Council

NATIONAL ACADEMY PRESS
1991

National Academy Press • 2101 Constitution Avenue, N.W. • Washington, D.C. 20418

NOTICE: The project that is the subject of this report was approved by the Governing Board of the National Research Council, whose members are drawn from the councils of the National Academy of Sciences, the National Academy of Engineering, and the Institute of Medicine. The members of the committee responsible for the report were chosen for their special competences and with regard for appropriate balance.

This report has been reviewed by a group other than the authors according to procedures approved by a Report Review Committee consisting of members of the National Academy of Sciences, the National Academy of Engineering, and the Institute of Medicine.

The National Academy of Sciences is a private, nonprofit, self-perpetuating society of distinguished scholars engaged in scientific and engineering research, dedicated to the furtherance of science and technology and to their use for the general welfare. Upon the authority of the charter granted to it by the Congress in 1863, the Academy has a mandate that requires it to advise the federal government on scientific and technical matters. Dr. Frank Press is president of the National Academy of Sciences.

The National Academy of Engineering was established in 1964, under the charter of the National Academy of Sciences, as a parallel organization of outstanding engineers. It is autonomous in its administration and in the selection of its members, sharing with the National Academy of Sciences the responsibility for advising the federal government. The National Academy of Engineering also sponsors engineering programs aimed at meeting national needs, encourages education and research, and recognizes the superior achievements of engineers. Dr. Robert M. White is president of the National Academy of Engineering.

The Institute of Medicine was established in 1970 by the National Academy of Sciences to secure the services of eminent members of appropriate professions in the examination of policy matters pertaining to the health of the public. The Institute acts under the responsibility given to the National Academy of Sciences by its congressional charter to be an adviser to the federal government and, upon its own initiative, to identify issues of medical care, research, and education. Dr. Samuel O. Thier is president of the Institute of Medicine.

The National Research Council was organized by the National Academy of Sciences in 1916 to associate the broad community of science and technology with the Academy's purposes of furthering knowledge and advising the federal government. Functioning in accordance with general policies determined by the Academy, the Council has become the principal operating agency of both the National Academy of Sciences and the National Academy of Engineering in providing services to the government, the public, and the scientific and engineering communities. The Council is administered jointly by both Academies and the Institute of Medicine. Dr. Frank Press and Dr. Robert M. White are chairman and vice chairman, respectively, of the National Research Council.

Support for this project was provided by the Defense Advanced Research Projects Agency under Contract No. N00014-89-J-1731. However, the content does not necessarily reflect the position or the policy of the Defense Advanced Research Projects Agency or the government, and no official endorsement should be inferred.

Library of Congress Cataloging-in-Publication Data
Computers at risk : safe computing in the information age / System
    Security Study Committee, Computer Science and Telecommunications Board,
    Commission on Physical Sciences, Mathematics, and Applications,
    National Research Council.
        p.   cm.
    Includes bibliographical references.
    ISBN 0-309-04388-3
    1. Computer security.   I. National Research Council (U.S.).
    Computer Science and Telecommunications Board.   System Security Study
    Committee.
    QA76.9.A25C6663    1990
    005.8—dc20                                             90-22329
                                                              CIP

Printed in the United States of America

First Printing, December 1990
Second Printing, March 1991
Third Printing, April 1991

---

*The project that is the subject of this report was initiated under the predecessor group of the Commission on Physical Sciences, Mathematics, and Applications, which was the Commission on Physical Sciences, Mathematics, and Resources, whose members are listed in Appendix G.

*v*

# Preface

The Computer Science and Technology Board, which became the Computer Science and Telecommunications Board in September 1990, formed the System Security Study Committee in response to a fall 1988 request from the Defense Advanced Research Projects Agency (DARPA) to address the security and trustworthiness of U.S. computing and communications systems. The committee was charged with developing a national research, engineering, and policy agenda to help the United States achieve a more trustworthy computing technology base by the end of the century. DARPA asked the committee to take a broad outlook—to consider the interrelationship of security and other qualities (e.g., safety and reliability), commercialization as well as research, and the diverse elements of the research and policy communities. In keeping with DARPA's initial request, the committee focused on security aspects but related them to other elements of trustworthiness.

The System Security Study Committee was composed of sixteen individuals from industry and academia, including computer and communications security researchers and practitioners and software engineers. It met in May, August, and November of 1989 and in February, April, and July of 1990. Its deliberations were complemented by briefings from and interviews with a variety of federal government researchers and officials and security experts and others from industry. A central feature of the committee's work was the forging of a consensus in the face of different technical and professional perspectives. While the committee drew on both the research literature and publications aimed at security practitioners, it sought to combine the research and practitioner perspectives to provide a more unified assessment than might perhaps be typical. Given the goal of producing an unclassified report, the committee focused on the protection of sensitive but unclassified information in computer and communications systems. The orientation toward an unclassified report also limited the extent to which the committee could probe tensions in federal policy between intelligence-gathering and security-providing objectives.

This report of the System Security Study Committee presents its assessment of key computer and communications security issues and its recommendations for enhancing the security and trustworthiness of the U.S. computing and communications infrastructure.

David D. Clark, *Chairman*
System Security Study Committee

# Acknowledgments

The System Security Study Committee appreciates the generous assistance provided by Carl Landwehr of the Naval Research Laboratory and a group of federal liaisons that he coordinated, including Anthony Adamski of the Federal Bureau of Investigation, Dennis Branstad of the National Institute of Standards and Technology, Leon Breault of the Department of Energy, Richard Carr of the National Aeronautics and Space Administration, Richard DeMillo of the National Science Foundation (preceded by John Gannon), C. Terrance Ireland of the National Security Agency, Stuart Katzke of the National Institute of Standards and Technology, Robert Morris of the National Security Agency, Karen Morrissette of the Department of Justice, Mark Scher of the Defense Communications Agency, and Kermith Speierman of the National Security Agency. These individuals made themselves and their associates available to the committee to answer questions, provide briefings, and supply valuable reference materials.

The committee is grateful for special briefings provided by William Vance of IBM, John Michael Williams of Unisys, and Peter Wild of Coopers and Lybrand. Additional insight into specific issues was provided by several individuals, including in particular Mark Anderson of the Australian Electronics Research Laboratory, Carolyn Conn of GE Information Services, Jay Crawford of the Naval Weapons Center at China Lake, California, George Dinolt of Ford Aerospace Corporation, Morrie Gasser and Ray Modeen of Digital Equipment Corporation, James Giffin of the Federal Trade Commission, J. Thomas Haigh of Secure Computing Technology Corporation, James Hearn of the National Security Agency, Frank Houston of the Food and Drug Administration, Christian Jahl of the German Industrie Anlagen Betriebs

Gesellschaft, Ian King of the U.K. Communications-Electronics Security Group, Stewart Kowalski of the University of Stockholm, Milan Kuchta of the Canadian Communications Security Establishment, Timothy Levin of Gemini Computers, Inc., Michael Nash representing the U.K. Department of Trade and Industry, Stephen Purdy and James Bauer of the U.S. Secret Service, John Shore of Entropic Research Laboratory, Inc., Linda Vetter of Oracle Corporation, Larry Wills of IBM, and the group of 30 corporate security officers who participated in a small, informal survey of product preferences.

The committee appreciates the encouragement and support of Stephen Squires and William Scherlis of DARPA, who provided guidance, insights, and motivation. It is particularly grateful for the literally hundreds of suggestions and criticisms provided by the ten anonymous reviewers of an early draft. Those inputs helped the committee to tighten and strengthen its presentation, for which it, of course, remains responsible.

Finally, the committee would like to acknowledge the major contribution that the staff of the Computer Science and Telecommunications Board has made to this report, in particular thanking Marjory Blumenthal, Damian Saccocio, Frank Pittelli, and Catherine Sparks. They supplied not only very capable administrative support, but also substantial intellectual contributions to the development of the report. The committee also received invaluable assistance from its editor, Susan Maurizi, who labored under tight time constraints to help it express its ideas on a complex and jargon-filled subject. It could not have proceeded effectively without this level of support from the National Research Council.

David D. Clark, *Chairman*
System Security Study Committee

# Contents

# Executive Summary

Computer systems are coming of age. As computer systems become more prevalent, sophisticated, embedded in physical processes, and interconnected, society becomes more vulnerable to poor system design, accidents that disable systems, and attacks on computer systems. Without more responsible design and use, system disruptions will increase, with harmful consequences for society. They will also result in lost opportunities from the failure to put computer and communications systems to their best use.

Many factors support this assessment, including the proliferation of computer systems into ever more applications, especially applications involving networking; the changing nature of the technology base; the increase in computer system expertise within the population, which increases the potential for system abuse; the increasingly global environment for business and research; and the global reach and interconnection of computer networks, which multiply system vulnerabilities. Also relevant are new efforts in Europe to promote and even mandate more trustworthy computer systems; European countries are strengthening their involvement in this arena, while the United States seems caught in a policy quagmire. Although recent and highly publicized abuses of computer systems may seem exceptional today, each illustrates potential problems that may be undetected and that are expected to become more common and even more disruptive. The nature and the magnitude of computer system problems are changing dramatically.

The nation is on the threshold of achieving a powerful information infrastructure that promises many benefits. But without adequate safeguards, we risk intrusions into personal privacy (given the growing electronic storage of personal information) and potential disasters that can cause economic and even human losses. For example, new vulnerabilities are emerging as computers become more common as components of medical and transportation equipment or more interconnected as components of domestic and international financial systems. Many disasters may result from intentional attacks on systems, which can be prevented, detected, or recovered from through better security. *The nation needs computer technology that supports substantially increased safety, reliability, and, in particular, security.*

Security refers to protection against unwanted disclosure, modification, or destruction of data in a system and also to the safeguarding of systems themselves. Security, safety, and reliability together are elements of system trustworthiness—which inspires the confidence that a system will do what it is expected to do.

In many ways the problem of making computer and communications systems more secure is a technical problem. Unlike a file cabinet, a computer system can help to protect itself; there exists technology to build a variety of safeguards into computer systems. As a result, software, hardware, and system development presents opportunities for increasing security. Yet known techniques are not being used, and development of better techniques is lagging in the United States. From a technical perspective, making computer system technology more secure and trustworthy involves assessing what is at risk, articulating objectives and requirements for systems, researching and developing technology to satisfy system requirements, and providing for independent evaluation of the key features (to assess functionality) and their strength (to provide assurance). All of these activities interact.

Attaining increased security, in addition to being a technical matter is also a management and social problem: what is built and sold depends on how systems are designed, purchased, and used. In today's market, demand for trustworthy systems is limited and is concentrated in the defense community and industries, such as banking, that have very high levels of need for security. That today's commercial systems provide only limited safeguards reflects limited awareness among developers, managers, and the general population of the threats, vulnerabilities, and possible safeguards. Most consumers have no real-world understanding of these concepts and cannot choose products wisely or make sound decisions about how to use them. Practical security specialists and professional societies have emerged and have begun to affect security practice from inside organizations, but their impact is constrained by lack of both management awareness and public awareness of security risks and options. Even when consumers do try to protect their own systems, they may be connected via networks to others with weaker safeguards—like a polluting factory in a densely populated area, one person's laxness in managing a computer system can affect many. As long as demand remains at best inconsistent, vendors have few incentives to make system products more secure, and there is little evidence of the kind of fundamental new system development necessary to make systems highly trustworthy. The market does not work well enough to raise the security of computer systems at a rate fast enough to match the apparent growth in threats to systems.

The U.S. government has been involved in developing technology for computer and communications security for some time. Its efforts have related largely to preserving national security and, in particular, to meeting one major security requirement, confidentiality (preserving data secrecy). But these programs have paid little attention to the other two major computer security requirements, integrity (guarding against improper data modification or destruction) and availability (enabling timely use of systems and the data they hold). These requirements are important to government system users, and they are particularly and increasingly important to users of commercial systems. Needed is guidance that is more wide-ranging and flexible than that offered by the so-called Orange Book published by the National Security Agency, and it should be guidance that stimulates the production of more robust, trustworthy systems at all levels of protection.

Overall, the government's efforts have been hamstrung by internecine conflict and underfunding of efforts aimed at civilian environments. These problems currently appear to be exacerbated, at precisely the time that decisive and concerted action is needed. A coherent strategy must be established now, given the time, resources, planning, and coordination required to achieve adequate system security and trustworthiness. The reorganization of and perceived withdrawal from relevant computer security-related activities at the National Security Agency and the repeated appropriations of minimal funding for relevant activities at the National Institute of Standards and Technology are strong indications of a weak U.S. posture in this area. A weak posture is especially troubling today, because of the momentum that is building overseas for a new set of criteria and associated system evaluation schemes and standards. Influencing what can be sold or may be required in overseas markets, these developments and the U.S. response will affect the competitiveness of U.S. vendors and the

options available to users of commercial computer systems worldwide. They will also affect the levels of general safety and security
experienced by the public.

This report characterizes the computer security problem and advances recommendations for containing it (Chapter 1). It examines
concepts of and requirements for computer security (Chapter 2), the
technology necessary to achieve system security and trustworthiness,
and associated development issues (Chapter 3), programming methodology (Chapter 4), the design and use of criteria for secure computer system development and evaluation of computer system security relative to a set of criteria (Chapter 5), and problems constraining
the market for trustworthy systems (Chapter 6). *The System Security
Study Committee concluded that several steps must be taken to achieve
greater computer system security and trustworthiness, and that the best
approach to implementing necessary actions is to establish a new organization, referred to in the report as the Information Security Foundation (ISF).*
The concept of the ISF and the roles and limitations of organizations
that currently have significant responsibilities in the computer security arena are discussed together (Chapter 7). Topics and tactics for
research to enable needed technology development are outlined (Chapter
8). Supporting the individual chapters are appendixes that provide
further details on selected technical and conceptual points.

The committee urges that its recommendations be considered together as integral to a coherent national effort to encourage the widespread development and deployment of security features in computer
systems, increase public awareness of the risks that accompany the
benefits of computer systems, and promote responsible use and
management of computer systems. Toward the end of increasing the
levels of security in new and existing computer and communications
systems, the committee developed recommendations in six areas. These
are outlined below and developed further in the full report.

**1. Promulgation of a comprehensive set of Generally Accepted
System Security Principles, referred to as GSSP, which would provide a clear articulation of essential security features, assurances,
and practices.** The committee believes that there is a basic set of
security-related principles for the design, use, and management of
systems that are of such broad applicability and effectiveness that
they ought to be a part of any system with significant operational
requirements. This set will grow with research and experience in
new areas of concern, such as integrity and availability, and can also
grow beyond the specifics of security to deal with other related aspects
of system trust, such as safety. GSSP should enunciate and codify

these principles. Successful GSSP would establish a set of expectations about and requirements for good practice that would be well understood by system development and security professionals, accepted by government, and recognized by managers and the public as protecting organizational and individual interests against security breaches and associated lapses in the protection of privacy. GSSP, which can be built on existing material (e.g., the Orange Book), would provide a basis for resolving differences between U.S. and other national and transnational criteria for trustworthy systems and for shaping inputs to international security and safety standards discussions.

2. **A set of short-term actions for system vendors and users that build on readily available capabilities and would yield immediate benefits,** including (for users) formation of security policy frameworks and emergency response teams, and (for vendors) universal implementation of specific minimal acceptable protections for discretionary and mandatory control of access to computing resources, broader use of modern software development methodology, implementation of security standards and participation in their further development, and procedures to prevent or anticipate the consequences of inadvisable actions by users (e.g., systems should be shipped with security features turned on, so that explicit action is needed to disable them).

3. **Establishment of a system-incident data repository and appropriate education and training programs to promote public awareness.**

4. **Clarification of export control criteria and procedures for secure or trusted systems and review for possible relaxation of controls on the export of implementations of the Data Encryption Standard (DES).**

5. **Funding and directions for a comprehensive program of research.**

6. **Establishment of a new organization to nurture the development, commercialization, and proper use of trust technology, referred to as the Information Security Foundation, or ISF.** The committee concludes that existing organizations active in the security arena have made important contributions but are not able to make the multifaceted and large-scale efforts that are needed to truly advance the market and the field. The proposed ISF would be a private, not-for-profit organization. It would be responsible for implementing much of what the committee has recommended, benefiting from the inherent

synergies: ISF should develop GSSP, develop flexible evaluation techniques to assess compliance with GSSP, conduct research related to GSSP and evaluation, develop and maintain an incident-tracking system, provide education and training services, broker and enhance communications between commercial and national security interests, and participate in international standardization and harmonization efforts for commercial security practice. In doing these things it would have to coordinate its activities with agencies and other organizations significantly involved in computer security. The ISF would need the highest level of governmental support; the strongest expression of such support would be a congressional charter.

Although the System Security Study Committee focused on computer and communications security, its recommendations would also support efforts to enhance other aspects of systems such as reliability and safety. It does not make sense to address these problems separately. Many of the methods and techniques that make systems more secure make them more trustworthy in general. The committee has framed several of its recommendations so as to recognize the more general objective of making systems more trustworthy, and specifically to accommodate safety as well as security. The committee believes it is time to consider all of these issues together, to benefit from economies in developing multipurpose safeguards, and to minimize any trade-offs.

With this report, the committee underscores the need to launch now a process that will unfold over a period of years, and that, by limiting the incidence and impact of disruptions, will help society to make the most of computer and communications systems.

# 1

# Overview and Recommendations

We are at risk. Increasingly, America depends on computers. They control power delivery, communications, aviation, and financial services. They are used to store vital information, from medical records to business plans to criminal records. Although we trust them, they are vulnerable—to the effects of poor design and insufficient quality control, to accident, and perhaps most alarmingly, to deliberate attack. The modern thief can steal more with a computer than with a gun. Tomorrow's terrorist may be able to do more damage with a keyboard than with a bomb.

To date, we have been remarkably lucky. Yes, there has been theft of money and information, although how much has been stolen is impossible to know.[1] Yes, lives have been lost because of computer errors. Yes, computer failures have disrupted communication and financial systems. But, as far as we can tell, there has been no successful systematic attempt to subvert any of our critical computing systems. Unfortunately, there is reason to believe that our luck will soon run out. Thus far we have relied on the absence of malicious people who are both capable and motivated. We can no longer do so. We must instead attempt to build computer systems that are secure and trustworthy.

In this report, the committee considers the degree to which a computer system and the information it holds can be protected and preserved. This requirement, which is referred to here as computer security, is a broad concept; security can be compromised by bad system design, imperfect implementation, weak administration of procedures, or through accidents, which can facilitate attacks. Of course, if we are to trust our systems, they must survive accidents as

7

well as attack. Security supports overall trustworthiness, and vice versa.

## COMPUTER SYSTEM SECURITY CONCERNS

Security is a concern of organizations with assets that are controlled by computer systems. By accessing or altering data, an attacker can steal tangible assets or lead an organization to take actions it would not otherwise take. By merely examining data, an attacker can gain a competitive advantage, without the owner of the data being any the wiser.

Computer security is also a concern of individuals, including many who neither use nor possess computer systems (Box 1.1). If data can be accessed improperly, or if systems lack adequate safeguards, harm may come not only to the owner of the data, but also to those to whom the data refers. The volume and nature of computerized databases mean that most of us run the risk of having our privacy violated in serious ways. This is particularly worrisome, since those in a position to protect our privacy may have little incentive to do so (Turn, 1990).

The threats to U.S. computer systems are international, and sometimes also political. The international nature of military and intelligence threats has always been recognized and addressed by the U.S. government. But a broader international threat to U.S. information resources is emerging with the proliferation of international computer networking—involving systems for researchers, companies, and other organizations and individuals—and a shift from conventional military conflict to economic competition.[2] The concentration of information and economic activity in computer systems makes those systems an attractive target to hostile entities. This prospect raises questions about the intersection of economic and national security interests and the design of appropriate security strategies for the public and private sectors. Finally, politically motivated attacks may also target a new class of system that is neither commercial nor military: computerized voting systems.[3]

Outside of the government, attention to computer and communications security has been episodic and fragmented. It has grown by spurts in response to highly publicized events, such as the politically motivated attacks on computer centers in the 1960s and 1970s and the more recent rash of computer viruses and penetrations of networked computer systems.[4] Commercial organizations have typically concentrated on abuses by individuals authorized to use their systems, which typically have a security level that prevents only the most straightforward of attacks.

BOX 1.1  SAMPLER OF COMPUTER SYSTEM PROBLEMS:
EVIDENCE OF INADEQUATE TRUSTWORTHINESS

Failures of system reliability, safety, or security are increasingly serious—and apparently increasing in number.  Notable are the following:

- A $259 million Volkswagen currency exchange scam involving phony transactions;
- The nearly successful attempt to use thousands of phony Bank of America automatic teller machine cards fabricated with personal identification numbers pirated from an on-line database;
- An almost-successful $15.2 million Pennsylvania Lottery fraud attempt in which the database of unclaimed ticket numbers was used in the fabrication of a ticket about to expire; and
- Thousands of reported virus attacks and hundreds of different viruses identified (e.g., Stoned, Devil's Dance, 1260, Jerusalem, Yankee Doodle, Pakistani Brain, Icelandic-2, Ping Pong, December 24, to cite just a few).

Penetrations and disruptions of communication systems appear to be increasing:

- A software design error freezing much of AT&T's long-distance network;
- The German Chaos Computer Club break-ins to the National Aeronautics and Space Administration's Space Physics Analysis Network;
- The West German Wily Hacker attacks (involving international espionage) on Lawrence Berkeley Laboratory;
- The Internet worm incident in which several thousand computers were penetrated; and
- Several takeovers of TV satellite up-links.

Individual privacy has been compromised.  For example, deficient security measures at major credit agencies have allowed browsing and surreptitious assignment of thousands of individuals' credit histories to others.

Health care has been jeopardized by inadequate system quality as well as by breaches of security:

- An error in the computer software controlling a radiation therapy machine, a Therac 25 linear accelerator, resulted in at least three separate patient deaths when doses were administered that were more than 100 times the typical treatment dose.
- A Michigan hospital reported that its patient information had been scrambled or altered by a virus that came with a vendor's image display system.
- A Cleveland man allegedly mailed over 26,000 virus-infected diskettes with AIDS prevention information to hospitals, businesses, and government agencies worldwide.

NOTE:  None of the cases cited above involved any classified data.  References to all of them can be found in Neumann (1989).

While weak computer security obviously affects direct and indirect users of computer systems, it may have less obvious but still important impacts on vendors of computer systems. The role of security and trust in product development and marketing should grow, and not only because it is in the public interest. In particular, failure to supply appropriate security may put vendors at a serious competitive disadvantage. Even though U.S. firms lead overall in the computer and communications market, several European governments are now promoting product evaluation schemes and standards that integrate other elements of trust, notably safety, with security. These developments may make it difficult for American industry to sell products in the European market.[5]

Although the committee focuses on technical, commercial, and related social concerns, it recognizes that there are a number of related legal issues, notably those associated with the investigation and prosecution of computer crimes, that are outside of its scope. It is important to balance technical and nontechnical approaches to enhancing system security and trust. Accordingly, the committee is concerned that the development of legislation and case law is being outpaced by the growth of technology and changes in our society. In particular, although law can be used to encourage good practice, it is difficult to match law to the circumstances of computer system use. Nevertheless, attacks on computer and communication systems are coming to be seen as punishable and often criminal acts (Hollinger and Lanza-Kaduce, 1988) within countries, and there is a movement toward international coordination of investigation and prosecution. However, there is by no means a consensus about what uses of computers are legitimate and socially acceptable. Free speech questions have been raised in connection with recent criminal investigations into dissemination of certain computer-related information.[6] There are also controversies surrounding the privacy impacts of new and proposed computer systems, including some proposed security safeguards. Disagreement on these fundamental questions exists not only within society at large but also within the community of computer specialists.[7]

## TRENDS—THE GROWING POTENTIAL
## FOR SYSTEM ABUSE

Overall, emerging trends, combined with the spread of relevant expertise and access within the country and throughout the world, point to growth in both the level and the sophistication of threats to major U.S. computer and communications systems. There is reason to believe that we are at a discontinuity: with respect to computer security, the past is not a good predictor of the future. Several trends underlie this assessment:

• Networking and embedded systems are proliferating, radically changing the installed base of computer systems and system applications.[8]

• Computers have become such an integral part of American business that computer-related risks cannot be separated from general business risks.

• The widespread use of databases containing information of a highly personal nature, for example, medical and credit records, leaves the privacy of individuals at risk.

• The increased trust placed in computers used in safety-critical applications (e.g., medical instruments) increases the likelihood that accidents or attacks on computer systems can cost people their lives.

• The ability to use and abuse computer systems is becoming widespread. In many instances (e.g., design of computer viruses, penetration of communications systems, credit card system fraud) attacks are becoming more sophisticated.

• The international political environment is unstable, raising questions about the potential for transnational attacks at a time when international corporate, research, and other computer networks are growing.

## THE NEED TO RESPOND

Use of computer systems in circumstances in which we must trust them is widespread and growing. But the trends identified above suggest that whatever trust was justified in the past will not be justified in the future unless action is taken now. (Box 1.2 illustrates how changing circumstances can profoundly alter the effective trustworthiness of a system designed with a given set of expectations about the world.) Computer system security and trustworthiness must become higher priorities for system developers and vendors, system administrators, general management, system users, educators, government, and the public at large.

This observation that we are at a discontinuity is key to understanding the focus and tone of this report. In a time of slow change, prudent practice may suggest that it is reasonable to wait for explicit evidence of a threat before developing a response. Such thinking is widespread in the commercial community, where it is hard to justify expenditures based on speculation. However, in this period of rapid change, significant damage can occur if one waits to develop a countermeasure until after an attack is manifest. On the one hand, it may

BOX 1.2   PERSONAL COMPUTERS:
SECURITY DETERIORATES WITH CIRCUMSTANCES

Personal computers (PCs), such as the popular IBM PC running the MS/DOS operating system, or those compatible with it, illustrate that what was once secure may no longer be. Security was not a major consideration for developers and users of early PCs. Data was stored on floppy disks that could be locked up if necessary, and information stored in volatile memory disappeared once the machine was turned off. Thus the operating system contained no features to ensure the protection of data stored in the computer. However, the introduction of hard disks, which can store large amounts of potentially sensitive information in the computer, introduced new vulnerabilities. Since the hard disk, unlike the floppy disk, cannot be removed from the computer to protect it, whoever turns on the PC can have access to the data and programs stored on the hard disk. This increased risk can still be countered by locking up the entire machine. However, while the machine is running, all the programs and data are subject to corruption from a malfunctioning program, while a dismounted floppy is physically isolated.

The most damaging change in the operating assumptions underlying the PC was the advent of network attachment. External connection via networks has created the potential for broader access to a machine and the data it stores. So long as the machine is turned on, the network connection can be exercised by a remote attacker to penetrate the machine. Unfortunately, MS/DOS does not contain security features that, for example, can protect against unwanted access to or modification of data stored on PCs.

A particularly dangerous example of compromised PC security arises from the use of telecommunication packages that support connecting from the PC to other systems. As a convenience to users, some of these packages offer to record and remember the user's password for other systems. This means that any user penetrating the PC gains access not only to the PC itself but also to all the systems for which the user has stored his password. The problem is compounded by the common practice of attaching a modem to the PC and leaving it turned on at night to permit the user to dial up to the PC from home: since the PC has no access control (unless the software supporting the modem provides the service), any attacker guessing the telephone number can attach to the system and steal all the passwords.

Storing passwords to secure machines on a machine with no security might seem the height of folly. However, major software packages for PCs invite the user to do just that, a clear example of how vendors and users ignore security in their search for ease of use.

take years to deploy a countermeasure that requires a major change to a basic system. Thus, for example, the current concern about virus attacks derives not from the intrinsic difficulty of resisting the attacks, but from the total lack of a countermeasure in such popular systems as MS/DOS and the Apple Macintosh operating system. It will take years to upgrade these environments to provide a technical means to resist virus attacks. Had such attacks been anticipated, the means to resist them could have been intrinsic to the systems. On the other hand, the threats are changing qualitatively; they are more likely to be catastrophic in impact than the more ordinary threat familiar to security officers and managers. This report focuses on the newer breed of threat to system trustworthiness.

The committee concludes, for the various reasons outlined above and developed in this report, that we cannot wait to see what attackers may devise, or what accident may happen, before we start our defense. We must develop a long-term plan, based on our predictions of the future, and start now to develop systems that will provide adequate security and trustworthiness over the next decade.

## TOWARD A PLANNED APPROACH

Taking a coherent approach to the problem of achieving improved system security requires understanding the complexity of the problem and a number of interrelated considerations, balancing the sometimes conflicting needs for security and secrecy, building on groundwork already laid, and formulating and implementing a new plan for action.

### Achieving Understanding

*The Nature of Security: Vulnerability, Threat, and Countermeasure*

The field of security has its own language and mode of thought, which focus on the processes of attack and on preventing, detecting, and recovering from attacks. In practice, similar thinking is accorded to the possibility of accidents that, like attacks, could result in disclosure, modification, or destruction of information or systems or a delay in system use. Security is traditionally discussed in terms of vulnerabilities, threats, and countermeasures. A *vulnerability* is an aspect of some system that leaves it open to attack. A *threat* is a hostile party with the potential to exploit that vulnerability and cause damage. A *countermeasure* or *safeguard* is an added step or improved design that eliminates the vulnerability and renders the threat impotent.

A safe containing valuables, for example, may have a noisy combination lock—a vulnerability—whose clicking can be recorded and analyzed to recover the combination. It is surmised that safecrackers can make contact with experts in illegal eavesdropping—a threat. A policy is therefore instituted that recordings of random clicking must be played at loud volume when the safe is opened—a countermeasure.

Threats and countermeasures interact in intricate and often counterintuitive ways: a threat leads to a countermeasure, and the countermeasure spawns a new threat. Few countermeasures are so effective that they actually eliminate a threat. New means of attack are devised (e.g., computerized signal processing to separate "live" clicks from recorded ones), and the result is a more sophisticated threat.

The interaction of threat and countermeasure poses distinctive problems for security specialists: the attacker must find but one of possibly multiple vulnerabilities in order to succeed; the security specialist must develop countermeasures for all. The advantage is therefore heavily to the attacker until very late in the mutual evolution of threat and countermeasure.[9]

If one waits until a threat is manifest through a successful attack, then significant damage can be done before an effective countermeasure can be developed and deployed. Therefore countermeasure engineering must be based on speculation. Effort may be expended in countering attacks that are never attempted.[10] The need to speculate and to budget resources for countermeasures also implies a need to understand what it is that should be protected, and why; such understanding should drive the choice of a protection strategy and countermeasures. This thinking should be captured in security policies generated by management; poor security often reflects both weak policy and inadequate forethought.[11]

Security specialists almost uniformly try to keep the details of countermeasures secret, thus increasing the effort an attacker must expend and the chances that an attack will be detected before it can succeed. Discussion of countermeasures is further inhibited because a detailed explanation of sophisticated features can be used to infer attacks against lesser systems.[12] As long as secrecy is considered important, the dissemination, without motivation, of guidelines developed by security experts will be a key instrument for enhancing secure system design, implementation, and operation. The need for secrecy regarding countermeasures and threats also implies that society must trust a group of people, security experts, for advice on how to maintain security.

Confidence in countermeasures is generally achieved by submitting them for evaluation by an independent team; this process increases the lead times and costs of producing secure systems. The existence of a successful attack can be demonstrated by an experiment, but the adequacy of a set of countermeasures cannot. Security specialists must resort to analysis, yet mathematical proofs in the face of constantly changing systems are impossible.

In practice, the effectiveness of a countermeasure often depends on how it is used; the best safe in the world is worthless if no one remembers to close the door. The possibility of legitimate users being hoodwinked into doing what an attacker cannot do for himself cautions against placing too much faith in purely technological countermeasures.

The evolution of countermeasures is a dynamic process. Security requires ongoing attention and planning, because yesterday's safeguards may not be effective tomorrow, or even today.

## Special Security Concerns Associated with Computers

Computerization presents several special security challenges that stem from the nature of the technology, including the programmability of computers, interconnection of systems, and the use of computers as parts of complex systems. A computing system may be under attack (e.g., for theft of data) for an indefinite length of time without any noticeable effects, attacks may be disguised or may be executed without clear traces being left, or attacks may be related to seemingly benign events. Thus "no danger signals" does not mean that everything is in order.[13] A further complication is the need to balance security against other interests, such as impacts on individual privacy. For example, automated detection of intrusion into a system, and other safeguards, can make available to system administrators significant information about the behavior of individual system users.

To some extent, those attributes of computing that introduce vulnerabilities can also be used to implement countermeasures. A computer system (unlike a file cabinet) can take active measures in its defense, by monitoring its activity and determining which user and program actions should be permitted (Anderson, 1980). Unfortunately, as discussed later in this report, this potential is far from realized.

*Programmability* The power of a general-purpose computer lies in its ability to become an infinity of different machines through programming.[14] This is also a source of great vulnerability, because if a system can be programmed, it can be programmed to do bad things.

Thus by altering program text a computer virus can transform a familiar and friendly machine into something else entirely (Cohen, 1984).

The vulnerability introduced by programmability is compounded by the degree to which the operation of a computer is hidden from its user. Whereas an individual concerned about security can inspect a mechanical typewriter and safely conclude that the effects of pressing a key are the appearance of a letter on the paper and the imprint of a letter on the ribbon, he can gain no such confidence about the operation of a word processor. It is clear that the pressing of a word processor's key causes the appearance of a letter on the screen. It is in no sense clear what else is happening—whether, for instance, the letters are being saved for subsequent transmission or the internal clock is being monitored for a "trigger date" for the alteration or destruction of files.

*Embeddedness and Interconnection*  The potential for taking improper irreversible actions increases with the degree to which computers are embedded in processes.[15]  The absence of human participation removes checks for the reasonableness of an action. And the time scale of automatic decisions may be too short to allow intervention before damage is done.

Interconnection enables attacks to be mounted remotely, anonymously, and against multiple vulnerabilities concurrently, creating the possibility of overwhelming impacts if the attacks are successful. This risk may not be understood by managers and system users. If a particular node on a massive, heterogeneous network does not contain any sensitive information, its owners may not be motivated to install any countermeasures. Yet such "wide-open" nodes can be used to launch attacks on the network as a whole, and little can be done in response, aside from disconnecting. The "Wily Hacker," for example, laundered his calls to defense-related installations through various university computers, none of which suffered any perceptible loss from his activities. The Internet worm of November 1988 also showed how networking externalizes risk. Many of the more than 2,000 affected nodes were entered easily once a "neighbor" node had been entered, usually through the electronic equivalent of an unlocked door.

In many cases, communication and interconnection have passed well beyond the simple exchange of messages to the creation of controlled opportunities for outsiders to access an organization's systems to facilitate either organization's business. On-line access by major telephone customers to telephone system management data and by large businesses to bank systems for treasury management functions are two examples of this phenomenon. A related development is electronic data interchange (EDI), in which companies have computer-communications links with suppliers and customers to automate ordering, queries about the status of orders, inventory management, market research, and even electronic funds transfer (EFT). EDI and EFT may add an additional system layer or interconnection where systems are mediated by third-party suppliers that collect, store, and forward messages between various parties in various organizations. This situation illustrates the need for trustworthiness in common carriage. In short, a wide range of organizations are connected to each other through computer systems, sometimes without knowing they are interconnected.

Interconnection gives an almost ecological flavor to security; it creates dependencies that can harm as well as benefit the community of those who are interconnected. An analogy can be made to pollution: the pollution generated as a byproduct of legitimate activity causes damage external to the polluter. A recognized public interest in eliminating the damage may compel the installation of pollution control equipment for the benefit of the community, although the installation may not be justified by the narrow self-interest of the polluter. Just as average citizens have only a limited technical understanding of their vulnerability to pollution, so also individuals and organizations today have little understanding of the extent to which their computer systems are put at risk by those systems to which they are connected, or vice versa. The public interest in the safety of networks may require some assurances about the quality of security as a prerequisite for some kinds of network connection.

### Security Must Be Holistic—Technology, Management, and Social Elements

Computer security does not stop or start at the computer. It is not a single feature, like memory size, nor can it be guaranteed by a single feature or even a set of features. It comprises at a minimum computer hardware, software, networks, and other equipment to which the computers are connected, facilities in which the computer is housed, and persons who use or otherwise come into contact with the computer. Serious security exposures may result from any weak technical or human link in the entire complex. For this reason, security is only partly a technical problem: it has significant procedural, administrative, physical facility, and personnel components as well. The General Accounting Office's recent criticisms of financial computer systems, for example, highlighted the risks associated with poor physical

---

BOX 1.3   SECURITY VS. RELIABILITY:
A TELEPHONE BILLING SYSTEM AS AN EXAMPLE

Consider, for example, a telephone billing system that computes the duration of a call by recording the time but not the date at the start and end of a call. The system cannot bill calls over 24 hours. Thus a call of 24 hours and 3 minutes would be billed for 3 minutes. In the normal course of events, such calls are very rare, and in the absence of an active threat it is possible to visualize an analysis whose conclusion is that the error is not worth fixing. That is, the revenue lost from that tiny number of calls that "naturally" last more than 24 hours would not cover the cost of making the fix. But the discovery of this error by an active threat (e.g., bookies) turns it immediately into a vulnerability that will be exploited actively and persistently until it is fixed. The tolerance for error is therefore very much less when one considers "security" than it is when one is simply concerned with "reliability."

---

and administrative security (GAO, 1990a), which sets the stage for even amateur attacks on critical systems.

Paralleling concerns about security are concerns about system safety and the need for assurance that a system will not jeopardize life or limb. Steps that enhance computer security will enhance safety, and vice versa.[16] Mechanisms used to achieve security are often similar to those used to achieve safety, reliability, and predictability. For example, contingency planning (which may involve system backup activities and alternative equipment and facilities) can protect an organization from the disruption associated with fires and other natural disasters, and it can help an organization to recover from a security breach.

Nevertheless, the environment in which those mechanisms operate differs when the principal concern is security. In particular, traditional risk analysis relies on statistical models that assume that unlikely events remain unlikely after they have occurred once. Security analyses cannot include such assumptions (see Box 1.3). Security is also distinguished from safety in that it involves protection against a conscious action rather than random unfortunate circumstances.[17]

*Commercial and Military Needs Are Different*

There has been much debate about the difference between military and commercial needs in the security area. Some analyses (OTA, 1987b) have characterized so-called military security policies (i.e., those concerned with national security or classified data) as being largely or exclusively concerned with secrecy, and commercial security policies (i.e., those of interest to the private sector) as being concerned with the integrity or reliability of data. This distinction is both superficial and misleading. National security activities, such as military operations, rely heavily on the integrity of data in such contexts as intelligence reports, targeting information, and command and control systems, as well as in more mundane applications such as payroll systems. Private sector organizations are concerned about protecting the confidentiality of merger and divestiture plans, personnel data, trade secrets, sales and marketing data and plans, and so on. Thus there are many common needs in the defense and civilian worlds.

Commonalities are especially strong when one compares the military to what could be called infrastructural industries—banking, the telephone system, power generation and distribution, airline scheduling and maintenance, and securities and commodities exchanges. Such industries both rely on computers and have strong security programs because of the linkage between security and reliability. Nonsecure systems are also potentially unreliable systems, and unreliability is anathema to infrastructure.

Nevertheless, specific military concerns affect the tack taken to achieve security in military contexts. Thus far, system attacks mounted by national intelligence organizations have been qualitatively different from attacks mounted by others (see Appendix E). This qualitative difference has led to basic differences in system design methodology, system vulnerability assessment, requirements for secrecy vs. openness in system design, and so on.

Other differences stem from the consequences of a successful attack. National security countermeasures stress prevention of attack, and only secondarily investigation and pursuit of the attackers, since the concept of compensatory or punitive damages is rarely meaningful in a national security context. Private sector countermeasures, however, are frequently oriented toward detection—developing audit trails and other chains of evidence that can be used to pursue attackers in the courts.

A final set of differences stem from variations in the ability to control who has access to computer systems. Threats can come from outsiders, individuals who have little or no legitimate access to the systems they are attacking, or from insiders, individuals who abuse their right to legitimate access. Embezzlement and theft of trade secrets by employees are familiar insider threats. Effective attacks often combine the two forms: a determined and competent group of outsiders aided by a subverted insider (Early, 1988).

The national security community conducts extensive background checks on individuals before it grants access to systems or information. Its countermeasures, therefore, tend to emphasize attacks by outsiders. Nonetheless, recognition of its own insider threats has led to an increased emphasis on accountability, auditing, and other measures to follow up on improper as well as accidental incidents. The private sector, by contrast, is limited by privacy and civil rights legislation in its ability to deny employment to individuals based on in-depth background investigations. This situation, together with the fact that most commercial applications are wide open to simple physical attacks and also have lacked external system connections, contributes to the private sector's historic emphasis on the threats posed by insiders (employees). Of course, the increasing interconnection and globalization of business, research, and other activities should raise the level of concern felt by all segments of the economy about outside threats.

The security needs of both commercial and defense sectors are matters of public interest. Partly because understanding of security is uneven, the computer and communications market has moved slowly and unevenly. Like other complex and sophisticated products, computer software and systems are difficult for the average consumer to understand and evaluate. This situation has depressed potential demand for security, and it has resulted in public and private efforts to stimulate and guide the market that, while well intended, fall short of what is needed. This is one area where it is generally agreed that some form of institutional support is not only desirable but also most valuable.

## Putting the Need for Secrecy into Perspective

There is a tension between the need for prudent limits on the dissemination of information on vulnerabilities and the need to inform those at risk of specific security problems. The secrecy imperative has historically dominated the communications security field. Cryptology (the science of making and breaking codes), for instance, is one of two sciences (the other being atomic energy) that is given special status under federal statute (Kahn, 1967). Secrecy has also been self-imposed; government investigators, prosecutors, and insurance representatives have noted the reluctance of companies that have experienced computer system attacks to report their experiences.

Concern for secrecy affects the way computer systems are built and used. Open discussion of the design of a system offers the benefit of collegial review (see Chapter 4) but also involves the risk that attackers may be immediately informed of vulnerabilities. Evaluation and analysis may also yield a list of residual vulnerabilities that cannot be countered for technical or economic reasons, and these become the most important secrets associated with the system. The more complex the system, the more difficult the trade-off becomes because of the increased likelihood that those close to the system will overlook something. General education in the proper use of countermeasures leads to a better-informed user community, but it also leads to a better-informed community of potential attackers. Publicizing specific vulnerabilities will lead some users to correct them, but will also provide a cookbook for attacking sites that do not hear about or are not motivated to install the countermeasure.

Concern for secrecy also impedes technological progress in the security area. It has deterred research in the academic community, which places a premium on open discussion and publication. It increases the difficulties faced by people new to the field, who cannot readily find out what has been done and what the real problems are; there is much reinventing of wheels. Finally, concern for secrecy makes it hard for the few who are well informed to seek the counsel and collaboration of others.

Perhaps the most damaging aspect of the secrecy associated with computer and communications security is that it has led many to assume that no problems exist. "Tomorrow will be pretty much like today," is the rationale that guides most government, corporate, and individual activities. However, with respect to computer security, secrecy makes it extremely hard to know what today is really like.

## Building on Existing Foundations

A number of government agencies have addressed portions of the computer system security problem, either by developing relevant technology or applying relevant tools and practices (see Box 1.4). Two government agencies, the National Security Agency (NSA)—most recently through one of its arms, the National Computer Security Center (NCSC)—and the National Institute of Standards and Technology (NIST; formerly the National Bureau of Standards) have been particularly active for some 20 years, but neither is positioned to adequately address the nation's needs.

The National Security Agency has been the more active of the two organizations. The establishment of the NCSC represented an effort to stimulate the commercial marketplace. Through the NCSC and the publication of the *Trusted Computer System Evaluation Criteria*, or Orange Book (U.S. DOD, 1985d), which outlines different levels of computer security and a process for evaluating the security of com-

---

BOX 1.4   RECENT MAJOR COMPUTER SECURITY INITIATIVES
UNDERTAKEN BY THE U.S. GOVERNMENT

• Establishment of the National Computer Security Center
• The Orange Book, Trusted Network Interpretation, related publications,
and the Trusted Products Evaluation Program
• National Security Decision Directive 145; revised and recast as NSD 42
• The Computer Fraud and Abuse Act of 1986
• The Computer Security Act of 1987
• National Telecommunications and Information System Security Policy
200—C2 by '92
• The Secure Data Network System project
• NIST's Integrity Workshop program
• DARPA's Computer Emergency Response Team program

---

puter systems (see Appendix A), the NSA has had a noticeable effect
(Box 1.5). Because of its defense-oriented charter, the NSA cannot,
however, more actively foster development or widespread dissemination of technology for use in the nonclassified or commercial world.
Indeed, its defense-related focus—specifically, a focus on systems that
process classified information—has been narrowed in recent years.

The National Institute of Standards and Technology's impact on
computer security has been concentrated within the federal government. NIST has limited technical expertise and funds; in FY 1990 its
appropriations for the computer security program totaled only $2.5
million. Although it can organize workshops, develop procedural
guidelines, and sanction standards efforts, it is not in a position to
develop technology internally or to provide direct support to external
technology development efforts. The newest (FY 1991) NIST budget
request called for a doubling of funds to support activities related to
computer security, and NIST has made plans to undertake some initiatives (e.g., an industry-oriented program to combat computer viruses).
However, the denial of NIST's FY 1990 request for modest additional
funds in this area is symptomatic of the lack of stability and predictability of the political process for government funding in general and
funding for NIST in particular.[18]

Tension between commercial and military interests dominated public
policymaking relating to computer security during the 1980s. National Security Decision Directive (NSDD) 145, the Computer Security
Act of 1987, and the mid-1990 revision of NSDD 145 (resulting in
NSD 42) have progressively restricted NSA to an emphasis on defense systems, leaving civilian (notably civil government) system se-

## BOX 1.5   THE RAINBOW SERIES

Since its formation in 1981, the National Computer Security Center has disseminated a collection of criteria and guidelines to assist developers, evaluators, and users in the development of trusted systems. This set of documents has become known as the Rainbow Series because of the different colors used for each volume's cover. Of these documents, perhaps the most widely known is the so-called Orange Book, which is formally known as the Department of Defense *Trusted Computer System Evaluation Criteria.* The following are brief descriptions of some of the documents that form the Rainbow Series:

Trusted Computer System Evaluation Criteria (TCSEC) (Orange)
> The TCSEC defines criteria for evaluating the security functionality and assurance provided by a computer system. The TCSEC formalizes the concept of a trusted computing base (TCB) and specifies how it should be constructed and used in order to ensure a desired level of trust.

Trusted Network Interpretation (TNI) (Red)
> The TNI interprets the TCSEC with regard to networked computer systems. The TNI has been particularly controversial due to the complex security issues that arise when computer networks are used. It has been undergoing revision.

Trusted Database Management System Interpretation (TDI) (forthcoming)
> The TDI interprets the TCSEC with regard to database management systems. The TDI is expected to be released in late 1990 or early 1991.

Password Management Guideline (Light Green)
> This document describes a set of good practices for using password-based authorization schemes. A similar set of guidelines has also been issued by the National Institute of Standards and Technology as a Federal Information Processing Standards publication.

Glossary of Computer Security Terms (Dark Green)
> This document defines the acronyms and terms used by computer security specialists, focusing on DOD contexts.

Magnetic Remanence Security Guidelines (Dark Blue)
> This document provides procedures and guidance for sanitizing magnetic storage media (e.g., disks and tapes) prior to their release to nonsecure environments.

Guidance for Applying the Department of Defense Trusted Computer System Evaluation Criteria in Specific Environments (Yellow)
> This volume provides guidance for applying the TCSEC to specific environments.

curity concerns to NIST. Partly as a result of the changing policy context, NSA has moved to diminish its interaction with commercial organizations, most notably by scaling back the NCSC. The full implications of these moves are yet to be appreciated at the time this report is being completed.

Meanwhile, no industry-based organization or professional association has stepped forward to play a leadership role in increasing computer system security, although the 1980s saw the birth or strengthening of a number of volunteer professional associations, and over the past couple of years major computer-related trade associations (e.g., the Computer and Business Equipment Manufacturers Association (CBEMA) and the computer software and services industry association ADAPSO) have begun to explore steps they can take to better track security problems, notably virus incidents, and to encourage better systems development. However valuable, these efforts are piecemeal.

Common technical interests, complementary objectives, and significant differences in resources combine to make the existing separate activities aimed at increasing computer security in commercial and military environments an incomplete solution to the problem of increasing the overall level of system security and trust. A more complete solution calls for the formulation and implementation of a new, more comprehensive plan that would inject greater resources into meeting commercial computer security needs.

## SCOPE, PURPOSE, CONTENTS, AND AUDIENCE

This report provides an agenda for public policy, computer and communications security research, technology development, evaluation, and implementation. It focuses on the broad base of deployed computers in the United States; it does not emphasize the special problems of government classified information systems. This committee is particularly concerned about raising the security floor, making sure that the commercial environment on which the economy and public safety depend has a better minimum level of protection.

A number of actions are needed to increase the availability of computer and communications systems with improved security, including:

• A clear articulation of essential security features, assurances, and practices;
• Enhanced institutional support and coordination for security; and
• Research and development of trustworthy computer-based technology.

This is the appropriate time to develop a new strategy that blends research, establishment of requirements and criteria, and commercial incentives. The committee's recommendations in each of the above areas are presented below in the "Recommendations" section of this chapter. These include recommendations for both short- and long-term actions.

This report is intended to address a variety of audiences, including government policymakers, vendors, managers responsible for the purchase and use of computer and communications systems, people involved in computer-related research and development, educators, and interested members of the general public. The chapters and appendixes that follow provide technical and analytical detail to further support the assertions, conclusions, and recommendations presented in this first chapter.

- Chapter 2 describes basic concepts of information security, including security policies and management controls.
- Chapter 3 describes technology associated with computer and communications security, relating technical approaches to security policies and management controls.
- Chapter 4 discusses methodological issues related to building secure software systems.
- Chapter 5 discusses system evaluation criteria, which provide yardsticks for evaluating the quality of systems. This topic is a current focus of much international concern and activity.
- Chapter 6 discusses why the marketplace has failed to substantially increase the supply of security technology and discusses options for stimulating the market.
- Chapter 7 discusses the need for a new institution, referred to as the Information Security Foundation.
- Chapter 8 outlines problems and opportunities in the research community and suggests topics for research and mechanisms for strengthening the research infrastructure.
- Appendixes provide further detail on the Orange Book (A), technology (B), emergency response teams (C), models for proposed guidelines (D), high-grade threats (E), and terminology (F).

The nature of the subject of security dictates some limits on the content of this report. Of necessity, this report anticipates threats in order to guide the development of effective security policy; it therefore inherently contains a degree of surmise. It leaves things unsaid so as not to act as a textbook for attackers, and therefore it may fail to inform or inspire some whose information is at risk. And finally, it may carry within it the seeds of its own failure, as the countermeasures it may inspire may also lead to new and more effective threats. Such is the nature of security.

## RECOMMENDATIONS

The central concern of this report is how to get more and better computer and communications security into use. Five of the committee's six recommendations endorse actions with medium- to long-range impacts. Another, Recommendation 2, outlines short-term actions aimed at immediately improving the security of computing systems. It is clear that system operators, users, and managers need to take effective steps now to upgrade and stabilize their operating environments; developers and vendors are likewise urged to use existing capabilities for immediate enhancement of computer security. Also of concern are a number of currently unfolding political developments (e.g., development of harmonized international criteria for trusted system design and evaluation) that call for immediate attention from both public policymakers and vendors in particular. The committee has addressed such developments within the body of the report as appropriate.

Although the committee focused on system security, its recommendations also serve other aspects of system trustworthiness, in particular safety and reliability. It does not make sense to address these issues separately. Many of the methods and techniques that make systems more secure make them more trustworthy in general. System safety is tied to security, both in method and in objective. The penetration of computing into the social and economic fabric means that, increasingly, what we may want to protect or secure is public safety.

Increasing the trustworthiness of computer systems requires actions on many fronts—developing technology and products, strengthening managerial controls and response programs, and enhancing public awareness. Toward that end, the committee recommends six sets of actions, summarized as follows:

1. Promulgating a comprehensive set of generally accepted system security principles, referred to as GSSP (see also Chapter 2);
2. Taking specific short-term actions that build on readily available capabilities (see also Chapter 6);
3. Establishing a comprehensive incident data repository and appropriate education programs to promote public awareness (see also Chapters 4 and 6);
4. Clarifying export control criteria and procedures (see also Chapter 6);

5. Securing funding for a comprehensive, directed program of research (see also Chapters 3, 4, and 8); and

6. Establishing a new organization to nurture the development, commercialization, and proper use of trust technology, referred to as the Information Security Foundation, or ISF (see also Chapters 5, 6, and 7).

## Recommendation 1
### Promulgate Comprehensive Generally Accepted System Security Principles (GSSP)

**1a. Establish a set of Generally Accepted System Security Principles, or GSSP, for computer systems.** Because of widely varying understanding about vulnerabilities, threats, and safeguards, system vendors and users need guidance to develop and use trusted systems. It is neither desirable nor feasible to make all who come into contact with computers experts in computer and communications security. It is, however, both desirable and feasible to achieve a general expectation for a minimum level of protection. Otherwise, responses to security problems will continue to be fragmented and often ineffective.

The committee believes it is possible to enunciate a basic set of security-related principles that are so broadly applicable and effective for the design and use of systems that they ought to be a part of any system with significant operational requirements. This set will grow with research and experience in new areas of concern, such as integrity and availability, and can also grow beyond the specifics of security to deal with other related aspects of system trust, such as safety. GSSP should articulate and codify these principles.

Successful GSSP would establish a set of expectations about and requirements for good practice that would be well understood by system developers and security professionals, accepted by government, and recognized by managers and the public as protecting organizational and individual interests against security breaches and lapses in the protection of privacy. Analogous broad acceptance has been accorded to financial accounting standards (what have been called the Generally Accepted Accounting Principles, or GAAP) and building codes,[19] both of which contain principles defined with industry input and used or recognized by government as well. To achieve a similar level of consensus, one that builds on but reaches beyond that accorded to the Orange Book (see Appendix A), the GSSP development process should be endorsed by and accept input from all relevant communities, including commercial users, vendors, and interested agencies of the U.S. government. The development of GSSP would

BOX 1.6    POTENTIAL ELEMENTS OF GENERALLY ACCEPTED
SYSTEM SECURITY PRINCIPLES

The following set of examples is intended to illustrate the kinds of principles and considerations that might be embodied in GSSP. The committee emphasizes security-related issues but believes that GSSP should also stress safety-related practices.

• *Quality control*—A system is safe and secure only to the extent that it can be trusted to provide the functionality it is intended to supply. At a minimum, the best known industrial practice must be used for system development, and some recognized means for potential purchasers or users to obtain independent evaluation must be provided. A stronger requirement would specify that every procedure in the software be accompanied by text specifying its potential impact on safety and security and arguing that those specifications imply the desired properties.* Chapter 5 discusses specific proposals for evaluation of systems relative to GSSP.

• *Access control on code as well as data*—Every system must have the means to control which users can perform operations on which pieces of data, and which particular operations are possible. A minimum mechanism has a fixed set of operations (for example read, write, and execute) and may only associate permission with static groups of users, but stronger means, such as the ability to list particular users, are recommended.

• *User identification and authentication*—Every system must assign an unambiguous identifier to each separate user and must have the means to assure that any user is properly associated with the correct identifier. A minimum mechanism for this function is passwords, but stronger means, such as challenge-response identity checks, are recommended.

• *Protection of executable code*—Every system must have the means to ensure that programs cannot be modified or replaced improperly. Mechanisms stronger than customary access control are recommended, such as a basic system function to recognize certain programs as "installed" or "production" or "trusted," and to restrict the access to specified data to only this class of program.

• *Security logging*—Every system must have the means to log for later audit all security-relevant operations on the system. At a minimum, this must include all improper attempts to authenticate a user or to access data, all changes to the list of authorized users, and (if appropriate) all successful

*Continued*

require a level of effort and community participation that is well beyond the scope either of this report or of organizations currently active in the security arena. The committee therefore recommends that the process of establishing GSSP be spearheaded by a new organization discussed below in recommendation 6.

Presented in Box 1.6 are some potential GSSP elements that in

*BOX 1.6  Continued*

security-related operations (user authentications, file opens, and so on). The log must be implemented in such a way that it cannot be altered or deleted after being written. A stronger version would also prevent the security administrator from deleting the log.

• *Security administrator*—All systems must support the concept of a special class of users who are permitted to perform actions that change the security state of the system, such as adding users or installing trusted programs. They must control system code and data sources in appropriate off-line facilities. They must employ standard procedures for system initialization, backup, and recovery from "crashes."

• *Data encryption*—While data encryption is not, in itself, an application-level security requirement, it is currently recognized as the method of choice for protecting communication in distributed systems. Any system that can be attached to a network must support some standard means for data encryption. A stronger version would forbid software encryption.

• *Operational support tools*—Every system must provide tools to assist the user and the security administrator in verifying the security state of the system. These include tools to inspect security logs effectively, tools to provide a warning of unexpected system behavior, tools to inspect the security state of the system, and tools to control, configure, and manage the off-line data and code storage and hardware inventory.

• *Independent audit*—At some reasonable and regular interval, an independent unannounced audit of the on-line system, operation, administration, configuration control, and audit records should be invoked by an agency unrelated to that responsible for the system design and/or operations. Such an audit should be analogous to an annual business audit by accounting firms.

• *Hazard analysis*—A hazard analysis must be done for every safety-critical system. This analysis must describe those states of the system that can lead to situations in which life is endangered and must estimate the probability and severity of each under various conditions of usage. It should also categorize the extent to which hazards are independent of each other.

*Note that the Internet Engineering Advisory Board has begun to contemplate "security impact statements" for proposed modifications to the large and complex Internet.

fully developed GSSP would be elaborated in greater detail. The committee expects that GSSP would also cover matters of safety that fall outside the scope of this report.

Comprehensive GSSP must reflect the needs of the widest possible spectrum of computer users. Although some groups with particular responsibilities (e.g., in banking) might be tempted to reject GSSP in favor of defining practices specific to their sectors, the committee believes that this would be unfortunate. Base-level security requirements of the sort outlined above are broadly applicable and ought to be defined in common (see Chapter 2), so that the features required to support GSSP can become a part of general-purpose computing. Only as a part of mainstream computing products will they become available at reasonable cost.

In order to serve a wide range of users, GSSP must allow variation with circumstances. The committee concludes (see Chapter 5) that GSSP should be organized in a somewhat more unbundled manner than is the Orange Book.

The process of motivating the adoption of GSSP could and probably should differ across sectors. For example, where computers are used to help manage assets, cooperation with the American Institute of Certified Professional Accountants or the Financial Accounting Standards Board might lead to incorporation of GSSP into the larger body of standard practice for accounting. In systems used for health care, GSSP might become a part of the Food and Drug Administration's regulations governing medical equipment. GSSP could also be directly incorporated into government requests for proposals (RFPs) and other procurement actions. During the development of GSSP it would be necessary to consider mechanisms and options for motivating adoption of GSSP.

The committee expects natural forces, such as customers' expectations, requirements for purchasing insurance, vendors' concerns about liability, industry associations, and advertising advantage, to instill GSSP in the marketplace. Nevertheless it is possible to imagine that in some circumstances, such as for life-critical systems, certain aspects of GSSP might become mandatory. Serious consideration of regulation or other mechanisms for enforcement is both premature and beyond the scope of this report. However, the process implied by the committee's set of recommendations could force such consideration in a few years. That process entails establishing a new organization, developing GSSP, and beginning the dissemination of GSSP through voluntary means.

**1b. Consider the system requirements specified by the Orange Book for the C2 and B1 levels as a short-term definition of Generally Accepted System Security Principles and a starting point for more extensive definitions.** To date and by default, the principal vehicle in the United States for raising the level of practice in computer and communications security has been the National Computer Security Center's Orange Book and its various interpretations. Although the Orange Book is not a full set of GSSP (see Appendix A), it is a major step that is currently molding the market and is clearly consonant with GSSP.

The C2 and B1 ratings describe systems that provide base-line levels of acceptable discretionary security (C2) and systems that provide minimal levels of acceptable mandatory multilevel security (B1).[20] However, the Orange Book is not adequate to meet the public's long-term needs, largely because it is incomplete. GSSP would provide fuller treatment of integrity, availability, and advanced techniques for assurance and software development.[21] It must address distributed systems and evolving architectures (as well as change in the underlying technologies generally), which means that it should go beyond trusted computing bases as currently defined.

**1c. Establish methods, guidelines and facilities for evaluating products for conformance to GSSP.** A mechanism for checking conformance to GSSP is required for GSSP to have its fullest impact and to protect both vendors and consumers. As with technical standards, it is possible to claim conformance, but conformance must be genuine for benefits, such as interoperability, to be realized. Conformance evaluation is already becoming a prominent issue across the industry because of the proliferation of standards.[22] Evaluation of security and safety properties is generally recognized as more difficult than evaluation of conformance to interoperability standards. Therefore, methods for evaluating conformance should be considered for each element of GSSP.

It will also be necessary both to train evaluators and to establish the extent and timing of independent evaluation. The details of the evaluation process affect costs to vendors and users as well as the confidence of both in the performance or quality of a system. In Chapter 5 the committee recommends that the minimal GSSP evaluation include two parts, an explicit design evaluation performed by an outside team, and a coordinated process of tracking field experience with the product and tracking and reporting security faults. This process ought to be less costly and time-consuming than the current NCSC process, thus improving the chances of its widespread acceptance.

Experience with the current NCSC evaluation process suggests that individual products can be evaluated somewhat formally and objectively. However, a system composed of evaluated components may not provide the security implied by component ratings. Achieving overall system security requires more objective, uniform, and rigorous standards for system certification. The committee recommends that GSSP include guidelines for system certification, again building on existing methodology.

**1d. Use GSSP as a basis for resolving differences between U.S. and foreign criteria for trustworthy systems and as a vehicle for shaping inputs to international discussions of security and safety standards.** With the current emergence of national evaluation criteria and the proposed harmonized *Information Technology Security Evaluation Criteria* (ITSEC; Federal Republic of Germany, 1990) developed by the United Kingdom, France, Germany, and the Netherlands, the Orange Book is no longer the only game in town. Just as GSSP would serve to extend the Orange Book criteria to cover integrity and availability and advanced system development and assurance techniques, it should also serve as the basis for resolving the differences between the Orange Book and international criteria such as the ITSEC. In the ongoing process of reconciling international criteria and evaluations, U.S. interests may be inadequately served if the comparatively narrowly focused Orange Book is the sole basis for U.S. positions.

The committee supports a move already under discussion to conduct simultaneous evaluations of products against the Orange Book and international criteria to improve the understanding of the relationships among different criteria and to enhance reciprocity. A concerted effort to simultaneously evaluate a series of trusted products can, over a reasonable period of time, bring the criteria (eventually including GSSP) to a common level of understanding and promote the development of reciprocity in ratings.

Similar concerns pertain to U.S. participation in international standards-setting committees. U.S. participation is often constrained by concerns about international technology transfer or by limited technical support from industry. The cost of weak participation may be the imposition on the marketplace of standards that do not fully reflect U.S. national or industrial interests.

## Recommendation 2
### Take Specific Short-term Actions That Build on
### Readily Available Capabilities

System users and vendors can take a number of actions that will immediately improve the security of computing systems.

**2a. Develop security policies.** Computer system users should think through their security needs, establish appropriate policies and associated procedures, and ensure that everyone in a given organization knows those policies and procedures and has some understanding of security risks and safe computing practices. Many organizations have taken these common-sense steps; many others have not or could do so more effectively.[23] At the highest level, these policies provide directions for programs that affect physical security, contingency planning, electronic access, networking, security awareness, and so on. Within each of these general security areas, policies should be developed to identify the specific controls or mechanisms needed to satisfy organizational objectives.

It should be understood that planning and setting policies and procedures need not result in wholesale changes to installed systems. Many of the most effective management controls relate to system operation rather than to functional changes to system design, both because operational changes can be accomplished quickly and because operational weaknesses in computer systems are among the most severe practical problems today. Such changes may not decrease vulnerabilities, but they can reduce a potential threat by imposing controls on potential abusers. Two obvious techniques are upgrading the quality of security administration (e.g., password management, audit analysis, and configuration management) and educating individual users about the risks of importing software (e.g., contamination by viruses).

**2b. Form computer emergency response teams.** The committee recommends that all organizations dependent on proper operation of computer systems form or obtain access to computer emergency response teams (CERTs) trained to deal with security violations (see Appendix C). These teams should be prepared to limit the impact of successful attacks, provide guidance in recovering from attacks, and take measures to prevent repetition of successful attacks.

For security problems arising from basic design faults, such as the lack of security in MS/DOS, little remedy can be expected in the short term. However, for problems resulting from implementation flaws, a CERT can help by informing the vendor of the fault, ensuring that the fault receives sufficient attention, and helping to ensure that upgraded software is distributed and installed. DARPA's CERT and other, smaller efforts have demonstrated the potential of emergency response teams.

**2c. Use as a first step the Orange Book's C2 and B1 criteria.** Until GSSP can be articulated and put in place, industry needs some guidance for raising the security floor in the marketplace. The Orange Book's C2 and B1 criteria provide such guidance, which should be valuable not only to conventional computer system vendors (hardware and software) but also to vendors of computer-based medical systems, specialized database management systems, and other computer-based products. Vendors who have not already done so should move to meet C2 and B1 criteria as a conservative step toward instituting GSSP.

**2d. Use sound methodology and modern technology to develop high-quality software.** The committee recommends that developers of security-relevant software use current-generation tools for software engineering. The development of high-quality software, clearly a paramount goal for any project, often is not achieved because of various real-world pressures and constraints (e.g., competitive need for fast release, or customer demand for enhanced performance). Although the development of more trustworthy systems in general is a concern, security in particular can suffer if systems are not constructed in a methodical and controlled way.

Poor development practices can have several consequences. First, they may lead to a system with vulnerabilities that result directly from undetected errors in the software. (Although objective evidence is hard to gather, it seems that technical attacks on systems are targeted more to implementation faults than to design faults.) Second, such a system may be much harder to evaluate, since it is very difficult for an independent evaluator to understand or review the implementation. Third, the system may be harder to maintain or evolve, which means that with time, the security of the system may get worse, not better.

Conventional wisdom about sound development practices applies with special force where security is involved (see Box 1.7).

**2e. Implement emerging security standards and participate actively in their design.** The committee urges vendors to incorporate emerging security standards into their product planning and to participate more actively in the design of such standards. In particular, vendors should develop distributed system architectures compatible with evolving security standards.[24] Further, vendors and large-system users should make the setting of security standards a higher priority.

Current attempts to set standards raise two concerns. First, standards-setting committees should strive to make security standards simple, since complexity is associated with a greater potential for security problems. Achieving consensus typically results in a standard that combines the interests of diverse parties, a process that promotes complexity. Second, because there are hundreds of computing-related standards groups, setting security standards gets rela-

---

BOX 1.7   SOUND DEVELOPMENT METHODOLOGY FOR
SECURE SOFTWARE AND SYSTEMS

• Strive for simplicity and smallness where feasible.

• Use software configuration management and control systems for all source and object code, specifications, documents, test plans and results, version control, and release tracking.

• Reduce exposure to failure of security. For example, validated copies of vital data should be kept off-line, and contingency plans for extended computer outages should be in place.

• Restrict general access to software development tools and products, and to the physical environment.

• Develop generally available components with well-documented program-level interfaces that can be incorporated into secure software. Among these should be standardized interfaces to security services (e.g., cryptography) that may have hardware implementations.

• Provide excess memory and computing capacity relative to the intended functionality. This reduces the need to solve performance problems by introducing complexity into the software.

• Use higher-level languages. (This suggestion may not apply to intelligence threats.)

• Aim for building secure software by extending existing secure software. Furthermore, use mature product or development technology.

• Couple development of secure software with regular evaluation. If system evaluation is to be done by an outside organization, that organization should be involved in the project from it inception.

• Schedule more time and resources for assurance than are typical today.

• Design software to limit the need for secrecy. When a project attempts to maintain secrecy, it must take extraordinary measures, (e.g., cleared "inspectors general") to ensure that secrecy is not abused (e.g., to conceal poor-quality work).

---

tively limited attention and participation. Although NIST has supported the setting of such standards, emphasis in this country on standards development by the private sector makes active industry participation essential. Therefore, vendors should be encouraged to assign representatives to U.S. standards efforts to ensure that (1) the impact of standards that affect security is fully understood and (2) security standards can be implemented effectively.

**2f. Use technical aids to foster secure operations.** The committee recommends that vendors take technical steps that will help diminish the impact of user ignorance and carelessness and make it easier to administer systems in a secure manner. For example, systems should be shipped with security features turned on, so that explicit action is needed to disable them, and with default identifications and passwords turned off, so that a conscious effort is required to enable them. More efforts are needed to develop and market tools that could examine the state of a system and report on its security.[25] Such audit tools (e.g., MIT's Kuang tool (Baldwin, 1988), Digital Equipment Corporation's Inspect, Clyde Digital's Cubic, DEMAX's Securepack, and AT&T's Quest) have proved useful in assuring the continued operational security of running systems.

## Recommendation 3
## Gather Information and Provide Education

**3a. Build a repository of incident data.** The committee recommends that a repository of incident information be established for use in research, to increase public awareness of successful penetrations and existing vulnerabilities, and to assist security practitioners, who often have difficulty persuading managers to invest in security. This database should categorize, report, and track pertinent instances of system security-related threats, risks, and failures. Because of the need for secrecy and confidentiality about specific system flaws and actual penetrations, this information must be collected and disseminated in a controlled manner. One possible model for data collection is the incident reporting system administered by the National Transportation Safety Board; two directly relevant efforts are the incident tracking begun by DARPA's computer emergency response team and NIST's announced plans to begin to track incidents.

**3b. Foster education in engineering secure systems.** There is a dramatic shortage of people qualified to build secure software. Universities should establish software engineering programs that emphasize development of critical and secure software; major system users should likewise provide for continuing education that promotes expertise in setting requirements for, specifying, and building critical software. Effective work on critical software requires specialized knowledge of what can go wrong in the application domain. Competence in software that controls a nuclear reactor, for example, does not qualify one to work on flight-control software. Working on secure software requires yet more skills, including understanding the potential for attack, for software in general and for the application domain in particular.

Especially needed is a university-based program aimed at returning, graduate-level students who are already somewhat familiar with at least one application area. In addition to covering conventional software engineering, such a program would give special emphasis to topics related to critical software and security[26] and could best be developed at universities with strong graduate engineering and business programs. The committee envisions as an initial step approximately three such programs, each turning out perhaps 20 people a year.

Given the current shortage of qualified people and the time needed for universities to establish appropriate programs, those undertaking large security-related development efforts should deal explicitly with the need to educate project members. Both time and money for this should appear in project budgets.

**3c. Provide early training in security practices and ethics.** The committee recommends that security practices and ethics be integrated into the general process of learning about and using computers. Awareness of the importance of security measures should be integrated into early education about computing. Lessons about socially acceptable and unacceptable behavior (e.g., stealing passwords is not acceptable) should also be taught when students first begin to use computers, just as library etiquette (e.g., writing in library books is not acceptable) is taught to young readers—with the recognition, of course, that security is a more complex subject. This recommendation is aimed at teachers, especially those at the primary and secondary levels. Implementing it would require that organizations and professionals concerned with security get the word out, to organizations that customarily serve and inform teachers and directly to teachers in communities.

### Recommendation 4
### Clarify Export Control Criteria, and
### Set Up a Forum for Arbitration

The market for computer and communications security, like the computer market overall, is international. If the United States does not allow vendors of commercial systems to export security products and products with relatively effective security features, large multinational firms as well as foreign consumers will simply purchase equivalent systems from foreign manufacturers. At issue is the ability to export two types of products: (1) trusted systems and (2) encryption.

**4a. Clarify export controls on trusted systems and differentiate**

**them from Orange Book ratings.** Industry has complained for some time about current export controls on trusted systems. The requirement for case-by-case review of export licenses for trusted systems with Orange Book ratings of B3 and above adds to the cost of such systems, because sales may be restricted and extra time is needed to apply for and receive export approval. These prospects discourage industry from developing more secure systems; vendors do not want to jeopardize the exportability of their mainline commercial offerings.[27]

The committee recommends that Orange Book ratings not be used as export control criteria. It also recommends that the Department of Commerce, in conjunction with the Departments of Defense and State, clarify for industry the content of the regulations and the process by which they are implemented. Removal of Orange Book ratings as control parameters would also help to alleviate potential problems associated with multiple, national rating schemes (see Chapter 5).

The crux of the problem appears to be confusion among Orange Book ratings, dual-use (military and civilian) technology, and military-critical technology. Security technology intended to counter an intelligence-grade threat is considered military critical and not dual use—it is not aimed at commercial as well as military uses. Security technology intended to counter a lower, criminal-grade threat is of use to both defense and commercial entities, but it is not military critical. Since an Orange Book rating per se is not proof against an intelligence-grade threat, it does not alone signal military-critical technology that should be tightly controlled. Industry needs to know which features of a product might trigger export restrictions.

**4b. Review export controls on implementations of the Data Encryption Standard.** The growth of networked and distributed systems has created needs for encryption in the private sector. Some of that pressure has been seen in the push for greater exportability of products using the Data Encryption Standard (DES) and its deployment in foreign offices of U.S. companies.[28]

In principle, any widely available internationally usable encryption algorithm should be adequate. NIST, working with NSA, is currently trying to develop such algorithms. However, the committee notes that this effort may not solve industry's problems, for several reasons. The growing installed base of DES products cannot be easily retrofitted with the new products. The foreign supply of DES products may increase the appeal of foreign products. Finally, NSA-influenced alternatives may be unacceptable to foreign or even U.S. buyers, as evidenced by the American Banking Association's opposition to the NSA's proposals to effectively restrict banks to encryption algorithms designed and developed by NSA when the DES was last recertified, in 1988.

The committee has been apprised that NSA, because of classified national security concerns, does not support the removal of remaining restrictions on export of DES. However, there is a growing lack of sympathy in the commercial community with the NSA position on this matter. The committee recommends that the Administration appoint an arbitration group consisting of appropriately cleared individuals from industry and the Department of Commerce as well as the Department of Defense to impartially evaluate if there are indeed valid reasons at this time for limiting the export of DES.[29]

## Recommendation 5
## Fund and Pursue Needed Research

The dramatic changes in the technology of computing make it necessary for the computer science and engineering communities to rethink some of the current technical approaches to achieving security. The most dramatic example of the problem is the confusion about how best to achieve security in networked environments and embedded systems.

At present, there is no vigorous program to meet this need. Particularly worrisome is the lack of academic research in computer security, notably research relevant to distributed systems and networks.[30] Only in theoretical areas, such as number theory, zero-knowledge proofs, and cryptology, which are conducive to individual research efforts, has there been significant academic effort. Although it must be understood that many research topics could be pursued in industrial as well as academic research laboratories, the committee has focused on strengthening the comparatively weaker research effort in universities, since universities both generate technical talent and are traditionally the base for addressing relatively fundamental questions.

The committee recommends that government sponsors of computer science and technology research (in particular, DARPA and NSF) undertake well-defined and adequately funded programs of research and technology development in computer security. A key role for NSF (and perhaps DARPA), beyond specific funding of relevant projects, is to facilitate increased cross-coupling between security experts and researchers in related fields. The committee also recommends that NIST, in keeping with its interest in computer security and its charter to enhance security for sensitive unclassified data and systems, pro-

---

BOX 1.8   SECURITY RESEARCH AGENDA

• *Security modularity*—How can a set of system components with known security properties be combined or composed to form a larger system with known security properties? How can a system be decomposed into building blocks, units that can be used independently in other systems?

• *Security policy models*—Security requirements other than disclosure control, such as integrity, availability, and distributed authentication and authorization, are not easily modeled. There is also a need for better models that address protocols and other aspects of distributed systems.

• *Cost/benefit models for security*—How much does security (including also privacy protection) really cost, and what are its real benefits?

• *New security mechanisms*—As new requirements are proposed, as new threats are considered, and as new technologies become prevalent, new mechanisms are required to maintain effective security. Some current topics for research include mechanisms to support critical aspects of integrity (separation of duty, for example), distributed key management on low-security systems, multiway and transitive authentication, availability (especially in distributed systems and networks), privacy assurance, and access controllers in networks to permit interconnection of mutually suspicious organizations.

• *Increasing effectiveness of assurance techniques*—More needs to be known about the spectrum of analysis techniques, both formal and informal, and to what aspects of security they best apply. Also, tools are needed to support the generation of assurance evidence.

• *Alternative representations and presentations*—New representations of security properties may yield new analysis techniques. For example,

*Continued*

---

vide funding for research in areas of key concern to it, either internally or in collaboration with other agencies that support research.

The committee has identified several specific technical issues that justify research (see Box 1.8). Chapter 8 provides a fuller discussion; Chapters 3 and 4 address some underlying issues. The list, although by no means complete, shows the scope and importance of a possible research agenda.

The committee believes that greater university involvement in large-scale research-oriented system development projects (comparable to the old Arpanet and Multics programs) would be highly beneficial for security research. It is important that contemporary projects, both inside and outside universities, be encouraged to use state-of-the art software development tools and security techniques, in order to evaluate these tools and to assess the expected gain in system security. Also, while academic computer security research traditionally has been

---

BOX 1.8 *Continued*

graphics tools that allow system operators to set, explore, and analyze proposed policies (who should get access to what) and system configurations (who has access to what) may help identify weaknesses or unwanted restrictions as policies are instituted and deployed systems used.

• *Automated security procedures*—Research is needed in automating critical aspects of system operation, to assist the system manager in avoiding security faults in this area. Examples include tools to check the security state of a system, models of operational requirements and desired controls, and threat assessment aids.

• *Nonrepudiation*—To protect proprietary rights it may be necessary to record user actions so as to bar the user from later repudiating these actions. Doing this in a way that respects the privacy of users is difficult.

• *Resource control*—Resource control is associated with the prevention of unauthorized use of proprietary software or databases legitimately installed in a computing system. It has attracted little research and implementation effort, but it poses some difficult technical problems and possibly problems related to privacy as well.

• *Systems with security perimeters*—Network protocol design efforts have tended to assume that networks will provide general interconnection. However, as observed in Chapter 3, a common practical approach to achieving security in distributed systems is to partition the system into regions that are separated by a security perimeter. This may cause a loss of network functionality. If, for example, a network permits mail but not directory services (because of security concerns about directory searches), less mail may be sent because no capability exists to look up the address of a recipient.

---

performed in computer science departments, several study areas are clearly appropriate for researchers based in business schools, including assessing the actual value to an organization of information technology and of protecting privacy.

DARPA has a tradition of funding significant system development projects of the kind that can be highly beneficial for security research. Examples of valuable projects include:

• Use of state-of-the-art software development techniques and tools to produce a secure system. The explicit goal of such an effort should be to evaluate the development process and to assess the expected gain in system quality. The difficulty of uncovering vulnerabilities through testing suggests that a marriage of traditional software engineering techniques with formal methods is needed.

• Development of distributed systems with a variety of security properties. A project now under way, with DARPA funding, is the development of encryption-based private electronic mail. Another such project could focus on decentralized, peer-connected name servers.

• Development of a system supporting some approach to data integrity. There are now some proposed models for integrity, but without worked examples it will be impossible to validate them. This represents an opportunity for DARPA-NIST cooperation.

In addition to funding specific relevant projects, both DARPA and NSF should encourage collaboration across research fields. Cross-disciplinary research in the following areas would strengthen system trustworthiness:

• *Safety:* There is growing concern about and interest in the safety-related aspects of computer processing both in the United States and internationally.

• *Fault-tolerant computing:* Much research has been directed at the problem of fault-tolerant computing, and an attempt should be made to extend this work to other aspects of security.

• *Code analysis:* People working on optimizing and parallelizing compilers have extensive experience in analyzing both source and object code for a variety of properties. An attempt should be made to see if similar techniques can be used to analyze code for properties related to security.

• *Security interfaces:* People working in the area of formal specification should be encouraged to specify standardized interfaces to security services and to apply their techniques to the specification and analysis of high-level security properties.

• *Theoretical research:* Theoretical work needs to be properly integrated in actual systems. Often both theoreticians and system practitioners misunderstand the system aspects of security or the theoretical limitations of secure algorithms.

• *Programming language research:* New paradigms require new security models, new design and analysis techniques, perhaps additional constructs, and persuasion of both researchers and users that security is important before too many tools proliferate.

• *Software development environments:* Myriad tools (e.g., theorem provers, test coverage monitors, object managers, and interface packages) continue to be developed by researchers, sometimes in collaborative efforts such as Arcadia. Some strategy for integrating such tools is needed to drive the research toward more system-oriented solutions.[31]

Again, much of this research is appropriate for both commercial and academic entities, and it might require or benefit from industry-university collaboration. Certainly, joint industry-university efforts may facilitate the process of technology transfer. NSF and DARPA have a tradition of working with the broad science community and could obviously take on programs to facilitate needed collaboration. Some possible specific actions are suggested in Chapter 8.

### Recommendation 6
### Establish an Information Security Foundation

The public needs an institution that will accelerate the commercialization and adoption of safer and more secure computer and communications systems. To meet that need, the committee recommends the establishment of a new private organization—a consortium of computer users, vendors, and other interested parties (e.g., property and casualty insurers). This organization must not be, or even be perceived to be, a captive of government, system vendors, or individual segments of the user community.

The committee recommends a new institution because it concludes that pressing needs in the following areas are not likely to be met adequately by existing entities:

- Establishment of Generally Accepted System Security Principles, or GSSP;
- Research on computer system security, including evaluation techniques;
- System evaluation;
- Development and maintenance of an incident, threat, and vulnerability tracking system;
- Education and training;
- Brokering and enhancing communications between commercial and national security interests; and
- Focused participation in international standardization and harmonization efforts for commercial security practice.

Why should these functions be combined in a single organization? Although the proposed organization would not have a monopoly on all of these functions, the committee believes that the functions are synergistic. For example, involvement in research would help the organization recruit technically talented staff; involvement in research and the development of GSSP would inform the evaluation effort; and involvement in GSSP development and evaluation would inform education, training, and contributions to international criteria-setting and evaluation schemes. Further, a new organization would have more flexibility than those currently focused on security to build strong bridges to other aspects of trust, notably safety.

In the short run, this organization, called the Information Security Foundation (ISF) in this report, would act to increase awareness and expectations regarding system security and safety. The pressure provided by organized tracking and reporting of faults would encourage vendors and users to pay greater attention to system quality; the development and promulgation of GSSP should cause users and vendors to focus on an accepted base of prudent practice.

In the longer term, a major activity of the ISF would be product evaluation. The complex and critical nature of security products makes independent evaluation essential. The only current official source of evaluations, the NCSC, has been criticized as poorly suited to meeting industry's needs, and changes in its charter and direction are reducing its role in this area. The process of evaluation described in Chapters 5 and 7 is intended to address directly industry's concerns with the current process and to define a program that can be a success in the commercial marketplace. The committee concludes that some form of system evaluation is a critical aspect of achieving any real improvement in computer security.

Also in the longer term, the ISF would work to bridge the security and safety arenas, using as vehicles GSSP and evaluation as well as the other activities. The ISF could play a critical role in improving the overall quality and trustworthiness of computer systems, using the need for better security as an initial target to motivate its activities.

The organization envisioned must be designed to interact closely with government, specifically the NCSC and NIST, so that its results can contribute to satisfying government needs. Similarly, it would coordinate with operational organizations such as DARPA's CERT, especially if the CERT proceeds with its plans to develop an emergency-incident tracking capability. The government may be the best vehicle to launch the ISF, but it should be an independent, private organization once functional.

As discussed in detail in Chapter 7, the committee concludes that the ISF would need the highest level of governmental support; the strongest expression of such support would be a special congressional charter. Such a charter would define ISF's role and its relation to the government. At the same time, the organization should be outside of the government to keep it separate from the focus on intragovernmental security needs, internecine political squabbles, and the hiring and resource limitations that constrain NCSC and NIST. Its major source of funds should be member subscriptions and fees for services such as evaluation. It must not depend on government funding for its viability.

Note that the mission outlined above is much more challenging than defining standards or providing evaluation of consumer durables (e.g., as done by Underwriters Laboratories, Inc.). The committee does not know of any existing private organization that could take on these tasks.

Although it recognizes that any proposal for establishing a new institution faces an uphill battle, the committee sees this proposal as a test of commitment for industry, which has complained loudly about the existing institutional infrastructure. Commitment to an organization like that proposed can facilitate self-regulation and greatly diminish the likelihood of explicit government regulation.

If a new organization is not established—or if the functions proposed for it are not pursued in an aggressive and well-funded manner, the most immediate consequence will be the further discouraging of efforts by vendors to develop evaluated products, even though evaluation is vital to assuring that products are indeed trustworthy; the continuation of a slow rate of progress in the market, leaving many system users unprotected and unaware of the risks they face; and the prospect that U.S. vendors will become less competitive in the international systems market. Without aggressive action to increase system trustworthiness, the national exposure to safety and security catastrophes will increase rapidly.

## CONCLUSION

Getting widely deployed and more effective computer and communications security is essential if the United States is to fully achieve the promise of the Information Age. The technology base is changing, and the proliferation of networks and distributed systems has increased the risks of threats to security and safety. The computer and communications security problem is growing. Progress is needed on many fronts—including management, development, research, legal enforcement, and institutional support—to integrate security into the development and use of computer and communications technology and to make it a constructive and routine component of information systems.

## NOTES

1.   Losses from credit card and communications fraud alone investigated by the Secret Service range into the millions. See Box 1.1 for other examples.

2. This growth may be aided by recent political changes in Eastern Europe and the Soviet Union, which are believed to be freeing up intelligence resources that analysts suggest may be redirected toward economic and technological targets (Safire, 1990).

3. Voting systems present special challenges: First, the data is public property. Second, voting systems are information systems deployed to strange locations, handled by volunteers, abused by the media ("got to know the results by 8 p.m."), and offered by specialty vendors. Third, the openness issue can be evaded by vendors promoting proprietary approaches, in the absence of any organized screening or regulatory activity. Fourth, the security overhead in the system cannot get in the way of the operations of the system under what are always difficult conditions. Voting system technology makes an interesting case study because it is inherently system-oriented: ballot preparation, input sensing, data recording and transmission, pre-election testing, intrusion prevention, result preservation, and reporting. The variety of product responses are therefore immense, and each product must fit as wide a range of voting situations as possible, and be attractive and cost-effective. Anecdotal evidence suggests a range of security problems for this comparatively new application. (Hoffman, 1988; ECRI, 1988b; Saltman, 1988; miscellaneous issues of RISKS.)

4. Viruses can spread by means of or independently of networks (e.g., via contaminated diskettes).

5. The committee did not find evidence of significant Japanese activity in computer security, although viruses have begun to raise concern in Japan as evidenced by Japanese newspaper articles, and Japanese system development interests provide a foundation for possible eventual action. For competitive reasons, both Japanese and European developments should be closely monitored.

6. A new organization, the Electronic Frontiers Foundation, has recently been launched to defend these free speech aspects.

7. For example, professional journals and meetings have held numerous debates over the interpretation of the Internet worm and the behavior of its perpetrator; the Internet worm also prompted the issuance or reissuance of codes of ethics by a variety of computer specialist organizations.

8. Two recent studies have pointed to the increased concern with security in networks: The congressional Office of Technology Assessment's *Critical Connections: Communication for the Future* (OTA, 1990) and the National Research Council's *Growing Vulnerability of the Public Switched Networks* (NRC, 1989b).

9. This evolution took roughly two centuries in the case of safecracking, a technology whose systems consist of a box, a door, and a lock.

10. This does not mean that the effort was wasted. In fact, some would argue that this is the height of success (Tzu, 1988).

11. For example, a California prosecutor recently observed that "We probably turn down more cases [involving computer break-ins] than we charge, because computer-system proprietors haven't made clear what is allowed and what isn't" (Stipp, 1990).

12. For example, a description of a magnetic door sensor that is highly selective about the magnetic field it will recognize as indicating "door closed" can indicate to attackers that less sophisticated sensors can be misled by placing a strong magnet near them before opening the door.

13. For example, the GAO recently noted in connection with the numerous penetrations of the Space Physics Analysis Network in the 1980s that, "Skillful, unauthorized users could enter and exit a computer without being detected. In such cases and even in those instances where NASA has detected illegal entry, data could have been copied, altered, or destroyed without NASA or anyone else knowing" (GAO, 1989e, p. 1).

14. "Programming" is to be understood in a general sense—anything that modifies or extends the capabilities of a system is programming. Modification of controls on access to a system, for example, is a type of programming with significant security implications. Even special-purpose systems with no access to programming languages, not even to a "shell" or command language, are usually programmable in this sense.

15. "Embeddedness" refers to the extent to which a computer system is embedded in a process, and it correlates with the degree to which the process is controlled by the computer. Computer-controlled X-ray machines and manufacturing systems, avionics systems, and missiles are examples of embedded systems. Higher degrees of embeddedness, generated by competitive pressures that drive the push for automation, shorten the link between information and action and increase the potential for irreversible actions taken without human intervention. By automating much of a process, embeddedness increases the leverage of an attacker.

16. However, sometimes there will be trade-offs between security or safety and other characteristics, like performance. Such trade-offs are not unique to computing, although they may be comparatively more recent.

17. It is worth noting, however, that "safety factors" play a role in security. Measures such as audit trails are included in security systems as a safety factor; they provide a backup mechanism for detection when something else breaks.

18. Even NSA is confronting budget cuts in the context of overall cuts in defense spending.

19. For example, the American Institute of Certified Public Accountants promulgates Statements on Auditing Standards (SAS), and the Financial Accounting Standards Board (FASB) promulgates what have been called Generally Accepted Accounting Principles (GAAP). Managers accept the importance of both the standards and their enforcement as a risk management tool. Adherence to these standards is also encouraged by laws and regulations that seek to protect investors and the public. (See Appendix D.)

20. B1 is also the highest level to which systems can effectively be retrofitted with security features.

21. An effort by several large commercial users to list desired computer and communications system security features demonstrates the importance of greater integrity protection and the emphasis on discretionary access control in that community. This effort appears to place relatively limited emphasis on assurance and evaluation, both of which the committee deem important to GSSP and to an ideal set of criteria. The seed for that effort was a project within American Express Travel Related Services to define a corporate security standard called C2-Plus and based, as the name suggests, on the Orange Book's C2 criteria (Cutler and Jones, 1990).

22. In the past decade, a number of organizations (e.g., Corporation for Open Systems and the formerly independent Manufacturing Automation Protocol/Technical Office Protocol Users Group) have emerged with the goal of influencing the development of industry standards for computing and communications technology and promoting the use of official standards, in part by facilitating conformance testing (Frenkel, 1990).

23. The Computer Security Act of 1987, for example, set in motion a process aimed at improving security planning in federal agencies. The experience showed that it was easier to achieve compliance on paper than to truly strengthen planning and management controls (GAO, 1990c).

24. Examples include ISO 7498-2 (ISO, 1989), CCITT X.509 (CCITT, 1989b), and the NSA-launched Secure Data Network System (SDNS) standardization program.

25. The very availability of such tools puts an extra responsibility on management to eliminate the kinds of vulnerabilities the tools reveal.

26. For example, discussions of different project management structures would

deal with their impact not only on productivity but also on security. Discussions of quality assurance would emphasize safety engineering more than might be expected in a traditional software engineering program.

27.   It is expensive for vendors to maintain two versions of products—secure and regular. Thus, all else being equal, regular versions can be expected to be displaced by secure versions. But if sales are restricted, then only the regular version will be marketed, to the detriment of security.

28.   As this report goes to press, a case is under consideration at the Department of State that could result in liberalized export of DES chips, although such an outcome is considered unlikely.

29.   As of this writing, similar actions may also be necessary in connection with the RSA public-key encryption system, which is already available overseas (without patent protection) because its principles were first published in an academic journal (Rivest et al., 1978).

30.   The paucity of academic effort is reflected by the fact that only 5 to 10 percent of the attendees at recent IEEE Symposiums on Security and Privacy have been from universities.

31.   For vendors, related topics would be trusted distribution and trusted configuration control over the product life cycle.

# 2

# Concepts of Information Security

This chapter discusses security policies in the context of requirements for information security and the circumstances in which those requirements must be met, examines common principles of management control, and reviews typical system vulnerabilities, in order to motivate consideration of the specific sorts of security mechanisms that can be built into computer systems—to complement nontechnical management controls and thus implement policy—and to stress the significance of establishing GSSP. Additional information on privacy issues and detailing the results of an informal survey of commercial security officers is provided in the two chapter appendixes.

Organizations and people that use computers can describe their needs for information security and trust in systems in terms of three major requirements:

- Confidentiality: controlling who gets to read information;
- Integrity: assuring that information and programs are changed only in a specified and authorized manner; and
- Availability: assuring that authorized users have continued access to information and resources.

These three requirements may be emphasized differently in various applications. For a national defense system, the chief concern may be ensuring the confidentiality of classified information, whereas a funds transfer system may require strong integrity controls. The requirements for applications that are connected to external systems will differ from those for applications without such interconnection. Thus the specific requirements and controls for information security can vary.

The framework within which an organization strives to meet its needs for information security is codified as security policy. A *security policy* is a concise statement, by those responsible for a system (e.g., senior management), of information values, protection responsibilities, and organizational commitment. One can implement that policy by taking specific actions guided by management control principles and utilizing specific security standards, procedures, and mechanisms. Conversely, the selection of standards, procedures, and mechanisms should be guided by policy to be most effective.

To be useful, a security policy must not only state the security need (e.g., for confidentiality—that data shall be disclosed only to authorized individuals), but also address the range of circumstances under which that need must be met and the associated operating standards. Without this second part, a security policy is so general as to be useless (although the second part may be realized through procedures and standards set to implement the policy). In any particular circumstance, some threats are more probable than others, and a prudent policy setter must assess the threats, assign a level of concern to each, and state a policy in terms of which threats are to be resisted. For example, until recently most policies for security did not require that security needs be met in the face of a virus attack, because that form of attack was uncommon and not widely understood. As viruses have escalated from a hypothetical to a commonplace threat, it has become necessary to rethink such policies in regard to methods of distribution and acquisition of software. Implicit in this process is management's choice of a level of residual risk that it will live with, a level that varies among organizations.

*Management controls* are the mechanisms and techniques—administrative, procedural, and technical—that are instituted to implement a security policy. Some management controls are explicitly concerned with protecting information and information systems, but the concept of management controls includes much more than a computer's specific role in enforcing security. Note that management controls not only are used by managers, but also may be exercised by users. An effective program of management controls is needed to cover all aspects of information security, including physical security, classification of information, the means of recovering from breaches of security, and above all training to instill awareness and acceptance by people. There are trade-offs among controls. For example, if technical controls are not available, then procedural controls might be used until a technical solution is found.

Technical measures alone cannot prevent violations of the trust people place in individuals, violations that have been the source of much of the computer security problem in industry to date (see Chapter 6). Technical measures may prevent people from doing unauthorized things but cannot prevent them from doing things that their job functions entitle them to do. Thus, to prevent violations of trust rather than just repair the damage that results, one must depend primarily on human awareness of what other human beings in an organization are doing. But even a technically sound system with informed and watchful management and users cannot be free of all possible vulnerabilities. The residual risk must be managed by auditing, backup, and recovery procedures supported by general alertness and creative responses. Moreover, an organization must have administrative procedures in place to bring peculiar actions to the attention of someone who can legitimately inquire into the appropriateness of such actions, and that person must actually make the inquiry. In many organizations, these administrative provisions are far less satisfactory than are the technical provisions for security.

A major conclusion of this report is that the lack of a clear articulation of security policy for general computing is a major impediment to improved security in computer systems. Although the Department of Defense (DOD) has articulated its requirements for controls to ensure confidentiality, there is no articulation for systems based on other requirements and management controls (discussed below)—individual accountability, separation of duty, auditability, and recovery. This committee's goal of developing a set of Generally Accepted System Security Principles, GSSP, is intended to address this deficiency and is a central recommendation of this report.

In computing there is no generally accepted body of prudent practice analogous to the Generally Accepted Accounting Principles promulgated by the Financial Auditing Standards Board (see Appendix D). Managers who have never seen adequate controls for computer systems may not appreciate the capabilities currently available to them, or the risks they are taking by operating without these controls. Faced with demands for more output, they have had no incentive to spend money on controls. Reasoning like the following is common: "Can't do it and still stay competitive"; "We've never had any trouble, so why worry"; "The vendor didn't put it in the product; there's nothing we can do."

On the basis of reported losses, such attitudes are not unjustified (Neumann, 1989). However, computers are active entities, and programs can be changed in a twinkling, so that past happiness is no predictor of future bliss. There has to be only one Internet worm incident to signal a larger problem. Experience since the Internet worm involving copy-cat and derivative attacks shows how a possibility once demonstrated can become an actuality frequently used.[1]

Some consensus does exist on fundamental or minimum-required security mechanisms. A recent informal survey conducted on behalf of the committee shows a widespread desire among corporate system managers and security officers for the ability to identify users and limit times and places of access, particularly over networks, and to watch for intrusion by recording attempts at invalid actions (see Chapter Appendix 2.2). Ad hoc virus checkers, well known in the personal computer market, are also in demand. However, there is little demand for system managers to be able to obtain positive confirmation that the software running on their systems today is the same as what was running yesterday. Such a simple analog of hardware diagnostics should be a fundamental requirement; it may not be seen as such because vendors do not offer it or because users have difficulty expressing their needs.

Although threats and policies for addressing them are different for different applications, they nevertheless have much in common, and the general systems on which applications are built are often the same. Furthermore, basic security services can work against many threats and support many policies. Thus there is a large core of policies and services on which most of the users of computers should be able to agree. On this basis the committee proposes the effort to define and articulate GSSP.

## SECURITY POLICIES—RESPONDING TO REQUIREMENTS FOR CONFIDENTIALITY, INTEGRITY, AND AVAILABILITY

The weight given to each of the three major requirements describing needs for information security—confidentiality, integrity, and availability—depends strongly on circumstances. For example, the adverse effects of a system not being available must be related in part to requirements for recovery time. A system that must be restored within an hour after disruption represents, and requires, a more demanding set of policies and controls than does a similar system that need not be restored for two to three days. Likewise, the risk of loss of confidentiality with respect to a major product announcement will change with time. Early disclosure may jeopardize competitive advantage, but disclosure just before the intended announcement may be insignificant. In this case the information remains the same, while the timing of its release significantly affects the risk of loss.

### Confidentiality

*Confidentiality* is a requirement whose purpose is to keep sensitive information from being disclosed to unauthorized recipients. The secrets might be important for reasons of national security (nuclear weapons data), law enforcement (the identities of undercover drug agents), competitive advantage (manufacturing costs or bidding plans), or personal privacy (credit histories) (see Chapter Appendix 2.1).

The most fully developed policies for confidentiality reflect the concerns of the U.S. national security community, because this community has been willing to pay to get policies defined and implemented (and because the value of the information it seeks to protect is deemed very high). Since the scope of threat is very broad in this context, the policy requires systems to be robust in the face of a wide variety of attacks. The specific DOD policies for ensuring confidentiality do not explicitly itemize the range of expected threats for which a policy must hold. Instead, they reflect an operational approach, expressing the policy by stating the particular management controls that must be used to achieve the requirement for confidentiality. Thus they avoid listing threats, which would represent a severe risk in itself, and avoid the risk of poor security design implicit in taking a fresh approach to each new problem.

The operational controls that the military has developed in support of this requirement involve automated mechanisms for handling information that is critical to national security. Such mechanisms call for information to be classified at different levels of sensitivity and in isolated compartments, to be labeled with this classification, and to be handled by people cleared for access to particular levels and/or compartments. Within each level and compartment, a person with an appropriate clearance must also have a "need to know" in order to gain access. These procedures are mandatory: elaborate procedures must also be followed to declassify information.[2]

Classification policies exist in other settings, reflecting a general recognition that to protect assets it is helpful to identify and categorize them. Some commercial firms, for instance, classify information as restricted, company confidential, and unclassified (Schmitt, 1990). Even if an organization has no secrets of its own, it may be obliged by law or common courtesy to preserve the privacy of information about individuals. Medical records, for example, may require more careful protection than does most proprietary information. A hospital must thus select a suitable confidentiality policy to uphold its fiduciary responsibility with respect to patient records.

In the commercial world confidentiality is customarily guarded by security mechanisms that are less stringent than those of the national security community. For example, information is assigned to an "owner" (or guardian), who controls access to it.[3] Such security mechanisms are capable of dealing with many situations but are not as resistant to certain attacks as are mechanisms based on classification and mandatory labeling, in part because there is no way to tell where copies of information may flow. With Trojan horse attacks, for example, even legitimate and honest users of an owner mechanism can be tricked into disclosing secret data. The commercial world has borne these vulnerabilities in exchange for the greater operational flexibility and system performance currently associated with relatively weak security.

## Integrity

*Integrity* is a requirement meant to ensure that information and programs are changed only in a specified and authorized manner. It may be important to keep data consistent (as in double-entry bookkeeping) or to allow data to be changed only in an approved manner (as in withdrawals from a bank account). It may also be necessary to specify the degree of the accuracy of data.

Some policies for ensuring integrity reflect a concern for preventing fraud and are stated in terms of management controls. For example, any task involving the potential for fraud must be divided into parts that are performed by separate people, an approach called separation of duty. A classic example is a purchasing system, which has three parts: ordering, receiving, and payment. Someone must sign off on each step, the same person cannot sign off on two steps, and the records can be changed only by fixed procedures—for example, an account is debited and a check written only for the amount of an approved and received order. In this case, although the policy is stated operationally—that is, in terms of specific management controls—the threat model is explicitly disclosed as well.

Other integrity policies reflect concerns for preventing errors and omissions, and controlling the effects of program change. Integrity policies have not been studied as carefully as confidentiality policies. Computer measures that have been installed to guard integrity tend to be ad hoc and do not flow from the integrity models that have been proposed (see Chapter 3).

## Availability

*Availability* is a requirement intended to ensure that systems work promptly and service is not denied to authorized users. From an operational standpoint, this requirement refers to adequate response time and/or guaranteed bandwidth. From a security standpoint, it represents the ability to protect against and recover from a damaging event. The availability of properly functioning computer systems (e.g., for routing long-distance calls or handling airline reservations) is essential to the operation of many large enterprises and sometimes for preserving lives (e.g., air traffic control or automated medical systems). Contingency planning is concerned with assessing risks and developing plans for averting or recovering from adverse events that might render a system unavailable.

Traditional contingency planning to ensure availability usually includes responses only to acts of God (e.g., earthquakes) or accidental anthropogenic events (e.g., a toxic gas leak preventing entry to a facility). However, contingency planning must also involve providing for responses to malicious acts, not simply acts of God or accidents, and as such must include an explicit assessment of threat based on a model of a real adversary, not on a probabilistic model of nature.

For example, a simple availability policy is usually stated like this: "On the average, a terminal shall be down for less than 10 minutes per month." A particular terminal (e.g., an automatic teller machine or a reservation agent's keyboard and screen) is up if it responds correctly within one second to a standard request for service; otherwise it is down. This policy means that the up time at each terminal, averaged over all the terminals, must be at least 99.98 percent.

A security policy to ensure availability usually takes a different form, as in the following example: "No inputs to the system by any user who is not an authorized administrator shall cause the system to cease serving some other user." Note that this policy does not say anything about system failures, except to the extent that they can be caused by user actions. Instead, it identifies a particular threat, a malicious or incompetent act by a regular user of the system, and requires the system to survive this act. It says nothing about other ways in which a hostile party could deny service, for example, by cutting a telephone line; a separate assertion is required for each such threat, indicating the extent to which resistance to that threat is deemed important.

## Examples of Security Requirements for Different Applications

The exact security needs of systems will vary from application to application even within a single application. As a result, organizations must both understand their applications and think through the relevant choices to achieve the appropriate level of security.

An automated teller system, for example, must keep personal identification numbers (PINs) confidential, both in the host system and during transmission for a transaction. It must protect the integrity of account records and of individual transactions. Protection of privacy is important, but not critically so. Availability of the host system is important to the economic survival of the bank, although not to its fiduciary responsibility. As compared to the availability of the host system, the availability of individual teller machines is of less concern.

A telephone switching system, on the other hand, does not have high requirements for integrity on individual transactions, as lasting damage will not be incurred by occasionally losing a call or billing record. The integrity of control programs and configuration records, however, is critical. Without these, the switching function would be defeated and the most important attribute of all—availability—would be compromised. A telephone switching system must also preserve the confidentiality of individual calls, preventing one caller from overhearing another.

Security needs are determined more by what a system is used for than by what it is. A typesetting system, for example, will have to assure confidentiality if it is being used to publish corporate proprietary material, integrity if it is being used to publish laws, and availability if it is being used to publish a daily paper. A general-purpose time-sharing system might be expected to provide confidentiality if it serves diverse clientele, integrity if it is used as a development environment for software or engineering designs, and availability to the extent that no one user can monopolize the service and that lost files will be retrievable.

## MANAGEMENT CONTROLS—CHOOSING THE MEANS TO SECURE INFORMATION AND OPERATIONS

The setting of security policy is a basic responsibility of management within an organization. Management has a duty to preserve and protect assets and to maintain the quality of service. To this end it must assure that operations are carried out prudently in the face of realistic risks arising from credible threats. This duty may be fulfilled by defining high-level security policies and then translating these policies into specific standards and procedures for selecting and nurturing personnel, for checking and auditing operations, for establishing contingency plans, and so on. Through these actions, management may prevent, detect, and recover from loss. Recovery depends on various forms of insurance: backup records, redundant systems and service sites, self-insurance by cash reserves, and purchased insurance to offset the cost of recovery.

### Preventing Breaches of Security—Basic Principles

Management controls are intended to guide operations in proper directions, prevent or detect mischief and harmful mistakes, and give early warning of vulnerabilities. Organizations in almost every line of endeavor have established controls based on the following key principles:

- Individual accountability,
- Auditing, and
- Separation of duty.

These principles, recognized in some form for centuries, are the basis of precomputer operating procedures that are very well understood.

*Individual accountability* answers the question: Who is responsible for this statement or action? Its purpose is to keep track of what has happened, of who has had access to information and resources and what actions have been taken. In any real system there are many reasons why actual operation may not always reflect the original intentions of the owners: people make mistakes, the system has errors, the system is vulnerable to certain attacks, the broad policy was not translated correctly into detailed specifications, the owners changed their minds, and so on. When things go wrong, it is necessary to know what has happened, and who is the cause. This information is the basis for assessing damage, recovering lost information, evaluating vulnerabilities, and initiating compensating actions, such as legal prosecution, outside the computer system.

To support the principle of individual accountability, the service called *user authentication* is required. Without reliable identification, there can be no accountability. Thus authentication is a crucial underpinning of information security. Many systems have been penetrated when weak or poorly administered authentication services have been compromised, for example, by guessing poorly chosen passwords.

The basic service provided by authentication is information that a statement or action was made by a particular user. Sometimes, however, there is a need to ensure that the user will not later be able to claim that a statement attributed to him was forged and that he never made it. In the world of paper documents, this is the purpose of notarizing a signature; the notary provides independent and highly credible evidence, which will be convincing even after many years, that a signature is genuine and not forged. This more stringent form of authentication, called *nonrepudiation*, is offered by few computer systems today, although a legal need for it can be foreseen as computer-mediated transactions become more common in business.

*Auditing* services support accountability and therefore are valuable to management and to internal or external auditors. Given the reality that every computer system can be compromised from within, and that many systems can also be compromised if surreptitious access can be gained, accountability is a vital last resort. Auditing services make and keep the records necessary to support accountability. Usually they are closely tied to authentication and authorization (a service for determining whether a user or system is trusted for a given purpose—see discussion below), so that every authentication is recorded, as is every attempted access, whether authorized or not. Given the critical role of auditing, auditing devices are sometimes the first target of an attacker and should be protected accordingly.

A system's audit records, often called an audit trail, have other potential uses besides establishing accountability. It may be possible, for example, to analyze an audit trail for suspicious patterns of access and so detect improper behavior by both legitimate users and masqueraders. The main drawbacks are processing and interpreting the audit data.

Systems may change constantly as personnel and equipment come and go and applications evolve. From a security standpoint, a changing system is not likely to be an improving system. To take an active stand against gradual erosion of security measures, one may supplement a dynamically collected audit trail (which is useful in ferreting out what has happened) with static audits that check the configuration to see that it is not open for attack. Static audit services may check that software has not changed, that file access controls are properly set, that obsolete user accounts have been turned off, that incoming and outgoing communications lines are correctly enabled, that passwords are hard to guess, and so on. Aside from virus checkers, few static audit tools exist in the market.

The well-established practice of *separation of duty* specifies that important operations cannot be performed by a single person but instead require the agreement of (at least) two different people. Separation of duty thus strengthens security by preventing any single-handed subversion of the controls. It can also help reduce errors by providing for an independent check of one person's actions by another.

Separation of duty is an example of a broader class of controls that attempt to specify who is trusted for a given purpose. This sort of control is generally known as user *authorization*. Authorization determines whether a particular user, who has been authenticated as the source of a request to do something, is trusted for that operation. Authorization may also include controls on the time at which something can be done (only during working hours) or the computer terminal from which it can be requested (only the one on the manager's desk).

Just as the goal of individual accountability requires a lower-level mechanism for user authentication, so also do authorization controls such as separation of duty require a lower-level mechanism to ensure that users have access only to the correct objects. Inside the computer, these enforcement mechanisms are usually called *access control mechanisms*.

### Responding to Breaches of Security

*Recovery controls* provide the means to respond to, rather than prevent, a security breach. The use of a recovery mechanism does not necessarily indicate a system shortcoming; for some threats, detection and recovery may well be more cost-effective than attempts at total prevention. Recovery from a security breach may involve taking disciplinary or legal action, notifying incidentally compromised parties, or changing policies, for example. From a technical standpoint, a security breach has much in common with a failure that results from faulty equipment, software, or operations. Usually some work will have to be discarded, and some or all of the system will have to be rolled back to a clean state.

Security breaches usually entail more recovery effort than do acts of God. Unlike proverbial lightning, breaches of security can be counted on to strike twice unless the route of compromise has been shut off. Causes must be located. Were passwords compromised? Are backups clean? Did some user activity compromise the system by mistake? And major extra work—changing all passwords, rebuilding the system from original copies, shutting down certain communication links or introducing authentication procedures on them, or undertaking more user education—may have to be done to prevent a recurrence.

## DEVELOPING POLICIES AND APPROPRIATE CONTROLS

Ideally a comprehensive spectrum of security measures would ensure that the confidentiality, integrity, and availability of computer-based systems were appropriately maintained. In practice it is not possible to make ironclad guarantees. The only recipe for perfect security is perfect isolation: nothing in, nothing out. This is impractical, and so security policies will always reflect trade-offs between cost and risk. The assets to be protected should be categorized by value, the vulnerabilities by importance, and the risks by severity, and defensive measures should be installed accordingly. Residual vulnerabilities should be recognized.

Planning a security program is somewhat like buying insurance. An organization considers the following:

- The value of the assets being protected.
- The vulnerabilities of the system: possible types of compro-

mise, of users as well as systems. What damage can the person in front of the automated teller machine do? What about the person behind it?[4]

• Threats: do adversaries exist to exploit these vulnerabilities? Do they have a motive, that is, something to gain? How likely is attack in each case?

• Risks: the costs of failures and recovery. What is the worst credible kind of failure? Possibilities are death, injury, compromise to national security, industrial espionage, loss of personal privacy, financial fraud, election fraud.

• The organization's degree of risk aversion.

Thence follows a rough idea of expected losses. On the other side of the ledger are these:

• Available countermeasures (controls and security services),
• Their effectiveness, and
• Their direct costs and the opportunity costs of installing them.

The security plans then become a business decision, possibly tempered by legal requirements and consideration of externalities (see "Risks and Vulnerabilities," below).

Ideally, controls are chosen as the result of careful analysis.[5] In practice, the most important consideration is what controls are available. Most purchasers of computer systems cannot afford to have a system designed from scratch to meet their needs, a circumstance that seems particularly true in the case of security needs. The customer is thus reduced to selecting from among the various preexisting solutions, with the hope that one will match the identified needs.

Some organizations formalize the procedure for managing computer-associated risk by using a control matrix that identifies appropriate control measures for given vulnerabilities over a range of risks. Using such a matrix as a guide, administrators may better select appropriate controls for various resources. A rough cut at addressing the problem is often taken: How much business depends on the system? What is the worst credible kind of failure, and how much would it cost to recover? Do available mechanisms address possible causes? Are they cost-effective?

The computer industry can be expected to respond to clearly articulated security needs provided that such needs apply to a broad enough base of customers. This has happened with the Orange Book vis à vis the defense community—but slowly, because vendors were not convinced the customer base was large enough to warrant accelerated investments in trust technology.

However, for many of the management controls discussed above, there is not a clear, widely accepted articulation of how computer systems should be designed to support these controls, what sort of robustness is required in the mechanisms, and so on. As a result, customers for computer security are faced with a "take-it-or-leave-it" marketplace. For instance, customers appear to demand password-based authentication because it is available, not because analysis has shown that this relatively weak mechanism provides enough protection. This effect works in both directions: a service is not demanded if it is not available, but once it becomes available somewhere, it soon becomes wanted everywhere. See Chapter 6 for a discussion of the marketplace.

## RISKS AND VULNERABILITIES

Risks arise because an attack could exploit some system vulnerability (see, for example, Boxes 2.1 and 2.2). That is, each vulnerability of a system reflects a potential threat, with corresponding risks. In a sampling of a collection of over 3,000 cases of computer system abuse, drawn from the media and personal reporting, the following types of attack, listed roughly in order of decreasing frequency, predominated (Neumann and Parker, 1989):

• Misusing authority, through activities such as improper acquisition of resources (reading of data, theft of programs), surreptitious modification, and denials of service, apparently by authorized users.

• Masquerading, as in one user impersonating another.

• Bypassing intended controls, by means such as password attacks and exploitation of trapdoors. These attacks typically exploit system flaws or hidden circumventive "features."

• Setting up subsequent abuses such as Trojan horses, logic bombs, or viruses.

• Carrying out hardware and media abuses, such as physical attacks on equipment and scavenging of information from discarded media. (Electronic interference and eavesdropping also belong in this class but have not been widely detected.)

• Using a computer system as an indirect aid in committing a criminal act, as in auto-dialing telephone numbers in search of answering modems, cracking another system's encrypted password files, or running an illicit business. (For example, drug operations are becoming increasingly computerized.)

The cases considered in the sampling cited above often involved multiple classes of abuse. In attacking the National Aeronautics and Space Administration systems, the West German Chaos Computer

---

### BOX 2.1 THE WILY HACKER

In August 1986, Clifford Stoll, an astronomer working at the Lawrence Berkeley Laboratory, detected an intruder, nicknamed him the Wily Hacker, and began to monitor his intrusions. Over a period of 10 months, the Wily Hacker attacked roughly 450 computers operated by the U.S. military and its contractors, successfully gaining access to 30 of them. Prior to detection, he is believed to have mounted attacks for as long as a year.

Although originally thought to be a local prankster, the Wily Hacker turned out to be a competent and persistent computer professional in West Germany, with alleged ties to the Soviet KGB, and possibly with confederates in Germany.* It is assumed that the Wily Hacker was looking for classified or sensitive data on each of the systems he penetrated, although regulations prohibit the storage of classified data on the systems in question.

Looking for technological keywords and for passwords to other systems, the Wily Hacker exhaustively searched the electronic files and messages located on each system. He carefully concealed his presence on the computer systems and networks that he penetrated, using multiple entry points as necessary. He made long-term plans, in one instance establishing a trapdoor that he used almost a year later.

The most significant aspect of the Wily Hacker incident is that the perpetrator was highly skilled and highly motivated. Also notable is the involvement of a U.S. accomplice. Tracking the Wily Hacker required the cooperation of more than 15 organizations, including U.S. authorities, German authorities, and private corporations. The treatment of the Wily Hacker by German authorities left some in the United States unsatisfied, because under German law the absence of damage to German systems and the nature of the evidence available diminished sentencing options.

*He has been identified variously as Mathias Speer or Marcus Hess, a computer science student in Hanover.

SOURCES: Stoll (1988); Markoff (1988a).

---

Club masqueraded, bypassed access controls (partly by exploiting a subtle operating system flaw), and used Trojan horses to capture passwords. The Internet worm of November 1988 exploited weak password mechanisms and design and implementation flaws in mail-handling and information-service programs to propagate itself from machine to machine (Rochlis and Eichin, 1989; Spafford, 1989a,b). Personal computer pest programs typically use Trojan horse attacks, some with virus-like propagation.

The preceding summary of penetrations gives a good view of the present situation. However, it is unwise to extrapolate from the present to predict the classes of vulnerability that will be significant in the future. As expertise and interconnection increase and as control procedures improve, the risks and likely threats will change.[6] For example, given recent events, the frequency of Trojan horse and virus attacks is expected to increase.

Interconnection results in the vulnerability of weak links endangering other parts of an interconnected system. This phenomenon is particularly insidious when different parts of a system fall under different managements with different assessments of risk. For example, suppose computer center A used by students determines that the expected costs of recovery from plausible attacks do not justify the costs of protective measures. The center has data connections to a more sensitive government-sponsored research center B, to which some students have access. By computer eavesdropping at the student-center end, an invisible intruder learns passwords to the research installation. Somewhat paradoxically, the low guard kept at center A forces B to introduce more rigorous and costly measures to protect the supposedly innocuous communications with A than are necessary for genuinely sensitive communications with installations that are as cautious as B.

Such scenarios have been played out many times in real life. In saving money for itself, installation A has shifted costs to B, creating what economists call an externality. At the very least, it seems, installation B should be aware of the security state of A before agreeing to communicate.

System interconnection may even affect applications that do not involve communication at all: the risks of interconnection are borne not only by the applications they benefit, but also by other applications that share the same equipment. In the example given above, some applications at installation B may need to be apprised of the security state of installation A even though they never overtly communicate with A.

In some sectors, the recognition of interdependence has already affected the choice of safeguard. For example, a national funds transfer system may depend on communications lines provided by a common carrier. It is common commercial practice to trust that common carriers transmit faithfully, but for funds transfer such trust is judged to be imprudent, and cryptographic methods are used to ensure that the carrier need not be trusted for the integrity of funds transfer (although it is still trusted to ensure availability). The alternative would have been to include the carriers within the trusted funds transfer system, and work to ensure that they transmit faithfully.

## BOX 2.2 THE INTERNET WORM

The Internet, an international network of computer systems that has evolved over the last decade, provides electronic mail, file transfer, and remote log-in capabilities. Currently, the Internet interconnects several thousand individual networks (including government, commercial, and academic networks) that connect some 60,000 computers. The Internet has become the electronic backbone for computer research, development, and user communities.

On November 2, 1988, the Internet was attacked by a self-replicating program called a worm that spread within hours to somewhere between 2,000 and 6,000 computer systems—the precise number remains uncertain. Only systems (VAX and Sun 3) running certain types of Unix (variants of BSD 4) were affected.

The Internet worm was developed and launched by Robert T. Morris, Jr., who at the time was a graduate student at Cornell University. Morris exploited security weaknesses (in the fingerd, .rhosts, and sendmail programs) in the affected versions of Unix. The worm program itself did not cause any damage to the systems that it attacked in the sense that it did not steal, corrupt, or destroy data and did not alter the systems themselves; however, its rapid proliferation and the ensuing confusion caused severe degradation in service and shut down some systems and network connections throughout the Internet for two or three days, affecting sites that were not directly attacked. Ironically, electronic mail messages with guidance for containing the worm were themselves delayed because of network congestion caused by the worm's rapid replication.

Although Morris argued that the worm was an experiment unleashed without malice, he was convicted of a felony (the conviction may be appealed) under the Computer Fraud and Abuse Act (CFAA) of 1986, the first such conviction. Reflecting uncertainty about both the applicability of the CFAA and the nature of the incident, federal prosecutors were slow to investigate and bring charges in this case.

The Internet worm has received considerable attention by computing professionals, security experts, and the general public, thanks to the abundant publicity about the incident, the divided opinions within the computer community about the impact of the incident, and a general recognition that the Internet worm incident has illuminated the potential for damage from more dangerous attacks as society becomes more dependent on computer networks. The incident triggered the establishment of numerous computer emergency response teams (CERTs), starting with DARPA's CERT for the Internet; a reevaluation of ethics for computer professionals and users; and, at least temporarily, a general tightening of security in corporate and government networks.

SOURCES: Comer (1988); Spafford (1989a); Rochlis and Eichin (1989); and Neumann (1990).

In other sectors, including the research community, the design and the management of computer-mediated networks generate communication vulnerabilities. In these systems (e.g., Bitnet) messages travel lengthy paths through computers in the control of numerous organizations of which the communicants are largely unaware, and for which message handling is not a central business concern. Responsibility for the privacy and integrity of communications in these networks is so diffuse as to be nonexistent. Unlike common carriers, these networks warrant no degree of trust. This situation is understood by only some of these networks' users, and even they may gamble on the security of their transmissions in the interests of convenience and reduced expenses.

## SECURING THE WHOLE SYSTEM

Because security is a weak-link phenomenon, a security program must be multidimensional. Regardless of security policy goals, one cannot completely ignore any of the three major requirements—confidentiality, integrity, and availability—which support one another. For example, confidentiality is needed to protect passwords. Passwords in turn promote system integrity by controlling access and providing a basis for individual accountability. Confidentiality controls themselves must be immune to tampering—an integrity consideration. And in the event that things do go wrong, it must be possible for administrative and maintenance personnel to step in to fix things—an availability concern.

A system is an interdependent collection of components that can be considered as a unified whole. A computer operating system, an application such as a computerized payroll, a local network of engineering workstations, or the nationwide network for electronic funds transfer each can be considered as a system—and any one system may depend on others. All of these involve physical elements and people as well as computers and software. Physical protection includes environmental controls such as guards, locks, doors, and fences as well as protection against and recovery from fire, flood, and other natural hazards.

Although a security program must be designed from a holistic perspective, the program itself need not—indeed should not—be monolithic. It is best to operate on a divide-and-conquer principle, reflecting the classical management control principle of separation of duty. A system made of mutually distrustful parts should be stronger than a simple trusted system. On a large scale, communications links define natural boundaries of distrust. Within a single system extra strength may be gained by isolating authentication functions and auditing records in physically separate, more rigorously controlled hardware. Such isolation of function is universal in serious cryptography.

Technology alone cannot provide security. In particular, an information security program is of little avail if its users do not buy into it. The program must be realistic and maintain the awareness and commitment of all participants. Further, management actions must signal that security matters. When rewards go only to visible results (e.g., meeting deadlines or saving costs), attention will surely shift away from security—until disaster strikes.

## APPENDIX 2.1—PRIVACY

Concern for privacy arises in connection with the security of computer systems in two disparate ways:

• the need to protect personal information about people that is kept in computer systems; and
• the need to ensure that employees of an organization are complying with the organization's policies and procedures.

The first need supports privacy; the institution of policies and mechanisms for confidentiality should strengthen it. The second, however, is a case in which need is not aligned with privacy; strong auditing or surveillance measures may well infringe on the privacy of those whose actions are observed. It is important to understand both aspects of privacy.

### Protection of Information About Individuals

The need to protect personal information is addressed in several laws, notably including the Privacy Act of 1974 (P.L. 93-579), which was enacted during a period of international concern about privacy triggered by advancing computerization of personal data.[7] A number of authors who have written on the subject believe that privacy protections are stronger in other countries (Turn, 1990; Flaherty, 1990).

The Privacy Act is based on five major principles that have been generally accepted as basic privacy criteria in the United States and Europe:

1. There must be no personal data recordkeeping system whose very existence is secret.
2. There must be a way for individuals to find out what information about them is on a record and how it is used.
3. There must be a way for individuals to prevent information

obtained about them for one purpose from being used or made available for other purposes without their consent.

4. There must be a way for individuals to correct or amend a record of identifiable information about them.

5. Any organization creating, maintaining, using, or disseminating records of identifiable personal data must assure that data are used as intended and must take precautions to prevent misuse of the data.

Even where most organizations make a reasonable, conscientious effort to protect the privacy of personal information residing in their computing systems, compromisable system and data access controls often allow intruders to violate personal privacy. For example, a survey of 178 federal agencies by the General Accounting Office revealed 34 known breaches in computerized systems containing personal information in fiscal years 1988 and 1989; 30 of those incidents involved unauthorized access to the information by individuals otherwise authorized to use the systems (GAO, 1990e). Frequent reports of "hacker" invasions into credit-reporting databases and patients' medical records provide ample evidence of the general lack of appropriate protection of personal information in computer systems. Also, some applications in and of themselves appear to undermine the Privacy Act's principle that individuals should be able to control information about themselves.[8] As noted in a recent newspaper column,

> Most of us have no way of knowing all the databases that contain information about us. In short, we are losing control over the information about ourselves. Many people are not confident about existing safeguards, and few are convinced that they should have to pay for the benefits of the computer age with their personal freedoms. (Lewis, 1990)

Because of concerns about privacy, companies will increasingly need secure systems to store information. Indeed, in Canada, governmental regulation concerning the requirements for privacy of information about individuals contributed to an ongoing effort to extend the U.S. Orange Book to include specific support for privacy policy.

## Employee Privacy in the Workplace

An employer's need to ensure that employees comply with policies and procedures requires some checking by management on employees' activities involving the use of company computing resources; how much and what kind of checking are subject to debate.[9] A common management premise is that if a policy or procedure is not enforced, it will eventually not be obeyed, leading to an erosion of respect for and compliance with other policies and procedures. For instance, consider a policy stating that company computing resources will be used only for proper business purposes. Users certify upon starting their jobs (or upon introduction of the policy) that they understand and will comply with this policy and others. Random spot checks of user files by information security analysts may be conducted to ensure that personal business items, games, and so on, are not put on company computing resources. Disciplinary action may result when violations of policy are discovered.

The above situation does not, in itself, relate to security. However, one method proposed to increase the level of system security involves monitoring workers' actions to detect, for example, patterns of activity that suggest that a worker's password has been stolen. This level of monitoring provides increased opportunity to observe all aspects of worker activity, not just security-related activity, and to significantly reduce a worker's expectation for privacy at work.

Some managers argue that a worker, while performing work-related activity, should expect arbitrary supervisory observation and review and that there is no expectation of privacy in that context. This argument combines consideration of privacy with considerations of management style and philosophy, which are beyond the scope of this report. However, what is relevant to this report is the fact that computer and communications technologies facilitate greater monitoring and surveillance of employees and that needs for computer and communications security motivate monitoring and surveillance, some of which may use computer technology. As the congressional Office of Technology Assessment has noted, the effects of computer-based monitoring depend on the way it is used (OTA, 1987a).

There are complex trade-offs among privacy, management control, and more general security controls. How, for example, can management ensure that its computer facilities are being used only for legitimate business purposes if the computer system contains security features that limit access to the files of individuals? Typically, a system administrator has access to everything on a system. To prevent abuse of this privilege, a secure audit trail may be used. The goal is to prevent the interaction of the needs for control, security, and privacy from inhibiting the adequate achievement of any of the three.

Note that by tracing or monitoring the computer actions of individuals, one can violate the privacy of persons who are not in an employee relationship but are more generally clients of an organization or citizens of a country. For example, the *Wall Street Journal* reported recently that customer data entered by a travel agency into a major airline reservation system was accessible to and used by other travel service firms without the knowledge of the customer or the travel agency (Winans, 1990). Computer systems as a mechanism provide no protection for people in these situations; as was observed above, computers, even very secure computers, are only a mechanism, not a policy. Indeed, very secure systems may actually make the problem worse, if the presence of these mechanisms falsely encourages people to entrust critical information to such systems.

There is an important distinction between policy and mechanism. A computer system is a mechanism, but if there is no enforceable policy, a mechanism provides no protection. Only in the presence of an enforceable policy can any protection or assurance occur. While five basic principles that make up a recognized privacy policy are summarized above, security, as it is discussed in this report, does not provide or enforce such a policy, except in the narrow sense of protecting a system from hostile intruders. Protecting a system (or the information it contains) from the owner of the system is a totally different problem, which will become increasingly important as we proceed to a still greater use of computers in our society.

## APPENDIX 2.2—INFORMAL SURVEY TO ASSESS SECURITY REQUIREMENTS

In April 1989 informal telephone interviews were conducted by a committee member with the information security officers of 30 private companies in the aerospace, finance, food and beverage, manufacturing, petrochemical, retail, and utilities industries. Within these categories an even distribution of companies was achieved, and interviewees were distributed geographically. Individuals were asked what basic security features should be built into vendor systems (essential features)— what their requirements were and whether those requirements were being met. Their unanimous opinion was that current vendor software does not meet their basic security needs.

The survey addressed two categories of security measures: prevention and detection. Within the prevention category the focus was on three areas: computers, terminals, and telecommunications and networking.

Individuals were asked to consider 40 specific security measures. For each, they were asked whether the measure should be built into vendor systems as a mandatory (essential) item, be built in as an optional item, or not be built in.

### User Identification

All of the interviewees believed that a unique identification (ID) for each user and automatic suspension of an ID for a certain number of unauthorized access attempts were essential. The capability to prevent the simultaneous use of an ID was considered essential by 90 percent of the individuals interviewed. A comment was that this capability should be controllable based either on the ID or the source of the access.

Eighty-three percent of the interviewees agreed it is essential that the date, time, and place of last use be displayed to the user upon sign-on to the system. A comment was that this feature should also be available at other times. The same number required the capability to assign to the user an expiration date for authorization to access a system. Comments on this item were that the ability to specify a future active date for IDs was needed and that the capability to let the system administrator know when an ID was about to expire was required. Seventy-three percent thought that the capability to limit system access to certain times, days, dates, and/or from certain places was essential.

### User Verification or Authentication

All interviewees believed that preventing the reuse of expired passwords, having the system force password changes, having the password always prompted for, and having the ID and password verified at sign-on time were all essential security measures.

Ninety-seven percent judged as essential the capabilities to implement a password of six or more alphanumeric characters and to have passwords stored encrypted on the system. Eighty-seven percent believed that an automatic check to eliminate easy passwords should be an essential feature, although one individual thought that, in this case, it would be difficult to know what to check for.

Sixty percent saw the capability to interface with a dynamic password token as an essential feature. One recommendation was to investigate the use of icons that would be assigned to users as guides to selecting meaningful (easily remembered) passwords. Thirty-three percent considered a random password generator essential; 7 percent did not want one.

### File Access Control

All interviewees considered it essential to be able to limit access to files, programs, and databases. Only 60 percent thought that the capability to limit access to a specified time or day should be essential. Although all information security officers of financial organizations thought such a capability should be essential, at least some representatives from all other categories of businesses preferred that such a feature be optional.

Eighty-three percent agreed that a virus detection and protection capability and the ability to purge a file during deletion were essential features. An added comment was that vendors should be required to certify a product as being free of viruses or trapdoors. Seventy-three percent considered the capability to encrypt sensitive data to be mandatory, but one respondent was opposed to that feature because it could complicate disaster recovery (i.e., one might not be able to access such data in an emergency during processing at an alternate site). Ninety-five percent thought it should be essential to require the execution of production programs from a secure production library and also, if using encryption, to destroy the plaintext during the encryption process.

### Terminal Controls

All interviewees agreed that preventing the display of passwords on screens or reports should be essential. Ninety-five percent favored having an automated log-off/time-out capability as a mandatory feature. A comment was that it should be possible to vary this feature by ID.

Identification of terminals was a capability that 87 percent considered essential, but only two-thirds felt that a terminal lock should be included in the essential category.

An additional comment was that a token port (for dynamic password interface) should be a feature of terminals.

### Telecommunications and Networking

More than 95 percent of the interviewees believed that network security monitoring; bridge, router, and gateway filtering; and dial-in user authentication should be essential features. Also, 90 percent wanted a modem-locking device as a mandatory feature. Eighty-three to eighty-seven percent of interviewees wanted security modems (call-back authentication), data encryption, automated encryption and decryption capabilities, and the ability to automatically disconnect an unneeded modem to be regarded as essential.

Additional comments in this area addressed the need for message authentication and nonrepudiation as security features.

### Detection Measures

All interviewees believed that audit trails identifying invalid access attempts and reporting ID and terminal source identification related to invalid access attempts were essential security measures. Likewise, all agreed that violation reports (including date, time, service, violation type, ID, data sets, and so forth) and the capability to query a system's log to retrieve selected data were essential features.

Eighty-three percent were in favor of network intrusion detection, a relatively new capability, as an essential item. However, everyone also agreed on the need for improved reporting of intrusions.

### General Comments and Summary

General suggestions made in the course of the interviews included the following:

• Make requirements general rather than specific so that they can apply to all kinds of systems.
• Make security transparent to the user.
• Make sure that "mandatory" really means mandatory.
• Seek opinions from those who pay for the systems.

In summary, it was clearly the consensus that basic information security features should be required components that vendors build into information systems. Some control of the implementation of features should be available to organizations so that flexibility to accommodate special circumstances is available.

Interviewees indicated that listing essential (must-have and must-use) and optional security features in an accredited standards document would be very useful for vendors and procurement officers in the private sector. Vendors could use the criteria as a measure of how well their products meet requirements for information security and the needs of the users. Procurement officers could use the criteria as benchmarks in evaluating different vendors' equipment during the purchasing cycle. Vendors could also use the criteria as a marketing tool, as they currently use the Orange Book criteria. These comments are supportive of the GSSP concept developed by this committee.

### NOTES

1. Some documentation can be found in the Defense Advanced Research Projects Agency's Computer Emergency Response Team advisories, which are distributed to system managers and in a variety of electronic newsletters and bulletin boards.

2. The mechanisms for carrying out such procedures are called mandatory access controls by the DOD.

3. Such mechanisms are called discretionary access controls by the DOD, and user-directed, identity-based access controls by the International Organization for Standards. Also, the owner-based approach stands in contrast with the more formal, centrally administered clearance or access-authorization process of the national security community.

4. There are many kinds of vulnerability. Authorized people can misuse their authority. One user can impersonate another. One break-in can set up the conditions for others, for example, by installing a virus. Physical attacks on equipment can compromise it. Discarded media can be scavenged. An intruder can get access from a remote system that is not well secured, as happened with the Internet worm.

5. Although it might be comforting to commend the use of, or research into, quantitative risk assessment as a planning tool, in many cases little more than a semiquantitative or checklist-type approach seems warranted. Risk assessment is the very basis of the insurance industry, which, it can be noted, has been slow to offer computer security coverage to businesses or individuals (see Chapter 6, Appendix 6.2, "Insurance"). In some cases (e.g., the risk of damage to the records of a single customer's accounts) quantitative assessment makes sense. In general, however, risk assessment is a difficult and complex task, and quantitative assessment of myriad qualitatively different, low-probability, high-impact risks has not been notably successful. The nuclear industry is a case in point.

6. The extent of interconnection envisioned for the future underscores the importance of planning for interdependencies. For example, William Mitchell has laid out a highly interconnected vision:

> Through open systems interconnection (OSI), businesses will rely on computer networks as much as they depend on the global telecom network. Enterprise networks will meet an emerging need: they will allow any single computer in any part of the world to be as accessible to users as any telephone. OSI networking capabilities will give every networked computer a unique and easily accessible address. Individual computer networks will join into a single cohesive system in much the same way as independent telecom networks join to form one global service. (Mitchell, 1990, pp. 69-72)

7. Other federal privacy laws include the Fair Credit Reporting Act of 1970 (P.L. 91-508), the Family Educational Rights and Privacy Act of 1974 (20 U.S.C. 1232g), the Right of Financial Privacy Act of 1978 (11 U.S.C. 1100 et seq.), the Electronic Funds Transfer Act of 1978 (15 U.S.C. 1693, P.L. 95-200), the Cable Communications Policy Act of 1984 (48 U.S.C. 551), the Electronic Communications Privacy Act of 1986 (18 U.S.C. 2511), and the Computer Matching and Privacy Protection Act of 1988 (5 U.S.C. 552a Note) (Turn, 1990). States have also passed laws to protect privacy.

8. This point was made by the congressional Office of Technology Assessment in an analysis of federal agency use of electronic record systems for computer matching, verification, and profiling (OTA, 1986b).

9. Recent cases about management perusing electronic mail messages that senders and receivers had believed were private amplify that debate (Communications Week, 1990a).

# 3

# Technology to Achieve
# Secure Computer Systems

A reasonably complete survey of the technology needed to protect information and other resources controlled by computer systems, this chapter discusses how such technology can be used to make systems secure. It explains the essential technical ideas, gives the major properties of relevant techniques currently known, and tells why they are important. Suggesting developments that may occur in the next few years, it provides some of the rationale for the research agenda set forth in Chapter 8.

Appendix B of this report discusses in more detail several topics that are either fundamental to computer security technology or of special current interest—including how some important things (such as passwords) work and why they do not work perfectly.

This discussion of the technology of computer security addresses two major concerns:

1. What do we mean by security?
2. How do we get security, and how do we know when we have it?

The first involves specification of security and the services that computer systems provide to support security. The second involves implementation of security, and in particular the means of establishing confidence that a system will actually provide the security the specifications promise. Each topic is discussed according to its importance for the overall goal of providing computer security, and not according to how much work has already been done on that topic.

This chapter discusses many of the concepts introduced in Chapter 2, but in more detail. It examines the technical process of relating computer mechanisms to higher-level controls and policies, a process that requires the development of abstract security models and supporting mechanisms. Although careful analysis of the kind carried out in this chapter may seem tedious, it is a necessary prerequisite to ensuring the security of something as complicated as a computer system. Ensuring security, like protecting the environment, requires a holistic approach; it is not enough to focus on the problem that caused trouble last month, because as soon as that difficulty is resolved, another will arise.

## SPECIFICATION VS. IMPLEMENTATION

The distinction between what a system does and how it does it, between specification and implementation, is basic to the design and analysis of computer systems. A specification for a system is the meeting point between the customer and the builder. It says what the system is supposed to do. This is important to the builder, who must ensure that what the system actually does matches what it is supposed to do. It is equally important to the customer, who must be confident that what the system is supposed to do matches what he wants. It is especially critical to know exactly and completely how a system is supposed to support requirements for security, because any mistake can be exploited by a malicious adversary.

Specifications can be written at many levels of detail and with many degrees of formality. Broad and informal specifications of security are called security policies[1] (see Chapter 2), examples of which include the following: (1) "Confidentiality: Information shall be disclosed only to people authorized to receive it." (2) "Integrity: Data shall be modified only according to established procedures and at the direction of properly authorized people."

It is possible to separate from the whole the part of a specification that is relevant to security. Usually a whole specification encompasses much more than the security-relevant part. For example, a whole specification usually says a good deal about price and performance. In systems for which confidentiality and integrity are the primary goals of security policies, performance is not relevant to security because a system can provide confidentiality and integrity regardless of how well or badly it performs. But for systems for which availability and integrity are paramount, performance specifications may be relevant to security. Since security is the focus of this discussion, "specification" as used here should be understood to describe only what is relevant to security.

A secure system is one that meets the particular specifications meant to ensure security. Since many different specifications are possible, there cannot be any absolute notion of a secure system. An example from a related field clarifies this point. We say that an action is legal if it meets the requirements of the law. Since different jurisdictions can have different sets of laws, there cannot be any absolute notion of a legal action; what is legal under the laws of Britain may be illegal in the United States.

A system that is believed to be secure is called trusted. Of course, a trusted system must be trusted for something; in the context of this report it is trusted to meet security specifications. In some other context such a system might be trusted to control a shuttle launch or to retrieve all the 1988 court opinions dealing with civil rights.

Policies express a general intent. Of course, they can be more detailed than the very general ones given as examples above; for instance, the following is a refinement of the first policy: "Salary confidentiality: Individual salary information shall be disclosed only to the employee, his superiors, and authorized personnel people."

But whether general or specific, policies contain terms that are not precisely defined, and so it is not possible to tell with absolute certainty whether a system satisfies a policy. Furthermore, policies specify the behavior of people and of the physical environment as well as the behavior of machines, so that it is not possible for a computer system alone to satisfy them. Technology for security addresses these problems by providing methods for the following:

• Integrating a computer system into a larger system, comprising people and a physical environment as well as computers, that meets its security policies;
• Giving a precise specification, called a security model, for the security-relevant behavior of the computer system;
• Building, with components that provide and use security services, a system that meets the specifications; and
• Establishing confidence, or assurance, that a system actually does meet its specifications.

This is a tall order that at the moment can be only partially filled. The first two actions are discussed in the section below titled "Specification," the last two in the following section titled "Implementation." Services are discussed in both sections to explain both the functions being provided and how they are implemented.

## SPECIFICATION: POLICIES, MODELS, AND SERVICES

This section deals with the specification of security. It is based on the taxonomy of security policies given in Chapter 2. There are only a few highly developed security policies, and research is needed to develop additional policies (see Chapter 8), especially in the areas of integrity and availability. Each of the highly developed policies has a corresponding (formal) security model, which is a precise specification of how a computer system should behave as part of a larger system that implements a policy. Implementing a security model requires mechanisms that provide particular security services. A small number of fundamental mechanisms have been identified that seem adequate to implement most of the highly developed security policies currently in use.

The simple example of a traffic light illustrates the concepts of policy and model; in this example, safety plays the role of security. The light is part of a system that includes roads, cars, and drivers. The safety policy for the complete system is that two cars should not collide. This is refined into a policy that traffic must not move in two conflicting directions through an intersection at the same time. This policy is translated into a safety model for the traffic light itself (which plays a role analogous to that of a computer system within a complete system): two green lights may never appear in conflicting traffic patterns simultaneously. This is a simple specification. Observe that the complete specification for a traffic light is much more complex; it provides for the ability to set the duration of the various cycles, to synchronize the light with other traffic lights, to display different combinations of arrows, and so forth. None of these details, however, is critical to the safety of the system, because they do not bear directly on whether or not cars will collide. Observe also that for the whole system to meet its safety policy, the light must be visible to the drivers, and they must understand and obey its rules. If the light remains red in all directions it will meet its specification, but the drivers will lose patience and start to ignore it, so that the entire system may not support a policy of ensuring safety.

An ordinary library affords a more complete example (see Appendix B of this report) that illustrates several aspects of computer system security in a context that does not involve computers.

## Policies

A security policy is an informal specification of the rules by which people are given access to a system to read and change information and to use resources. Policies naturally fall into a few major categories:

1. *Confidentiality:* controlling who gets to read information;
2. *Integrity:* assuring that information and programs are changed only in a specified and authorized manner; and

3. *Availability:* assuring that authorized users have continued access to information and resources.

Two orthogonal categories can be added:

4. *Resource control:* controlling who has access to computing, storage, or communication resources (exclusive of data); and

5. *Accountability:* knowing who has had access to information or resources.

Chapter 2 describes these categories in detail and discusses how an organization that uses computers can formulate a security policy by drawing elements from all these categories. The discussion below summarizes this material and supplements it with some technical details.

Security policies for computer systems generally reflect long-standing policies for the security of systems that do not involve computers. In the case of national security these are embodied in the information classification and personnel clearance system; for commercial computing they come from established accounting and management control practices.

From a technical viewpoint, the most fully developed policies are those that have been developed to ensure confidentiality. They reflect the concerns of the national security community and are derived from Department of Defense (DOD) Directive 5000.1, the basic directive for protecting classified information.[2]

The DOD computer security policy is based on *security levels*. Given two levels, one may be lower than the other, or the two may not be comparable. The basic principle is that information can never be allowed to leak to a lower level, or even to a level that is not comparable. In particular, a program that has "read access" to data at a higher level cannot simultaneously have "write access" to lower-level data. This is a rigid policy motivated by a lack of trust in application programs. In contrast, a person can make an unclassified telephone call even though he may have classified documents on his desk, because he is trusted to not read the document over the telephone. There is no strong basis for placing similar trust in an arbitrary computer program.

A security level or compartment consists of an access level (either top secret, secret, confidential, or unclassified) and a set of categories (e.g., Critical Nuclear Weapon Design Information (CNWDI), North Atlantic Treaty Organization (NATO), and so on). The access levels are ordered (top secret, highest; unclassified, lowest). The categories, which have unique access and protection requirements, are not ordered, but sets of categories are ordered by inclusion: one set is lower than another if every category in the first is included in the second. One security level is lower than another, different level if it has an equal or lower access level and an equal or lower set of categories. Thus [confidential; NATO] is lower than both [confidential; CNWDI, NATO] and [secret; NATO]. Given two levels, it is possible that neither is lower than the other. Thus [secret; CNWDI] and [confidential; NATO] are not comparable.

Every piece of information has a security level (often called its label). Normally information is not permitted to flow downward: information at one level can be derived only from information at equal or lower levels, never from information that is at a higher level or is not comparable. If information is computed from several inputs, it has a level that is at least as high as any of the inputs. This rule ensures that if information is stored in a system, anything computed from it will have an equal or higher level. Thus the classification never decreases.

The DOD computer security policy specifies that a person is cleared to a particular security level and can see information only at that, or a lower, level. Since anything seen can be derived only from other information categorized as being at that level or lower, the result is that what a person sees can depend only on information in the system at his level or lower. This policy is *mandatory*: except for certain carefully controlled downgrading or declassification procedures, neither users nor programs in the system can break the rules or change the security levels. As Chapter 2 explains, both this and other confidentiality policies can also be applied in other settings.

Integrity policies have not been studied as carefully as confidentiality policies, even though some sort of integrity policy governs the operation of every commercial data-processing system. Work in this area (Clark and Wilson, 1987) lags work on confidentiality by about 15 years. Nonetheless, interest is growing in workable integrity policies and corresponding mechanisms, especially since such mechanisms provide a sound basis for limiting the damage caused by viruses, self-replicating software that can carry hidden instructions to alter or destroy data.

The most highly developed policies to support integrity reflect the concerns of the accounting and auditing community for preventing fraud. The essential notions are individual accountability, auditability, separation of duty, and standard procedures. Another kind of integrity policy is derived from the information-flow policy for confidentiality applied in reverse, so that information can be derived only from other information of the same or a higher integrity level (Biba, 1975). This particular policy is extremely restrictive and thus has not been applied in practice.

Policies categorized under accountability have usually been formulated as part of confidentiality or integrity policies. Accountability has not received independent attention.

In addition, very little work has been done on security policies related to availability. Absent this work, the focus has been on the practical aspects of contingency planning and recoverability.

## Models

To engineer a computer system that can be used as part of a larger system that implements a security policy, and to decide unambiguously whether such a computer system meets its specification, an informal, broadly stated policy must be translated into a precise model. A model differs from a policy in two ways:

1. It describes the desired behavior of a computer system's mechanisms, not that of the larger system that includes people.

2. It is precisely stated in formal language that resolves the ambiguities of English and makes it possible, at least in principle, to give a mathematical proof that a system satisfies the model.

Two models are in wide use. One, based on the DOD computer security policy, is the flow model; it supports a certain kind of confidentiality policy. The other, based on the familiar idea of stationing a guard at an entrance, is the access control model; it supports a variety of confidentiality, integrity, and accountability policies. There are no models that support availability policies.

### Flow Model

The flow model is derived from the DOD computer security policy described above. In this model (Denning, 1976) each piece of data in the system visible to a user or an application program is held in a container called an object. Each object has an associated security level. An object's level indicates the security level of the data it contains. Data in one object is allowed to affect another object only if the source object's level is lower than or equal to the destination object's level. All the data within a single object have the same level and hence can be manipulated freely.

The flow model ensures that information at a given security level flows only to an equal or higher level. Data is not the same as information; for example, an encrypted message contains data, but it conveys no information unless one knows the encryption key or can break the encryption system. Unfortunately, data is all the computer can understand. By preventing an object at one level from being affected in any way by data that is not at an equal or lower level, the flow model ensures that information can flow only to an equal or higher level inside the computer system. It does this very conservatively and thus forbids many actions that would not in fact cause any information to flow improperly.

A more complicated version of the flow model (which is actually the basis of the rules in the Orange Book) separates objects into active subjects that can initiate operations and passive objects that simply contain data, such as a file, a piece of paper, or a display screen. Data can flow only between an object and a subject; flow from object to subject is called a read operation, and flow from subject to object is called a write operation. Now the rules are that a subject can only read from an object at an equal or lower level, and can only write to an object at an equal or higher level.

Not all possible flows in a system look like read and write operations. Because the system is sharing resources among objects at different levels, it is possible for information to flow on what are known as covert channels (Lampson, 1973; IEEE, 1990a). For example, a high-level subject might be able to send a little information to a low-level subject by using up all the disk space if it learns that a surprise attack is scheduled for next week. When the low-level subject finds itself unable to write a file, it has learned about the attack (or at least received a hint). To fully realize the intended purpose of a flow model, it is necessary to identify and attempt to close all the covert channels, although total avoidance of covert channels is generally impossible due to the need to share resources.

To fit this model of a computer system into the real world, it is necessary to account for people. A person is cleared to some level of permitted access. When he identifies himself to the system as a user present at some terminal, he can set the terminal's level to any equal or lower level. This ensures that the user will never see information at a higher level than his clearance allows. If the user sets the terminal level lower than the level of his clearance, he is trusted not to take high-level information out of his head and introduce it into the system.

Although not logically required, the flow model policy has generally been viewed as *mandatory*; neither users nor programs in a system can break the flow rule or change levels. No real system can strictly follow this rule, since procedures are always needed for declassifying data, allocating resources, and introducing new users, for example. The access control model is used for these purposes, among others.

*Access Control Model*

The access control model is based on the idea of stationing a guard in front of a valuable resource to control who has access to it. This model organizes the system into

- *Objects:* entities that respond to operations by changing their state, providing information about their state, or both;
- *Subjects:* active objects that can perform operations on objects; and
- *Operations:* the way that subjects interact with objects.

The objects are the resources being protected; an object might be a document, a terminal, or a rocket. A set of rules specifies, for each object and each subject, what operations that subject is allowed to perform on that object. A reference monitor acts as the guard to ensure that the rules are followed (Lampson, 1985). An example of a set of access rules follows:

| Subject | Operation | Object |
|---|---|---|
| Smith | Read file | "1990 pay raises" |
| White | Send "Hello" | Terminal 23 |
| Process 1274 | Rewind | Tape unit 7 |
| Black | Fire three rounds | Bow gun |
| Jones | Pay invoice 432567 | Account Q34 |

There are many ways to express the access rules. The two most popular are to attach to each subject a list of the objects it can access (a capability list), or to attach to each object a list of the subjects that can access it (an access control list). Each list also identifies the operations that are allowed. Most systems use some combination of these approaches.

Usually the access rules do not mention each operation separately. Instead they define a smaller number of "rights" (often called permissions)—for example, read, write, and search—and grant some set of rights to each (subject, object) pair. Each operation in turn requires some set of rights. In this way a number of different operations, all requiring the right to read, can read information from an object. For example, if the object is a text file, the right to read may be required for such operations as reading a line, counting the number of words, and listing all the misspelled words.

One operation that can be done on an object is to change which subjects can access the object. There are many ways to exercise this control, depending on what a particular policy is. When a *discretionary* policy applies, for each object an "owner" or principal is identified who can decide without any restrictions who can do what to the object. When a *mandatory* policy applies, the owner can make these decisions only within certain limits. For example, a mandatory flow policy allows only a security officer to change the security level of an object, and the flow model rules limit access. The principal controlling the object can usually apply further limits at his discretion.

The access control model leaves open what the subjects are. Most commonly, subjects are users, and any active entity in the system is treated as acting on behalf of some user. In some systems a program can be a subject in its own right. This adds a great deal of flexibility, because the program can implement new objects using existing ones to which it has access. Such a program is called a protected subsystem; it runs as a subject different from the principal invoking it, usually one that can access more objects. The security services used to support creation of protected subsystems also may be used to confine suspected Trojan horses or viruses, thus limiting the potential for damage from such programs. This can be done by running a suspect program as a subject that is different from the principal invoking it, in this case a subject that can access fewer objects. Unfortunately, such facilities have not been available in most operating systems.

The access control model can be used to realize both secrecy and integrity policies, the former by controlling read operations and the latter by controlling write operations, and others that change the state. This model supports accountability, using the simple notion that every time an operation is invoked, the identity of the subject and the object as well as the operation should be recorded in an audit trail that can later be examined. Difficulties in making practical use of such information may arise owing to the large size of an audit trail.

### Services

Basic security services are used to build systems satisfying the policies discussed above. Directly supporting the access control model, which in turn can be used to support nearly all the policies discussed, these services are as follows:

• *Authentication:* determining who is responsible for a given request or statement,[3] whether it is, "The loan rate is 10.3 percent," or "Read file 'Memo to Mike,'" or "Launch the rocket."

• *Authorization:* determining who is trusted for a given purpose, whether it is establishing a loan rate, reading a file, or launching a rocket.

• *Auditing:* recording each operation that is invoked along with the identity of the subject and object, and later examining these records.

Given these services, it is easy to implement the access control model. Whenever an operation is invoked, the reference monitor uses authentication to find out who is requesting the operation and then uses authorization to find out whether the requester is trusted for that operation. If so, the reference monitor allows the operation to proceed; otherwise, it cancels the operation. In either case, it uses auditing to record the event.

## Authentication

To answer the question, Who is responsible for this statement?, it is necessary to know what sort of entities can be responsible for statements; we call these entities principals. It is also necessary to have a way of naming the principals that is consistent between authentication and authorization, so that the result of authenticating a statement is meaningful for authorization.

A principal is a (human) user or a (computer) system. A user is a person, but a system requires some explanation. A system comprises hardware (e.g., a computer) and perhaps software (e.g., an operating system). A system can depend on another system; for example, a user-query process depends on a database management system, which depends on an operating system, which depends on a computer. As part of authenticating a system, it may be necessary to verify that the systems it depends on are trusted.

In order to express trust in a principal (e.g., to specify who can launch the rocket), one must be able to give the principal a name. The name must be independent of any information (such as passwords or encryption keys) that may change without any change in the principal itself. Also, it must be meaningful, both when access is granted and later when the trust being granted is reviewed to see whether that trust is still warranted. A naming system must be:

- *Complete:* every principal has a name; it is difficult or impossible to express trust in a nameless principal.
- *Unambiguous:* the same name does not refer to two different principals; otherwise it is impossible to know who is being trusted.
- *Secure:* it is easy to tell which other principals must be trusted in order to authenticate a statement from a named principal.

In a large system, naming must be decentralized to be manageable. Furthermore, it is neither possible nor wise to rely on a single principal that is trusted by every part of the system. Since systems as well as users can be principals, systems as well as users must be able to have names.

One way to organize a decentralized naming system is as a hierarchy, following the model of a tree-structured file system like the one in Unix or MS/DOS, two popular operating systems. The Consultative Committee on International Telephony and Telegraphy (CCITT) X.500 standard for naming defines such a hierarchy (CCITT, 1989b); it is meant to be suitable for naming every principal in the world. In this scheme an individual can have a name like "US/GOV/State/James_Baker." Such a naming system can be complete; there is no shortage of names, and registration can be made as convenient as desired. It is unambiguous provided each directory is unambiguous.

The CCITT also defines a standard (X.509) for authenticating a principal with an X.500 name; the section on authentication techniques below discusses how this is done (CCITT, 1989b). Note that an X.509 authentication may involve more than one agent. For example, agent A may authenticate agent B, who in turn authenticates the principal.

A remaining issue is exactly who should be trusted to authenticate a given name. In the X.509 authentication framework, typically, principals trust agents close to them in the hierarchy. A principal is less likely to trust agents farther from it in the hierarchy, whether those agents are above, below, or in entirely different branches of the tree. If a system at one point in the tree wants to authenticate a principal elsewhere, and if there is no one agent that can authenticate both, then the system must establish a chain of trust through multiple agents.[4]

Often a principal wants to act with less than its full authority, in order to reduce the damage that can be done in case of a mistake. For this purpose it is convenient to define additional principals, called roles, to provide a way of authorizing a principal to play a role, and to allow the principal to make a statement using any role for which it is authorized. For example, a system administrator might have a "normal" role and a "powerful" role. The authentication service then reports that a statement was made by a role rather than by the original principal, after verifying both that the statement came from the original principal and that he was authorized to play that role. (It is critical to ensure that the use of such roles does not prevent auditing measures from identifying the individual who is ultimately responsible for actions.)

In general, trust is not simply a matter of trusting a single user or system principal. It is necessary to trust the (hardware and software) systems through which that user is communicating. For example, suppose that a user Alice running on a workstation B is entering a transaction on a transaction server C, which in turn makes a network access to a database machine D. D's authorization decision may need to take account not just of Alice, but also of the fact that B and C are involved and must be trusted. Some of these issues do not arise in a centralized system, where a single authority is responsible for all the authentication and provides the resources for all the applications, but even in a centralized system an operation on a file, for example, is often invoked through an application, such as a word-processing program, which is not part of the base system and perhaps should not be trusted in the same way.

Such rules may be expressed by introducing new, compound principals, such as "Smith ON Workstation 4," to represent the user acting through intermediaries. Then it becomes possible to express trust in the compound principal exactly as in any other. The name "Workstation 4" identifies the intermediate system, just as the name "Smith" identifies the user.

How do we authenticate such principals? When Workstation 4 says, "Smith wants to read the file 'pay raises,'" how do we know (1) that the request is really from that workstation and not somewhere else and (2) that it is really Smith acting through Workstation 4, and not Jones or someone else?

We answer the first question by authenticating the intermediate systems as well as the users. If the resource and the intermediate are on the same machine, the operating system can authenticate the intermediate to the resource. If not, we use the cryptographic methods discussed in the section below titled "Secure Channels."

To answer the second question, we need some evidence that Smith has delegated to Workstation 4 the authority to act on his behalf. We cannot ask for direct evidence that Smith asked to read the file—if we could have that, then he would not be acting through the workstation. We certainly cannot take the workstation's word for it; then it could act for Smith no matter who is really there. But we can demand a statement that we believe is from Smith, asserting that Workstation 4 can speak for him (probably for some limited time, and perhaps only for some limited purposes). Given that Smith says, "Workstation 4 can act for me," and Workstation 4 says, "Smith says to read the file 'pay raises,'" then we can believe that Smith on Workstation 4 says, "Read the file 'pay raises.'"

There is another authentication question lurking here, namely how do we know that the software in the workstation is correctly representing Smith's intended action? Unless the application program that Smith is using is itself trusted, it is possible that the action Smith has requested has been transformed by this program into another action that Smith is authorized to execute. Such might be the case if a virus were to infect the application Smith is running on his workstation. This aspect of the authentication problem can be addressed through the use of trusted application software and through integrity mechanisms as discussed in the section "Secure Channels" below.

To authenticate the delegation statement from Smith, "Workstation

4 can act for me," we need to employ the cryptographic methods described below.

The basic service provided by authentication is information that a statement was made by some principal. An aggressive form of authentication, called nonrepudiation, can be accomplished by a digital analog of notarizing, in which a trusted authority records the signature and the time it was made (see "Digital Signatures" in Appendix B).

## Authorization

Authorization determines who is trusted for a given purpose, usually for doing some operation on an object. More precisely, it determines whether a particular principal, who has been authenticated as the source of a request to do an operation on an object, is trusted for that operation on that object. (This object-oriented view of authorization also encompasses the more traditional implementations of file protection, and so forth.)

Authorization is customarily implemented by associating with the object an access control list (ACL) that tells which principals are authorized for which operations. The ACL also may refer to attributes of the principals, such as security clearances. The authorization service takes a principal, an ACL, and an operation or a set of rights, and returns "yes" or "no." This way of providing the service leaves the object free to store the ACL in any convenient place and to make its own decisions about how different parts of the object are protected. A database object, for instance, may wish to use different ACLs for different fields, so that salary information is protected by one ACL and address information by another, less restrictive one.

Often several principals have the same rights to access a number of objects. It is both expensive and unreliable to repeat the entire set of principals for each object. Instead, it is convenient to define a group of principals, give it a name, and give the group access to each of the objects. For instance, a company might define the group "executive committee." The group thus acts as a principal for the purpose of authorization, but the authorization service is responsible for verifying that the principal actually making the request is a member of the group.

In this section authorization has been discussed mainly from the viewpoint of an object, which must decide whether a principal is authorized to invoke a certain operation. In general, however, the subject doing the operation may also need to verify that the system implementing the object is authorized to do so. For instance, when logging in over a telephone line, a user may want to be sure that he has actually reached the intended system and not some other, hostile system that may try to spoof him. This process is usually called mutual authentication, although it actually involves authorization as well: statements from the object must be authenticated as coming from the system that implements the object, and the subject must have access rules to decide whether that system is authorized to do so.

## Auditing

Given the reality that every computer system can be compromised from within, and that many systems can also be compromised if surreptitious access can be gained, accountability is a vital last resort. Accountability policies were discussed above—and the point was made that, for example, all significant events should be recorded and the recording mechanisms should be nonsubvertible. Auditing services support these policies. Usually they are closely tied to authentication and authorization, so that every authentication is recorded, as is every attempted access, whether authorized or not.

In addition to establishing accountability, an audit trail may also reveal suspicious patterns of access and so enable detection of improper behavior by both legitimate users and masqueraders. However, limitations to this use of audit information often restrict its use to detecting unsophisticated intruders. In practice, sophisticated intruders have been able to circumvent audit trails in the course of penetrating systems. Techniques such as the use of write-once optical disks, cryptographic protection, and remote storage of audit trails can help counter some of these attacks on the audit database itself, but these measures do not address all the vulnerabilities of audit mechanisms. Even in circumstances where audit trail information could be used to detect penetration attempts, a problem arises in processing and interpreting the audit data. Both statistical and expert-system approaches are currently being tried, but their utility is as yet unproven (Lunt, 1988).

## IMPLEMENTATION: THE TRUSTED COMPUTING BASE

This section explores how to build a system that meets the kind of security specifications discussed earlier, and how to establish confidence that it does meet them. Systems are built of components; a system also depends on its components. This means that the components have to work (i.e., meet their specifications) for the system to work (i.e., meet its specification). Note, however, that not all components of a system have to work properly in order for a given aspect of the system to function properly. Thus security properties need not depend on all components of a system working correctly; rather, only the security-relevant components must function properly.

Each component is itself a system with specifications and implementation, and so the concept of a system applies at all levels. For example, a distributed system depends on a network, workstations, servers, mainframes, printers, and so forth. A workstation depends on a display, keyboard, disk, processor, network interface, operating system, and, for example, a spreadsheet application. A processor depends on integrated circuit chips, wires, circuit boards, and connectors. A spreadsheet depends on display routines, an arithmetic library, and a macro language processor, and so it goes down to the basic operations of the programming language, which in turn depend on the basic operations of the machine, which in turn depend on changes in the state of the chips and wires, for example. A chip depends on adders and memory cells, and so it goes down to the electrons and photons, whose behavior is described by quantum electrodynamics.

A component must be trusted if it has to work for the system to meet its security specification. The set of trusted hardware and software components is called the *trusted computing base* (TCB). If a component is in the TCB, so is every component that it depends on, because if they do not work, it is not guaranteed to work either. As was established previously, the concern in this discussion is security, and so the trusted components need to be trusted only to support security in this context.

Note that a system depends on more than its hardware and software. The physical environment and the people who use, operate, and manage it are also components of the system. Some of them must also be trusted. For example, if the power fails, a system may stop providing service; thus the power source must be trusted for availability. Another example: every system has security officers who set security levels, authorize users, and so on; they must be trusted to do this properly. Yet another: the system may disclose information only to authorized users, and they must be trusted not to publish the information in the newspaper. Thus when trust is assessed, the security of the entire system must be evaluated, using the basic principles of analyzing dependencies, minimizing the number and complexity of trusted components, and carefully analyzing each one.

From a TCB perspective, three key aspects of implementing a secure system are the following (derived from Anderson, 1972):

1. Keeping the TCB as small and simple as possible to make it amenable to detailed analysis;

2. Ensuring that the TCB mediates all accesses to data and programs that are to be protected; that is, it must not be possible to bypass the TCB; and

3. Making certain that the TCB itself cannot be tampered with, that is, that programs outside the TCB cannot maliciously modify the TCB software or data structures.

The basic method for keeping the TCB small is to separate out all the nonsecurity functions into untrusted components. For example, an elevator has a very simple braking mechanism whose only job is to stop the elevator if it starts to move at a speed faster than a fixed maximum, no matter what else goes wrong. The rest of the elevator control mechanism may be very complex, involving scheduling of several elevators or responding to requests from various floors, but none of this must be trusted for safety, because the braking mechanism does not depend on anything else. In this case, the braking mechanism is called the safety kernel.

A purchasing system may also be used to illustrate the relative smallness of a TCB. A large and complicated word processor may be used to prepare orders, but the TCB can be limited to a simple program that displays the completed order and asks the user to confirm it. An even more complicated database system may be used to find the order that corresponds to an arriving shipment, but the TCB can be limited to a simple program that displays the received order and a proposed payment authorization and asks the user to confirm them. If the order and authorization can be digitally signed (using methods described below), even the components that store them need not be in the TCB.

The basic method for finding dependencies, relevant to ensuring TCB access to protected data and programs and to making the TCB tamperproof, is careful analysis of how each step in building and executing a system is carried out. Ideally assurance for each system is given by a formal mathematical proof that the system satisfies its specification provided all its components do. In practice such proofs are only sometimes feasible, because it is hard to formalize the specifications and to carry out the proofs. Moreover, every such proof is conditioned on the assumption that the components work and have not been tampered with. (See the Chapter 4 section "Formal Specification and Verification" for a description of the state of the art.) In practice, assurance is also garnered by relying on components that have worked for many people, trusting implementors not to be malicious, carefully writing specifications for components, and carefully examining implementations for dependencies and errors. Because there are so many bases to cover, and because every base is critical to assurance, there are bound to be mistakes.

Hence two other important aspects of assurance are redundant checks like the security perimeters discussed below, and methods, such as audit trails and backup databases, for recovering from failures.

The main components of a TCB are discussed below in the sections headed "Computing" and "Communications." This division reflects the fact that a modern distributed system is made up of computers that can be analyzed individually but that must communicate with each other quite differently from the way each communicates internally.

## Computing

The computing part of the TCB includes the application programs, the operating system that they depend on, and the hardware (processing and storage) that both depend on.

### Hardware

Since software consists of instructions that must be executed by hardware, the hardware must be part of the TCB. The hardware is depended on to isolate the TCB from the untrusted parts of the system. To do this, it suffices for the hardware to provide for a "user state" in which a program can access only the ordinary computing instructions and restricted portions of the memory, as well as a "supervisor state" in which a program can access every part of the hardware. Most contemporary computers above the level of personal computers tend to incorporate these facilities. There is no strict requirement for fancier hardware features, although they may improve performance in some architectures.

The only essential, then, is to have simple hardware that is trustworthy. For most purposes the ordinary care that competent engineers take to make the hardware work is good enough. It is possible to get higher assurance by using formal methods to design and verify the hardware; this has been done in several projects, of which the VIPER verified microprocessor chip (for a detailed description see Appendix B) is an example (Cullyer, 1989). There is a mechanically checked proof to show that the VIPER chip's gate-level design implements its specification. VIPER pays the usual price for high assurance: it is several times slower than ordinary microprocessors built at the same time.

Another approach to using hardware to support high assurance is to provide a separate, simple processor with specialized software to implement the basic access control services. If this hardware controls the computer's memory access mechanism and forces all input/output data to be encrypted, that is enough to keep the rest of the hardware and software out of the TCB. (This requires that components upstream of the security hardware do not share information across security classes.) This approach has been pursued in the LOCK project, which is described in detail in Appendix B.

Unlike the other components of a computing system, hardware is physical and has physical interactions with the environment. For instance, someone can open a cabinet containing a computer and replace one of the circuit boards. If this is done with malicious intent, obviously all bets are off about the security of the computer. It follows that physical security of the hardware must be assured. There are less obvious physical threats. In particular, computer hardware involves changing electric and magnetic fields, and it therefore generates electromagnetic radiation (often called emanations)[5] as a byproduct of normal operation. Because this radiation can be a way for information to be disclosed, ensuring confidentiality may require that it be controlled. Similarly, radiation from the environment can affect the hardware.

## Operating System

The job of an operating system is to share the hardware among application programs and to provide generic security services so that most applications do not need to be part of the TCB. This layering of security services is useful because it keeps the TCB small, since there is only one operating system for many applications. Within the operating system itself the idea of layering or partitioning can be used to divide the operating system into a *kernel* that is part of the TCB and into other components that are not (Gasser, 1988). How to do this is well known.

The operating system provides an authorization service by controlling subjects' (processes) accesses to objects (files and communication devices such as terminals). The operating system can enforce various security models for these objects, which may be enough to satisfy the security policy. In particular it can enforce a flow model, which is sufficient for the DOD confidentiality policy, as long as it is able to keep track of security levels at the coarse granularity of whole files.

To enforce an integrity policy like the purchasing system policy described above, there must be some trusted applications to handle functions like approving orders. The operating system must be able to treat these applications as principals, so that they can access objects that the untrusted applications running on behalf of the same user cannot access. Such applications are protected subsystems.

*Applications and the Problem of Malicious Code*

Ideally applications should not be part of the TCB, since they are numerous, are often large and complicated, and tend to come from a variety of sources that are difficult to police. Unfortunately, attempts to build applications, such as electronic mail or databases that can handle multiple levels of classified information, on top of an operating system that enforces flow have had limited success. It is necessary to use a different operating system object for information at each security level, and often these objects are large and expensive. And to implement an integrity policy, it is always necessary to trust some application code. Again, it seems best to apply the kernel method, putting the code that must be trusted into separate components that are protected subsystems. The operating system must support this approach (Honeywell, 1985-1988).

In most systems any application program running on behalf of a user has full access to all that the user can access. This is considered acceptable on the assumption that the program, although it may not be trusted to always do the right thing, is unlikely to do an intolerable amount of damage. But suppose that the program does not just do the wrong thing, but is actively malicious? Such a program, which appears to do something useful but has hidden within it the ability to cause serious damage, is called a Trojan horse. When a Trojan horse runs, it can do a great deal of damage: delete files, corrupt data, send a message with the user's secrets to another machine, disrupt the operation of the host, waste machine resources, and so forth. There are many places to hide a Trojan horse: the operating system, an executable program, a shell command file, or a macro in a spreadsheet or word-processing program are only a few of the possibilities. Moreover, a compiler or other program development tool with a Trojan horse can insert secondary Trojan horses into the programs it generates.

The danger is even greater if the Trojan horse can also make copies of itself. Such a program is called a virus. Because it can spread quickly in a computer network or by copying disks, a virus can be a serious threat ("Viruses," in Appendix B, gives more details and describes countermeasures). Several examples of viruses have infected thousands of machines.

*Communications*

Methods for dealing with communications and security for distributed systems are less well developed than those for stand-alone centralized systems; distributed systems are both newer and more complex. There is no consensus about methods to provide security for distributed systems, but a TCB for a distributed system can be built out of suitable trusted elements running on the various machines that the system comprises. The committee believes that distributed systems are now well enough understood that this approach to securing such systems should also become recognized as effective and appropriate in achieving security.

A TCB for communications has two important aspects: secure channels for facilitating communication among the various parts of a system, and security perimeters for restricting communication between one part of a system and the rest.

## Secure Channels

The access control model describes the working of a system in terms of requests for operations from a subject to an object and corresponding responses, whether the system is a single computer or a distributed system. It is useful to explore the topic of secure communication separately from the discussions above of computers, subjects, or objects so as to better delineate the fundamental concerns that underlie secure channels in a broad range of computing contexts.

A channel is a path by which two or more principals communicate. A secure channel may be a physically protected path (e.g., a physical wire, a disk drive and associated disk, or memory protected by hardware and an operating system) or a logical path secured by encryption. A channel need not operate in real time: a message sent on a channel may be read much later, for instance, if it is stored on a disk. A secure channel provides integrity (a receiver can know who originally created a message that is received and that the message is intact (unmodified)), confidentiality (a sender can know who can read a message that is sent), or both.[6] The process of finding out who can send or receive on a secure channel is called authenticating the channel; once a channel has been authenticated, statements and requests arriving on it are also authenticated.

Typically the secure channels between subjects and objects inside a computer are physically protected: the wires in the computer are assumed to be secure, and the operating system protects the paths by which programs communicate with each other, using methods described above for implementing TCBs. This is one aspect of a broader point: every component of a physically protected channel is part of the TCB and must meet a security specification. If a wire connects two computers, it may be difficult to secure physically, especially if the computers are in different buildings.

To keep wires out of the TCB we resort to *encryption*, which makes it possible to have a channel whose security does not depend on the security of any wires or intermediate systems through which the messages are passed. Encryption works by computing from the data of the original message, called the clear text or plaintext, some different data, called the ciphertext, which is actually transmitted. A corresponding decryption operation at the receiver takes the ciphertext and computes the original plaintext. A good encryption scheme reflects the concept that there are some simple rules for encryption and decryption, and that computing the plaintext from the ciphertext, or vice versa, without knowing the rules is too difficult to be practical. This should be true even for one who already knows a great deal of other plaintext and its corresponding ciphertext.

Encryption thus provides a channel with confidentiality and integrity. All the parties that know the encryption rules are possible senders, and those that know the decryption rules are possible receivers. Obtaining many secure channels requires having many sets of rules, one for each channel, and dividing the rules into two parts, the algorithm and the key. The algorithm is fixed, and everyone knows it. The key can be expressed as a reasonably short sequence of characters, a few hundred at most. It is different for each secure channel and is known only to the possible senders or receivers. It must be fairly easy to generate new keys that cannot be easily guessed.

The two kinds of encryption algorithms are described below. It is important to have some understanding of the technical issues involved in order to appreciate the policy debate about controls that limit the export of popular forms of encryption (Chapter 6) and influence what is actually available on the market.[7]

1. Symmetric (secret or private) key encryption, in which the same key is used to send and receive (i.e., to encrypt and decrypt). The key must be known only to the possible senders and receivers. Decryption of a message using the secret key shared by a receiver and a sender can provide integrity for the receiver, assuming the use of suitable error-detection measures. The Data Encryption Standard (DES) is the most widely used, published symmetric encryption algorithm (NBS, 1977).

2. Asymmetric (public) key encryption, in which different keys are used to encrypt and decrypt. The key used to encrypt a message for confidentiality in asymmetric encryption is a key made publicly known by the intended receiver and identified as being associated with him, but the corresponding key used to decrypt the message is known only to that receiver. Conversely, a key used to encrypt a message for integrity (to digitally sign the message) in asymmetric

encryption is known only to the sender, but the corresponding key used to decrypt the message (validate the signature) must be publicly known and associated with that sender. Thus the security services to ensure confidentiality and integrity are provided by different keys in asymmetric encryption. The Rivest-Shamir-Adelman (RSA) algorithm is the most widely used form of public-key encryption (Rivest et al., 1978).

Known algorithms for asymmetric encryption run at relatively slow rates (a few thousand bits per second at most), whereas it is possible to buy hardware that implements DES at rates of up to 45 megabits per second, and an implementation at a rate of 1 gigabit per second is feasible with current technology. A practical design therefore uses symmetric encryption for handling bulk data and uses asymmetric encryption only for distributing symmetric keys and for a few other special purposes. Appendix B's "Cryptography" section gives details on encryption.

A digital signature provides a secure channel for sending a message to many receivers who may see the message long after it is sent and who are not necessarily known to the sender. Digital signatures may have many important applications in making a TCB smaller. For instance, in the purchasing system described above, if an approved order is signed digitally, it can be stored outside the TCB, and the payment component can still trust it. See the Appendix B section headed "Digital Signatures" for a more careful definition and some discussion of how to implement digital signatures.

## Authenticating Channels

Given a secure channel, it is still necessary to find out who is at the other end, that is, to authenticate it. The first step is to authenticate a channel from one computer system to another. The simplest way to do this is to ask for a password. Then if there is a way to match up the password with a principal, authentication is complete. The trouble with a password is that the receiver can misrepresent himself as the sender to anyone else who trusts the same password. As with symmetric encryption, this means that one needs a separate password to authenticate himself to every system that one trusts differently. Furthermore, anyone who can read (or eavesdrop on) the channel also can impersonate the sender. Popular computer network media such as Ethernet or token rings are vulnerable to such abuses.

The need for a principal to use a unique symmetric key to authenticate himself to every different system can be addressed by using a trusted third party to act as an intermediary in the cryptographic authentication process, a concept that has been understood for some time (Branstad, 1973; Kent, 1976; Needham and Schroeder, 1978). This approach, using symmetric encryption to achieve authentication, is now embodied in the Kerberos authentication system (Miller et al., 1987; Steiner et al., 1988). However, the requirement that this technology imposes, namely the need to trust a third party with keys that may be used (directly or indirectly) to encrypt the principal's data, may have hampered its widespread adoption.

Both of these problems can be overcome by challenge-response authentication schemes. These schemes make it possible to prove that a secret is known without disclosing it to an eavesdropper. The simplest scheme to explain as an example is based on asymmetric encryption, although schemes based on the use of symmetric encryption (Kent et al., 1982) have been developed, and zero-knowledge techniques have been proposed (Chaum, 1983). The challenger finds out the public key of the principal being authenticated, chooses a random number, and sends it to the principal encrypted using both the challenger's private key and the principal's public key. The principal decrypts the challenge using his private key and the public key of the challenger, extracts the random number, and encrypts the number with his private key and the challenger's public key and sends back the result. The challenger decrypts the result using his private key and the principal's public key; if he gets back the original number, he knows that the principal must have done the encrypting.[8]

How does the challenger learn the principal's public key? The CCITT X.509 standard defines a framework for authenticating a secure channel to a principal with an X.500 name; this is done by authenticating the principal's public key using certificates that are digitally signed. Such a certificate, signed by a trusted authority, gives a public key, K, and asserts that a message signed by K can be trusted to come from the principal. The standard does not define how other channels to the principal can be authenticated, but technology for doing this is well understood. An X.509 authentication may involve more than one agent. For example, agent A may authenticate agent B, who in turn authenticates the principal. (For a more thorough discussion of this sort of authentication, see X.509 (CCITT, 1989b) and subsequent papers that identify and correct a flaw in the X.509 three-way authentication protocol (e.g., Burrows et al., 1989).)

Challenge-response schemes solve the problem of authenticating one computer system to another. Authenticating a user is more difficult, since users are not good at doing encryption or remembering large, secret quantities. One can be authenticated by what one knows (a password), what one is (as characterized by biometrics), or what one has (a "smart card" or token).

The use of a password is the traditional method. Its drawbacks have already been explained and are discussed in more detail in the section titled "Passwords" in Appendix B.

Biometrics involves measuring some physical characteristic of a person—handwriting, fingerprints, or retinal patterns, for example—and transmitting this information to the system that is authenticating the person (Holmes et al., 1990). The problems are forgery and compromise. It may be easy to substitute a mold of someone else's finger, especially if the impersonator is not being watched. Alternatively, anyone who can bypass the physical reader and simply inject the bits derived from the biometric scanning can impersonate the person, a critical concern in a distributed system environment. Perhaps the greatest problem associated with biometric authentication technology to date has been the cost of equipping terminals and workstations with the input devices necessary for most of these techniques.[9]

By providing the user with a tiny computer that can be carried around and will act as an agent of authentication, a smart card or token reduces the problem of authenticating a user to the problem of authenticating a computer (NIST, 1988). A smart card fits into a special reader and communicates electrically with a system; a token has a keypad and display, and the user keys in a challenge, reads the response, and types it back to the system (see, for example, the product Racal Watchword). (At least one token authentication system (Security Dynamics' SecureID) relies on time as an implicit challenge, and thus the token used with this system requires no keypad.) A smart card or token is usually combined with a password to keep it from being easily used if it is lost or stolen; automatic teller machines require a card and a personal identification number (PIN) for the same reason.

## Security Perimeters

A distributed system can become very large; systems with 50,000 computers exist today, and they are growing rapidly. In a large system no single agent will be trusted by everyone; security must take account of this fact. Security is only as strong as its weakest link. To control the amount of damage that a security breach can do and to limit the scope of attacks, a large system may be divided into parts, each surrounded by a security perimeter. The methods described above can in principle provide a high level of security even in a very large system that is accessible to many malicious principals. But implementing these methods throughout a system is sure to be difficult and time-consuming, and ensuring that they are used correctly is likely to be even more difficult. The principle of "divide and conquer" suggests that it may be wiser to divide a large system into smaller parts and to restrict severely the ways in which these parts can interact with each other.

The idea is to establish a security perimeter around part of a system and to disallow fully general communication across the perimeter. Instead, carefully managed and audited gates in the perimeter allow only certain limited kinds of traffic (e.g., electronic mail, but not file transfers). A gate may also restrict the pairs of source and destination systems that can communicate through it.

It is important to understand that a security perimeter is not foolproof. If it allows the passing of electronic mail, then users can encode arbitrary programs or data in the mail and get them across the perimeter. But this is unlikely to happen by mistake, for it requires much more deliberate planning than do the more direct ways of communicating inside the perimeter using terminal connections. Furthermore, a mail-only perimeter is an important reminder of system security concerns. Users and managers will come to understand that it is dangerous to implement automated services that accept electronic mail requests from outside and treat them in the same fashion as communications originating inside the perimeter.

As with any security measure, a price is paid in convenience and flexibility for a security perimeter: it is difficult to do things across the perimeter. Users and managers must decide on the proper balance between security and convenience. See Appendix B's "Security Perimeters" section for more details.

## Methodology

An essential part of establishing trust in a computing system is ensuring that it was built according to proper methods. This important subject is discussed in detail in Chapter 4.

## CONCLUSION

The technical means for achieving greater system security and trust are a function of the policies and models that have been articulated and developed to date. Because most work to date has focused on confidentiality policies and models, the most highly developed services and the most effective implementations support requirements for confidentiality. What is currently on the market and known to users thus reflects only some of the need for trust technology. Research topics described in Chapter 8 provide some direction for redressing this imbalance, as does the process of articulating GSSP described in Chapter 1, which would both nourish and draw from efforts to develop a richer set of policies and models. As noted in Chapter 6, elements of public policy may also affect what technology is available to protect information and other resources controlled by computer systems—negatively, in the case of export controls, or positively, in the case of federal procurement goals and regulations.

## NOTES

1. Terminology is not always used consistently in the security field. Policies are often called "requirements"; sometimes the word "policy" is reserved for a broad statement and "requirement" is used for a more detailed statement.

2. DOD Directive 5200.28, "Security Requirements for Automatic Data Processing (ADP) Systems," is the interpretation of this policy for computer security (encompassing requirements for personnel, physical, and system security). The Trusted Computer Security Evaluation Criteria (TCSEC, or Orange Book, also known as DOD 5200.28-STD; U.S. DOD, 1985d) specifies security evaluation criteria for computers that are used to protect classified (or unclassified) data.

3. That is, who caused it to be made, in the context of the computer system; legal responsibility is a different matter.

4. The simplest such chain involves all the agents in the path, from the system up through the hierarchy to the first ancestor that is common to both the system and the principal, and then down to the principal. Such a chain will always exist if each agent is prepared to authenticate its parent and children. This scheme is simple to explain; it can be modified to deal with renaming and to allow for shorter authentication paths between cooperating pairs of principals.

5. The government's Tempest (Transient Electromagnetic Pulse Emanations Standard) program is concerned with reduction of such emanations. Tempest requirements can be met by using Tempest products or shielding whole rooms where unprotected products may be used. NSA has evaluated and approved a variety of Tempest products, although nonapproved products are also available.

6. In some circumstances a third secure channel property, availability, might be added to this list. If a channel exhibits secure availability, a sender can, with high probability, be confident that his message will be received, even in the face of malicious attack. Most communication channels incorporate some facilities designed to ensure availability, but most do so only under the assumptions of benign error, not in the context of malicious attack. At this time there is relatively little understanding of practical, generic methods of providing communication channels that offer availability in the face of attack (other than those approaches provided to deal with natural disasters or those provided for certain military communication systems).

7. For example, the Digital Equipment Corporation's development of an architecture for distributed system security was reportedly constrained by the availability of specific algorithms:

> The most popular algorithm for symmetric key encryption is the DES (Data Encryption Standard). . . . However, the DES algorithm is not specified by the architecture and, for export reasons, ability to use other algorithms is a requirement. The preferred algorithm for asymmetric key cryptography, and the only known algorithm with the properties required by the architecture, is RSA. . . . (Gasser et al., 1989, p. 308)

8. This procedure proves the presence of the principal but gives no assurance that the principal is actually at the other end of the channel; it is possible that an adversary controls the channel and is relaying messages from the principal. To provide this assurance, the principal should encrypt some unambiguous identification of the channel with his private key as well, thus certifying that he is at one end. If the channel is secured by encryption, the encryption key identifies it. Since the key itself must not be disclosed, a one-way hash (see Appendix B) of the key should be used instead.

9. Another problem with retina scans is that individuals concerned about potential health effects sometimes object to use of the technology.

# 4

# Programming Methodology

This chapter discusses issues pertinent to producing all high-quality software and, in particular, issues pertinent primarily to producing software designed to resist attack. Both application and system-level software are considered. Although there are differences between how the two are produced, the similarities dominate the differences.

Of the several factors that govern the difficulty of producing software, one of the most important is the level of quality to be attained, as indicated by the extent to which the software performs according to expectations. High-quality software does what it is supposed to do almost all the time, even when its users make mistakes. For the purposes of this study, software is classified according to four levels of quality: exploratory, production quality, critical, and secure. These levels differ according to what the software is expected to do (its functionality) and the complexity of the conditions under which the software is expected to be used (environmental complexity).

Exploratory software does not have to work; the chief issue is speed of development. Although it has uses, exploratory software is not discussed in this report.

Production-quality software needs to work reasonably well most of the time, and its failures should have limited effects. For example, we expect our spreadsheets to work most of the time but are willing to put up with occasional crashes, and even with occasional loss of data. We are not willing to put up with incorrect results.

Critical software needs to work very well almost all of the time, and certain kinds of failures must be avoided. Critical software is used in trusted and safety-critical applications, for example, medical instruments, where failure of the software can have catastrophic results.

In producing critical software the primary worries are minimizing bugs in the software and ensuring reasonable behavior when nonmalicious users do unexpected things or when unexpected combinations of external events occur. Producing critical software presents the same problems as producing production-quality software, but because the cost of failure is higher, the standards must be higher. In producing critical software the goal is to decrease risk, not to decrease cost.

Secure software is critical software that needs to be resistant to attack. Producing it presents the same problems as does producing critical software, plus some others. One of the key problems is analyzing the kinds of attacks that the software must be designed to resist. The level and kind of threat have a significant impact on how difficult the software is to produce. Issues to consider include the following:

• To what do potential attackers have access? The spectrum ranges from the keyboard of an automated teller machine to the object code of an operational system.

• Who are the attackers and what resources do they have? The spectrum ranges from a bored graduate student, to a malicious insider, to a knowledgeable, well-funded, highly motivated organization (e.g., a private or national intelligence-gathering organization).

• How much and what has to be protected?

In addition, the developers of secure software cannot adopt the various probabilistic measures of quality that developers of other software often can. For many applications, it is quite reasonable to tolerate a flaw that is rarely exposed and to assume that its having occurred once does not increase the likelihood that it will occur again (Gray, 1987; Adams, 1984). It is also reasonable to assume that logically independent failures will be statistically independent and not happen in concert. In contrast, a security vulnerability, once discovered, will be rapidly disseminated among a community of attackers and can be expected to be exploited on a regular basis until it is fixed.

In principle, software can be secure without being production quality. The most obvious problem is that software that fails frequently will result in denial of service. Such software also opens the door to less obvious security breaches. A perpetrator of an intelligence-grade attack (see Appendix E, "High-grade Threats") wants to avoid alerting the administrators of the target system while conducting an attack; a system with numerous low-level vulnerabilities provides a rich source of false alarms and diversions that can be used to cover up the actual attack or to provide windows of opportunity (e.g., when the system is recovering from a crash) for the subversion of hardware or software.

Low-quality software also invites attack by insiders, by requiring that administrative personnel be granted excessive privileges of access to manually repair data after software or system failures.

Another important factor contributing to the difficulty of producing software is the set of performance constraints the software is intended to meet, that is, constraints on the resources (usually memory or time) the software is permitted to consume during use. At one extreme, there may be no limit on the size of the software, and denial of service is considered acceptable. At the other extreme is software that must fit into limited memory and meet "hard" real-time constraints. It has been said that writing extremely efficient programs is an exercise in logical brinkmanship. Working on the brink increases the probability of faults and vulnerabilities. If one must work on the brink, the goals of the software should be scaled back to compensate.

Perhaps the most important factor influencing the difficulty of producing software is size. Producing big systems, for example, a global communication system, is qualitatively different from producing small ones. The reasons for this are well documented (NRC, 1989a).

In summary, simultaneous growth in level of quality, performance constraints, functionality, and environmental complexity results in a corresponding dramatic increase in the cost and risk of producing, and the risk of using, the software. There is no technology available to avoid this, nor is research likely to provide us with such a technology in the foreseeable future. If the highest possible quality is demanded for secure software, something else must give. Because security cannot be attained without quality and the environment in which a system is to run is usually hard to control, typically one must either remove performance constraints (perhaps by allocating extra resources) or reduce the intended functionality.

## SOFTWARE IS MORE THAN CODE

Good software is more than good code. It must be accompanied by high-quality documentation, including a requirements document, a design document, carefully written specifications for key modules, test plans, a maintenance plan, and so on.

Of particular importance for secure software is a guide to operations. More comprehensive than a user's manual, such a guide often calls for operational procedures that must be undertaken by people other than users of the software, for example, by system administrators. In evaluating software one must consider what it will do if the instructions in the guide to operations are followed, and what it will do if they are not. One must also evaluate how likely it is that capable people with good intentions will succeed in following the procedures laid down in the guide to operations.

For critical and secure software, a guide to operations is particularly important. In combination with the software it must provide for the following:

• *Auditing:* What information is to be collected, how it is to be collected, and what is to be done with it must be described. Those who have penetrated secure software cannot be expected to file a bug report, and so mechanisms for detecting such penetrations are needed. Reduction of raw audit data to intelligible form remains a complex and expensive process; a plan for secure software must include resources for the development of systems to reduce and display audit data.

• *Recovery:* Producing fault-free software of significant size is nearly impossible. Therefore one must plan for dealing with faults, for example, by using carefully designed recovery procedures that are exercised on a regular basis. When they are needed, it is important that such procedures function properly and that those who will be using them are familiar with their operation. If at all possible manual procedures should be in place to maintain operations in the absence of computing. This requires evaluating the risk of hardware or software crashes versus the benefits when everything works.

• *Operation in an emergency mode:* There may be provisions for bypassing some security features in times of extreme emergency. For example, procedures may exist that permit "breaking in" to protected data in critical circumstances such as incapacitation or dismissal of employees with special authorizations. However, the system design should treat such emergencies explicitly, as part of the set of events that must be managed by security controls.

Software should be delivered with some evidence that it meets its specifications (assurance). For noncritical software the good reputation of the vendor may be enough. Critical software should be accompanied by documentation describing the analysis the software has been subjected to. For critical software there must be no doubt about what configurations the conclusions of testing and validation apply to and no doubt that what is delivered is what was validated. Secure software should be accompanied by instructions and tools that make it possible to do continuing quality assurance in the field.

Software delivered without assurance evidence may provide only illusory security. A system that is manifestly nonsecure will generally inspire caution on the part of its users; a system that provides illusory security will inspire trust and then betray that trust when attacked.

Arrangements should be made to have the assurance evidence reviewed by a team of experts who are individually and organizationally independent from the development team.

Software should be delivered with a plan for its maintenance and enhancement. This plan should outline how various expected changes might be accomplished and should also make clear what kinds of changes might seriously compromise the software.

Secure software must be developed under a security plan. The plan should address what elements of the software are to be kept confidential, how to manage trusted distribution of software changes, and how authorized users can be notified of newly discovered vulnerabilities without having that knowledge fall into the wrong hands.

## SIMPLER IS BETTER

The best software is simple in two respects. It has a relatively simple internal structure, and it presents a relatively simple interface to the environment in which it is embedded.

Before deciding to incorporate a feature into a software system, one should attempt to understand all the costs of adding that feature and do a careful cost-benefit analysis. The cost of adding a feature to software is usually underestimated. The dominant cost is not that of the feature per se, but that of sorting out and controlling the interactions of that feature with all the others. In particular, underestimating cost results from a failure to appreciate the effects of scale. The other side of the coin is that the value of a new feature is usually overestimated. When features are added, a program becomes more complex for its users as well as for its developers. Furthermore, the interactions of features may introduce unexpected security risks. It is axiomatic among attackers that one does not break components but rather systems, by exploiting unanticipated combinations of features. It cannot be emphasized enough that truly secure systems are modest, straightforward, and understandable.

The best designs are straightforward. The more intricate the design and the greater the number of special-case features to accomplish a given functionality, the greater the scope for errors. Sometimes simple designs may be (or may appear to be) unacceptably inefficient. This can lead developers to compromise the structure or integrity of code or to employ intricate fast algorithms, responses that almost always make the software harder to produce and less reliable, and often make it more dependent on the precise characteristics of the input. Better hardware and less ambitious specifications deserve strong consideration before one ventures into such an exercise in software virtuosity. Such trade-offs deserve special attention by designers of secure systems, who too often accept the almost impossible requirements to preserve the full performance, function, and hardware of predecessor systems.

## THE ROLE OF PROGRAMMING LANGUAGES

An important threat to all software is bugs that have been accidentally introduced by programmers. It has been clearly demonstrated that higher-level programming languages tend to reduce the number of such bugs, for the following reasons:

• Higher-level languages reduce the total amount of code that must be written.

• Higher-level languages provide abstraction mechanisms that make programs easier to read. All higher-level languages provide procedures. The better languages provide mechanisms for data abstraction (e.g., packages) and for control abstraction (e.g., iterators).

• Higher-level languages provide checkable redundancy, such as type checking that can turn programs with unintended semantics into illegal programs that are rejected by the compiler. This helps turn errors that would otherwise occur while the program is running into errors that must be fixed before the program can run.

• Higher-level languages can eliminate the possibility of making certain kinds of errors. Languages with automatic storage management, for example, greatly reduce the likelihood of a program trying to use memory that no longer belongs to it. Much useful analysis can be done by the compiler, but there is usually ample opportunity to use other tools as well. Sometimes these tools—for example, various C preprocessors—make up for deficiencies in the programming language. Sometimes they enforce coding standards peculiar to an organization or project, for example, the standard that all types be defined in a separate repository. Sometimes they are primitive program verification systems that look for anomalies in the code, for example, code that cannot be reached.

A potential drawback to using higher-level programming languages in producing secure software is that they open up the possibility of certain kinds of "tunneling attacks." In a tunneling attack, the attacker attempts to exploit vulnerabilities at a level of abstraction beneath that at which the system developers were working. To avoid such attacks one must be able to analyze the software beneath the level of the source language. Higher-level languages often have large run-time packages (e.g., the Ada Run-Time Support Library). These run-time packages are often provided as black boxes by compiler vendors and are not subject to the requirements for independent examination and development of assurance evidence that the rest of the software must satisfy. They are, therefore, often a weak link in the security chain.

## THE ROLE OF SPECIFICATIONS

Specifications describe software components. They are written primarily to provide precise, easy-to-read, module-level documentation of interfaces. This documentation facilitates system design, integration, and maintenance, and it encourages reuse of modules. The most vexing problems in building systems involve overall system organization and the integration of components. Modularity is the key to effective integration, and specifications are essential for achieving program modularity. Abstraction boundaries allow one to understand programs one module at a time. However, an abstraction is intangible. Without a specification, there is no way to know what the abstraction is or to distinguish it from one of its implementations (i.e., executable code).

The process of writing a specification clarifies and deepens understanding of the object being specified by encouraging prompt attention to inconsistencies, incompletenesses, and ambiguities. Once written, specifications are helpful to auditors, implementors, and maintainers. A specification describes an agreement between clients and providers of a service. The provider agrees to write a module that meets a specification. The user agrees not to rely on any properties of the module that are not guaranteed by the specification. Thus specifications provide logical firewalls between providers and clients of abstractions.

During system auditing, specifications provide information that can be used to generate test data, build stubs, and analyze information flow. During system integration they reduce the number and severity of interfacing problems by reducing the number of implicit assumptions.

Specifications are usually much easier to understand than are implementations—thus combining specifications is less work than combining implementations. By relying only on those properties guaranteed by a specification, one makes the software easier to maintain because it is clear what properties must be maintained when an abstraction or its implementation is changed. By distinguishing abstractions from implementations, one increases the probability of building reusable components.

One of the most important uses of specifications is design verification. Getting a design "right" is often much more difficult than implementing the design.[1] Therefore, the ease and precision with which conjectures about a design can be stated and checked are of primary importance.

The kinds of questions one might ask about a design specification fall into a spectrum including two extremes: general questions relevant to any specification and problem-specific questions dealing with a particular application. The general questions usually deal with inconsistency (e.g., Does the specification contradict itself?) or incompleteness (e.g., Have important issues not been addressed?). Between the two extremes are questions related to a class of designs, for example, generic security questions. Design verification has enjoyed considerable success both inside and outside the security area. The key to this success has been that the conjectures to be checked and the specifications from which they are supposed to follow can both be written at the same relatively high level of abstraction.

## RELATING SPECIFICATIONS TO PROGRAMS

The preceding discussions of the roles of programming languages and specifications have emphasized the importance of separately analyzing both specifications and programs. Showing that programs meet their specifications is approached mainly by the use of testing and verification (or proving). Testing is a form of analysis in which a relatively small number of cases are examined. Verification deals with a potentially unbounded number of cases and almost always involves some form of inductive reasoning, either over the number of steps of a program (e.g., one shows that if some property holds after the program has executed $n$ steps, it will also hold after $n + 1$ steps) or over the structure of a data type (e.g., one shows that if some property holds for the first $n$ elements of an array, it will also hold for the first $n + 1$ elements).

The purpose of both kinds of analysis is to discover errors in programs and specifications, not to certify that either is error-free. Proponents of testing have always understood this. Testing cannot provide assurance that a property holds—there are simply too many cases to be examined in any realistic system. In principle, verification can be used to certify that a program satisfies its specification. In practice, this is not the case. As the history of mathematics makes clear, even the most closely scrutinized proofs may be flawed.

Testing techniques can be grouped roughly into three classes: (1) random testing involves selection of data across the environment, often with some frequency distribution; (2) structural testing involves generating test cases from a program itself, forcing known behavior onto the program; and (3) functional testing uses the specified functions of a program as the basis for defining test cases (Howden, 1987; Miller and Howden, 1981). These techniques are complementary and should be used in concert.

It is important that verification not be equated with formal proofs. Informal but rigorous reasoning about the relationships between implementations and specifications has proved to be an effective approach to finding errors (Solomon, 1982). People building concurrent programs frequently state key invariants and make informal arguments about their validity (Lamport, 1989; Wing, 1990).

Common sense and much empirical evidence make it clear that neither testing nor verification by itself is adequate to provide assurance for critical and secure software. In addition to being necessarily incomplete, testing is not a cheap process, often requiring that months be spent in grinding out test cases, running the system on them, and examining the results. These tests must be repeated whenever the code or operating environment is changed (a process called regressions testing). Testing software under actual operating conditions is particularly expensive.[2] Verification relies on induction to address multiple cases at once. However, discovering the appropriate induction hypotheses can be a difficult task. Furthermore, unless the proofs are machine checked they are likely to contain errors, and, as discussed in the following section, large machine-checked proofs are typically beyond the current state of the art.

Many views exist on how testing and proving can be combined. The IBM "cleanroom" approach (Linger and Mills, 1988; Selby et al., 1987) uses a form of design that facilitates informal proofs during an inspection process combined with testing to yield statistical evidence. Some parts of a system may be tested and others proved. The basic technique of proving—working a symbolic expression down a path of the program—may be used in either a testing or proving mode. This is especially applicable to secure systems when the symbolic expression represents an interesting security infraction, such as penetrating a communication system or faking an encryption key. Inductive arguments may be used to show that certain paths cannot be taken, thereby reducing the number of cases to be analyzed.

Real-time systems pose special problems. The current practice is to use information gathered from semiformal but often ad hoc analysis (e.g., design reviews, summation of estimated times for events along specific program paths, and simulation) to determine whether an implementation will meet its specified time deadlines with an acceptable degree of probability. More systematic methods for analyzing functional and performance properties of real-time software systems are needed.

## FORMAL SPECIFICATION AND VERIFICATION

In the computer science literature, the phrase "formal method" is often used to refer to any application of a mathematical technique to the development or analysis of hardware or software (IEEE, 1990b,c). In this report, "formal" is used in the narrower sense of "subject to symbolic reasoning." Thus, for example, a formal proof is a proof that can, at least in principle, be checked by machine.

The process of formally verifying that a program is correct with respect to its specification involves both generating and proving verification conditions. A verification-condition generator accepts as input a piece of code and formal specifications for that code, and then outputs a set of verification conditions, also called conjectures or proof obligations. These verification conditions are input to a theorem prover in an attempt to prove their validity using the underlying logic. If the conditions are all proved, then the program is said to satisfy its specification.

The security community has been interested for some time in the use of formal verification to increase confidence in the security of software (Craigen and Summerskill, 1990). While some success has been reported (Haigh et al., 1987), on the whole formal program verification has not proved to be a generally cost-effective technique. The major obstacles have been the following (Kemmerer, 1986):

- The difficulty of crossing the barrier between the level of abstraction represented by code and the level of abstraction at which specifications should be written.
- Limits on theorem-proving technology. Given the current state of theorem-proving technology, program verification entails extensive user interaction to prove relatively simple theorems.
- The lack of well-engineered tools.

The last obstacle is certainly surmountable, but whether the first two can be overcome is subject to debate.

There are fundamental limits to how good theorem provers can become. The basic problem is undecidable, but that is not relevant for most of the proof obligations that arise in program verification. A more worrisome fact is that reasoning about many relatively simple theories is inherently expensive,[3] and many of the formulas that arise in practice take a long time to simplify. Despite these difficulties, there has been enough progress in mechanical theorem proving in the last decade (Lindsay, 1988) to give some cause for optimism.

Whether or not the abstraction barrier can be gracefully crossed is the most critical question. The problem is that the properties people care about, for example, authentication of users, are most easily stated at a level of abstraction far removed from that at which the code is written. Those doing formal program verification spend most of their time mired in code-level details, for example, proving that two variables do not refer to the same piece of storage, and in trying to map those details onto the properties they really care about.

A formal specification is a prerequisite to formal program verification. However, as outlined above in the section titled "The Role of Specifications," specifications have an important role that is independent of program verification.

The potential advantages of formal over informal specifications are clear: formal specifications have an unambiguous meaning and are subject to manipulation by programs. To fully realize these advantages, one must have access to tools that support constructing and reasoning about formal specifications.

An important aspect of modern programming languages is that they are carefully engineered so that some kinds of programming errors are detected by either the compiler or the run-time system. Some languages use "specs" or "defs" modules (Mitchell et al., 1979), which can be viewed as a first step in integrating formal specifications into the programming process. However, experience with such languages shows that while programmers are careful with those parts (e.g., the types of arguments) that are checked by their programming environment, they are much less careful about those parts (e.g., constraints on the values of arguments) that are not checked. If the latter parts were checked as well, programmers would be careful about them, too.

Designs are expressed in a formal notation that can be analyzed, and formal statements about them can be proved. The process of formal design verification can be used to increase one's confidence that the specifications say "the right thing," for example, that they imply some security property.

Organizations building secure systems have made serious attempts to apply formal specification, formal design verification, and formal program verification. This committee interviewed members of several such organizations[4] and observed a consistent pattern:

• Writing formal specifications and doing design verification significantly increased people's confidence in the quality of their designs.
• Important flaws were found both during the writing of specifications and during the actual design verification. Although the majority of

the flaws were found as the specifications were written, the "threat" of design verification was an important factor in getting people to take the specification process seriously.

• Design-level verification is far more cost-effective than is program-level verification.

• Writing code-level entry/exit assertions is useful even if they are not verified.

• Although usable tools exist for writing and proving properties about specifications, better specification languages and tools are needed.

• More attention needs to be devoted to formalizing a variety of generally applicable security properties that can be verified at the design level.

• Little is understood about the formal specification and verification of performance constraints.

## HAZARD ANALYSIS

For critical and secure systems, hazard analysis is important. This involves the identification of environmental and system factors that can go wrong and the levels of concern that should be attached to the results. Environmental events include such actions as an operator mistyping a command or an earthquake toppling a disk drive. Systematic hazard analysis starts with a list of such events generated by experts in such domains as the application, the physics of the underlying technology, and the history of failures of similar systems. Each hazard is then traced into the system by asking pertinent questions: Is system behavior defined for this hazard? How will the system actually behave under these conditions? What can be done to minimize the effects of this hazard? Thus hazard analysis is a form of validation in assuring that the environment is well understood and that the product is being built to respond properly to expected events. Many forms of security breaches can be treated as hazards (U.K. Ministry of Defence, 1989b).

Physical system safety engineers have long used techniques such as failure-mode effects analysis and fault trees to trace the effects of hazards. Software is also amenable to analysis by such techniques, but additional problems arise (Leveson, 1986). First, the sheer complexity of most software limits the depth of analysis. Second, the failure modes of computer-controlled systems are not as intuitive as those for physical systems. By analogy, as radios with analog tuners age, the ability to separate stations slowly decreases. In contrast, radios with digital tuners tend to work well, or not at all.

## STRUCTURING THE DEVELOPMENT PROCESS

Some of the more popular approaches to software development have aspects that this committee believes are counterproductive.

Some approaches encourage organizations to ignore what they already have when starting a new software project. There seems to be an almost irresistible urge to start with a clean slate. While this offers the advantage of not having to live with past mistakes, it offers the opportunity to make a host of new ones. Most of the time, using existing software reduces both cost and risk. If software has been around for some time, those working with it already have a considerable investment in understanding it. This investment should not be discarded lightly. Finally, when the hazards of a system are well understood, it often becomes possible to devise operational procedures to limit their scope.

For similar reasons it is usually prudent to stick to established tools when building software that must be secure. Not only should programmers use programming languages they already understand, but they should also look for compilers that have been used extensively in similar projects. Although this is a conservative approach that over the long haul is likely to impede progress in the state of the art, it is clear that using new tools significantly increases risk.

The development process should not place unnecessary barriers between the design, implementation, and validation stages of an effort to produce software. Particularly dangerous in producing critical or secure software are approaches that rely primarily on ex post facto validation. Software should be evaluated as it is being built, so that the process as well as the product can be examined. The most reliable evaluations involve knowing what goes on while the system is being designed. Evaluation by outsiders is necessary but should not be the primary method of assurance.

Both software and the software development process should be structured so as to include incremental development based on alternation between relatively short design and implementation phases. This style of development has several advantages, among them the following:

• It helps to keep designers in touch with the real world by providing feedback.

• It tends to lead to a more modular design because designers are encouraged to invent coherent subsystems that can be implemented independently of other subsystems. (That is not to say that the various subsystems do not share code.)

• It leads to designs in which piecewise validation (usually by some combination of reasoning and testing) of the implementation is possible. At the same time it encourages designers to think of planning for validation as part of the design process.

• By encouraging designers to think of the design as something that changes rather than as a static entity that is done "correctly" once, it tends to lead to designs that can be more easily changed if the software needs to be modified.

## MANAGING SOFTWARE PROCUREMENT

Current trends in software procurement (particularly under government contracts) are rather disturbing:

1. It has become increasingly common for those buying software to develop an adversarial relationship with those producing it. Recent legislation (the Procurement Integrity Act of 1989, P.L. 100-679, Section 27) could be interpreted as virtually mandating such a relationship. If implemented, this act, which would stop the flow of "inside" information to potential vendors, might have the effect of stopping the flow of all information to potential vendors, thus significantly increasing the number of government software procurements that would overrun costs or fail to meet the customer's expectations.[5]

2. Purchasers of software have begun to take an increasingly narrow view of the cost of software. Procurement standards that require buying software from the lowest bidder tend to work against efforts to improve software quality. Likewise, the procurement of software by organizations that are separate from the end users typically leads to an emphasis on reduction of initial cost, with a corresponding increase in life-cycle expense.

3. Contractors often use their most talented engineers to procure contracts rather than to build systems.

The best software is produced when the customer and vendor have a cooperative relationship. In the beginning, this makes it possible for the customer to be frank about his needs and the vendor to be frank about the difficulty of meeting those needs. A negotiation can then follow as together the customer and vendor attempt to balance the customer's desires against implementation difficulties. As the project progresses, particularly if it is done in the incremental way suggested above, the vendor and customer must both feel free to revisit the definition of what the software is to do. Such a relationship, while still possible in the private sector, could become difficult in government procurements, owing to the difficulty of determining what is or is not illegal under the Procurement Integrity Act of 1989 (if it is actually implemented). Adaptation to changed circumstances and redirection of contracts to incorporate lessons learned could be difficult, because the law makes even preliminary discussion of such issues between customer and vendor a criminal offense. Thus increasingly the emphasis in the customer-vendor relationship could be on satisfaction of the letter of the contract. The sense of team ownership of a problem, so essential to success in an intangible field such as software development, would be lost completely.

Procurement standards that require software to be purchased from the lowest bidder often miss the point that the real cost of software is not the initial purchase price. The costs of porting, supporting, maintaining, and modifying the software usually dominate initial production costs. Furthermore the cost of using software that does not perform as well as it might can often outweigh any savings achieved at the time it is purchased. Finally, buying software from the lowest bidder encourages vendors to take a short-term approach to software development. In a well-run software organization, every significant software project should have as a secondary goal producing components that will be useful in other projects. This will not happen by accident, since it is more work and therefore more costly to produce components that are likely to be reusable.

## SCHEDULING SOFTWARE DEVELOPMENT

One of the reasons that software projects are chronically behind schedule and over budget is that they start with unrealistic requirements, schedules, and budgets. A customer's requirements are often vague wish lists, which are frequently interpreted as less onerous than they in fact prove to be when they are later clarified. The scheduled delivery date for software is often based on marketing considerations (e.g., winning a contract), rather than on a careful analysis of how much work is actually involved. An unrealistically optimistic schedule has many disadvantages:

• Decisions about what the software will do are made under crisis conditions and at the wrong time (near the end of a project) and for the wrong reasons (how hard something will be to implement given the current state of the software, rather than how important it is or how hard it would have been to implement from the starting point).

• Programmers who have worked hard trying to meet an impossible schedule will be demoralized when it becomes apparent that the schedule cannot be met. They will eventually begin to believe that missing deadlines is the norm.

• The whole development process is distorted. People may spend inordinate amounts of care on relatively unimportant pieces of the software that happen to be built early in the project and then race through important pieces near the end. Activities like quality assurance that typically occur near the end of the process get compressed and slighted.

Scheduling the development of critical or secure software is somewhat different from the scheduling for other kinds of software. Extra time and money must be allocated for extensive review and analysis. If an outside review is required, this must be taken into account from the beginning, since extra time and money must be allocated throughout the life of the project. One consequence of an extremely careful review process is the increased likelihood of uncovering problems. Time and money must be reserved for dealing with such problems prior to system delivery.

## EDUCATION AND TRAINING

There is a shortage of well-qualified people to work on production-quality software. There is a more serious shortage of those qualified to build critical software, and a dramatic shortage of people qualified to build secure software. A discussion of the general shortage of qualified technical people in this country is beyond the scope of this report. However, a few comments are in order about the narrower problems associated with the education and training of those working on critical and secure software.

Setting requirements for, specifying, and building critical software require specialized knowledge not possessed by typical software engineers. Over the years other engineering disciplines have developed specialized techniques—hazard analysis—for analyzing critical artifacts. Such techniques are not covered in most software engineering curricula, nor are they covered by most on-the-job training. Furthermore, working on critical software requires specialized knowledge of what can go wrong in the application domain.

Working on secure software requires yet more skills. Most notably, one must be trained to understand the potential for attack, for software in general and for the specific application domain in particular.

This committee advocates a two-pronged approach to addressing the shortage of people qualified to work on software: a new university-based program in combination with provisions for more on-the-job education as a part of current and future software projects.

The university-based program would be aimed at returning, graduate-level students who are already somewhat familiar with at least one application area. While the program would cover conventional software engineering, special emphasis would be given to topics related to critical and secure software. For example, different project management structures would be discussed in terms of their impact on both productivity and security. Discussions of quality assurance might emphasize safety engineering more than would be expected in a traditional software engineering program. Although careful consideration should be given to the specific content of such a curriculum, it seems clear that at least a one-year or perhaps even a two-year program is needed. Such a program could best be developed at universities with strong graduate engineering and business programs.

The committee envisions as an initial step approximately three such programs, each turning out perhaps 20 people a year. Over time, it would be necessary (and probably possible) to increase the number of graduates. Developing such a program would not be inexpensive: the committee estimates that the cost would be on the order of $1 million.

Given the current shortage and the time it will take to establish university programs that can increase the supply of qualified software engineers, managers of large security-related development efforts should deal explicitly with the need to educate project members. Both time and money for this should be appear in project budgets.

## MANAGEMENT CONCERNS IN PRODUCING SECURE SOFTWARE

Managing a project to produce secure software requires all the basic skills and discipline required to manage any substantial project. However, production of secure software typically differs from production of general high-quality software in one area, and that is in the heavy emphasis placed on assurance, and in particular on the evaluation of assurance conducted by an independent team.

Perhaps the most difficult, and certainly the most distinctive, management problem faced in the production of secure software is integrating the development and the assurance evaluation efforts. The two efforts are typically conducted by different teams that have different outlooks and use different notations. In general, the assurance team has an analytical outlook that is reflected in the notations it uses to describe a system; the development team focuses on the timely production of software, and accordingly emphasizes synthesis and creativity.

As a consequence it is very easy for an antagonistic relationship to develop between the two teams. One result is that what is analyzed (typically a description of a system) may bear little resemblance to the software that is actually produced. Geographic and organizational separation of the assurance and development teams compounds this problem. Ideally, the teams work side by side with the same material; as a practical matter, a jointly satisfactory "translation notation" may have to be devised so that the assurance team does not have to work with actual source code (which is typically not processable by their tools) and the development team does not have to program in an inappropriate language.

Scheduling of the various assurance and implementation milestones is typically a difficult process. Assurance technology is considerably less mature than implementation technology, and the tools it uses are often laboratory prototypes rather than production-quality software. Estimates of time and effort on the part of the assurance team are therefore difficult to make, and the various assurance milestones often become the "gating factor" in maintaining a project's schedule. Managers must make it clear from the outset, and maintain the posture, that assurance is an important aspect of the project and not just something that causes schedule slips and prevents programmers from doing things in otherwise reasonable ways. They must also recognize the fact that assurance will be a continuing cost. When a software system is modified, the assurance evidence must be updated. This means more than merely running regression tests. If, for example, assurance involves covert channel analyses, then those too must be redone.

The project plan must include a long, slow start-up in the beginning, with a higher percentage of time devoted to specification and analysis than is devoted to design. This lead time is required because the typical design team can devise mechanisms at a rate that greatly exceeds the ability of the assurance team to capture the mechanisms in their notations and to analyze them.

Managers should also cultivate a project culture in which assurance is viewed as everybody's problem and not just some mysterious process that takes place after the software is done. It is particularly necessary that the developers appreciate an attacker's mind-set, so that they themselves look at everything they do from the point of view of the threat. Information security (INFOSEC) attacks generally succeed because the attacker has embarked on an adventure, whereas the defenders are just working at a job. Management must instill the probing, skeptical, confident view of the attacker in each developer if the software is to be secure in fact as well as on paper.

## WHAT MAKES SECURE SOFTWARE DIFFERENT

From the perspective of programming methodology, the hardest part of producing secure software is producing good software. If one includes denial of service under the security rubric, producing secure software involves all the difficulties associated with building critical software, plus the additional difficulties associated with assuring integrity and confidentiality under the presumption of outside attack.

Some of the techniques generally considered useful in producing software have additional benefits in the security realm. People in the programming methodology field have long stressed the importance of modularity. In addition to making software easier to build, modularity helps to limit the scope of bugs and penetrations. Modularity may even be useful in reducing the impact of subverted developers.

There are also some apparent trade-offs between security concerns and other facets of good practice—"apparent" because most of the time one should opt for good software practice; without it one will not have anything useful.

Attempts to provide protection from high-grade threats by strictly limiting the number of people with access to various parts of the software may be self-defeating. The social process of the interaction of professionals on a project, conducted formally or casually, is a powerful tool for achieving correctness in fields like mathematics or software that deal with intangibles. Secrecy stops the social process in its tracks, and strict application of the "need-to-know" principle makes it very likely that system elements are subject to scrutiny only by insiders with a vested interest in the success of the project. Secrecy may also hinder the technical evolution of countermeasures; individuals assigned to the development of a given device or subsystem may not be aware of even the existence of predecessor devices, much less their specific strengths and weaknesses and mix of success and failure.

The inherent mutability of software conflicts with the requirements for achieving security. Consequently secure software is often deliberately made difficult to modify, for example, by burning code into read-only memory. Not only does this make it hard for attackers to subvert the software, but it also, unfortunately, makes it hard to make legitimate changes, for example, fixing a known vulnerability.

In resource-limited projects, any resources devoted to protecting those parts of a system deemed most vulnerable will detract from protecting other parts of the system. One must be careful to ensure that other parts of the system are not unduly impoverished.

## RECOMMENDED APPROACHES TO SOUND DEVELOPMENT METHODOLOGY

The recommendations that follow are broad directives intended to reflect general principles. Some are included in the fourth subset of the committee's recommendation 2, which calls for short-term actions that build on existing capabilities (see Chapter 1).

• *Finding:* What correlates most strongly with lack of vulnerabilities in software is simplicity. Furthermore, as complexity and size increase, the probability of serious vulnerabilities increases more than linearly. *Recommendation:* To produce software systems that are secure, structure systems so that security-critical components are simple and small.

• *Finding:* Software of significant size must be assumed to have residual errors that can compromise security. *Recommendation:* Reduce vulnerability arising from failure of security. Keep validated copies of vital data off-line. Establish contingency plans for extended computer outages.

• *Finding:* Extensive and extended use of software tends to reduce the number of residual errors, and hence the vulnerabilities. *Recommendation:* Encourage the development of generally available components with well-documented program-level interfaces that can be incorporated into secure software. Among these should be standardized interfaces to security services.

• *Finding:* Design-level verification using formal specifications has proved to be effective in the security area. *Recommendation:* Do more research on the development of tools to support formal design-level verification. Emphasize as a particularly important aspect of this research the identification of design-level properties to be verified.

• *Finding:* The most important bottleneck in reasoning about programs is the difficulty of dealing with multiple levels of abstraction. *Recommendation:* Conduct research on program verification so as to put greater emphasis on this problem.

• *Finding:* Software that taxes the resources of the computing environment in which it is run is likely to be complex and thus vulnerable. *Recommendation:* When building secure software, provide excess memory and computing capacity relative to the intended functionality.

• *Finding:* The use of higher-level programming languages reduces the probability of residual errors, which in turn reduces the probability of residual vulnerabilities. *Recommendation:* When tunneling attacks are not a major concern, use higher-level languages in building secure software.

• *Finding:* Using established software tends to reduce risk. *Recommendation:* In general, build secure software by extending existing software with which experience has been gained. Furthermore, use mature technology, for example, compilers that have been in use for some time.

• *Finding:* Ex post facto evaluation of software is not as reliable as evaluation that takes place during the construction of the software. *Recommendation:* Couple development of secure software with regular evaluation. If evaluation is to be done by an outside organization, involve that organization in the project from the start.

• *Finding:* There is a severe shortage of people qualified to build secure software. *Recommendation:* Establish educational programs that emphasize the construction of trusted and secure software in the context of software engineering.

• *Finding:* Adopting new software production practices involves a substantial risk that cannot usually be undertaken without convincing evidence that significant benefits are likely to result. This greatly inhibits the adoption of new and improved practice. *Recommendation:* Establish an organization for the purpose of conducting showcase projects to demonstrate the effectiveness of applying well-understood techniques to the development of secure software.

• *Finding:* Assurance is often the gating factor in maintaining a project schedule for producing secure software. This is particularly true during the design phase of a project. *Recommendation:* Build into schedules more time and resources for assurance than are currently typical.

• *Finding:* There is a trade-off between the traditional security technique of limiting access to information to those with a need to know and the traditional software engineering technique of extensively reviewing designs and code. Although there are circumstances in which it is appropriate to keep mechanisms secret, for most parts of most applications the benefits of secrecy are outweighed by the costs. When a project attempts to maintain secrecy, it must take extraordinary measures, for example, providing for cleared "inspectors general," to ensure that the need to maintain secrecy is not abused for other purposes, such as avoiding accountability on the part of developers. *Recommendation:* Design software so as to limit the need for secrecy.

## NOTES

1. For example, Jay Crawford of the Naval Weapons Center at China Lake, California, reports that the majority of errors in the production versions of the flight software managed there were classified as specification and design errors rather than coding errors.

2. The Navy estimates that testing software in an operating aircraft costs $10,000 per hour.

3. Checking the satisfiability of simple boolean formulas, for example, is an NP-complete problem; that is, the worst-case time required (probably) grows exponentially in the size of the formula.

4. Morrie Gasser and Ray Modeen, Secure Systems Group, Digital Equipment Corporation; Timothy E. Levin, Gemini Computers, Inc.; J. Thomas Haigh, Secure Computing

Technology Corporation (formerly Honeywell Secure Computing Technology Center); and George Dinolt, Ford Aerospace Corporation.

5.   Implementation of the Procurement Integrity Act of 1989 was suspended through November 30, 1990, and may be further suspended until May 31, 1991, to consider proposed changes by the Administration (see Congressional Record of June 21, 1990, and August 2, 1990).

# 5
# Criteria to Evaluate
# Computer and Network Security

Characterizing a computer system as being secure presupposes some criteria, explicit or implicit, against which the system in question is measured or evaluated. Documents such as the National Computer Security Center's (NCSC's) *Trusted Computer System Evaluation Criteria* (TCSEC, or Orange Book; U.S. DOD, 1985d) and its *Trusted Network Interpretation* (TNI, or Red Book; U.S. DOD, 1987), and the harmonized *Information Technology Security Evaluation Criteria* (ITSEC; Federal Republic of Germany, 1990) of France, Germany, the Netherlands, and the United Kingdom provide standards against which computer and network systems can be evaluated with respect to security characteristics. As described below in "Comparing National Criteria Sets," these documents embody different approaches to security evaluation, and the differences are a result of other, perhaps less obvious purposes that security evaluation criteria can serve.

This chapter describes the competing goals that influence the development of criteria and how current criteria reflect trade-offs among these goals. It discusses how U.S. criteria should be restructured to reflect the emergence of foreign evaluation criteria and the experience gained from the use of current NCSC criteria. While building on experience gained in the use of Orange Book criteria, the analysis contributes to the arguments for a new construct, Generally Accepted System Security Principles, or GSSP. As recommended by the committee, GSSP would provide a broader set of criteria and drive a more flexible and comprehensive process for evaluating single-vendor (and conglomerate) systems.

## SECURITY EVALUATION CRITERIA IN GENERAL

At a minimum, security evaluation criteria provide a standard language for expressing security characteristics and establish an objective basis for evaluating a product relative to these characteristics. Thus one can critique such criteria based on how well security characteristics can be expressed and evaluated relative to the criteria. Security evaluation criteria also serve as frameworks for users (purchasers) and for vendors. Users employ criteria in the selection and acquisition of computer and network products, for example, by relying on independent evaluations to validate vendor claims for security and by using ratings as a basis for concisely expressing computer and network security requirements. Vendors rely on criteria for guidance in the development of products and use evaluations as a means of product differentiation. Thus it is also possible to critique security evaluation criteria based on their utility to users and vendors in support of these goals.

These goals of security evaluation criteria are not thoroughly complementary. Each of the national criteria sets in use (or proposed) today reflects somewhat different goals and the trade-offs made by the criteria developers relative to these goals. A separate issue with regard to evaluating system security is how applicable criteria of the sort noted above are to complete systems, as opposed to individual computer or network products. This question is addressed below in "System Certification vs. Product Evaluation." Before discussing in more detail the goals for product criteria, it is useful to examine the nature of the security characteristics addressed in evaluation criteria.

### Security Characteristics

Most evaluation criteria reflect two potentially independent aspects of security: functionality and assurance. Security functionality refers to the facilities by which security services are provided to users. These facilities may include, for example, various types of access control mechanisms that allow users to constrain access to data, or authentication mechanisms that verify a user's claimed identity. Usually it is easy to understand differences in security functionality, because they are manifested by mechanisms with which the user interacts (perhaps indirectly). Systems differ in the number, type, and combination of security mechanisms available.

In contrast, security assurance often is not represented by any user-visible mechanisms and so can be difficult to evaluate. A product rating intended to describe security assurance expresses an evaluator's degree of confidence in the effectiveness of the implementation of security functionality. Personal perceptions of "degree of confidence" are relative, and so criteria for objectively assessing security assurance are based primarily on requirements for increasingly rigorous development practices, documentation, analysis, configuration management, and testing. Relative degrees of assurance also may be indicated by rankings based on the relative strength of the underlying mechanisms (e.g., cryptographic algorithms).

Thus two products that appear to provide the same security functionality to a user may actually provide different levels of assurance because of the particulars (e.g., relative strength or quality) of the mechanisms used to implement the functionality or because of differences in the development methodology, documentation, or analysis accorded each implementation. Such differences in the underlying mechanisms of implementation should be recognized in an evaluation of security. Their significance can be illustrated by analogy: two painted picnic tables may appear to be identical outwardly, but one is constructed of pressure-treated lumber and the other of untreated lumber. Although the functionality of both with regard to table size and seating capacity is identical, the former table may be more durable than the latter because of the materials used to construct (implement) it.

Another example illustrates more subtle determinants of assurance. A product might be evaluated as providing a high level of assurance because it was developed by individuals holding U.S. government top-secret clearances and working in a physically secure facility, and because it came with reams of documentation detailing the system design and attesting to the rigorous development practices used. But an identical product developed by uncleared individuals in a nonsecured environment and not accompanied by equivalent documentation, would probably receive a much lower assurance rating. Although the second product in this example is not necessarily less secure than the first, an evaluator probably would have less confidence in the security of the second product due to the lack of supporting evidence provided by its implementors, and perhaps, less confidence in the trustworthiness of the implementors themselves.[1]

Somewhat analogous is the contrast between buying a picnic table from a well-known manufacturer with a reputation for quality (a member of the "Picnic Table Manufacturers of America") versus purchasing a table from someone who builds picnic tables as an avocation. One may have confidence that the former manufacturer will use good materials and construction techniques (to protect his corporate image), whereas the latter may represent a greater risk (unless one knows the builder or has references from satisfied customers), irrespective of the actual quality of materials and workmanship. For computers and networks, the technology is sufficiently complex that users cannot, in general, personally evaluate the security assurance and therefore the quality of the product as they might the quality of a picnic table. Even evaluators cannot thoroughly examine every aspect of a computer system to the depth one would prefer, hence the reliance on evidence of good development practices, extensive documentation, and so on.

Security assurance is evaluated in these indirect ways in part because testing, specification, and verification technology is not sufficiently mature to permit more direct rankings of assurance. In principle one could begin by specifying, using a formal specification language, the security policies that a target product should implement. Then one could use verification tools (programs) to establish the correspondence between this specification and a formal top-level specification (FTLS) for the product. This FTLS could, in turn, be shown to match the actual implementation of the product in a (high-level) programming language. The output of the compiler used to translate the high-level language into executable code would also have to be shown to correspond to the high-level language. This process could be continued to include firmware and hardware modules and logic design if one were to impose even more stringent assurance standards.

As described in Chapter 4 of this report, state-of-the-art specification and verification technology does not allow for such a thorough, computer-driven process to demonstrate that a computer or network correctly supports a security policy. Experience has shown that there are numerous opportunities for human subversion of such a process unless it is carried through to the step that includes examination of the executable code (Thompson, 1984), and unless extreme measures, currently beyond the state of the art, are taken to ensure the correctness of the verification tools, compilers, and so on. Testing is a useful adjunct to the process, but the interfaces to the products of interest are sufficiently complex so as to preclude exhaustive testing to detect security flaws. Thus testing can contribute to an evaluator's confidence that security functionality is correctly implemented, but it cannot be the sole basis for providing a rating based on assurance as well. This explains, in large part, the reliance on indirect evidence of assurance (e.g., documentation requirements, trusted developers, and use of a secure development environment).

## Assurance Evaluation

There are actually two stages of assurance evaluation: design evaluation and implementation evaluation. Design evaluation attempts to assure that a particular proposed system design actually provides the functionality it attempts rather than simply appearing to do so. Some early systems were constructed that associated passwords with files, rather than with users, as a form of access control. This approach gave the appearance of providing the required functionality but in fact failed to provide adequate accountability. This is an example of a design flaw that would likely be detected and remedied by a design evaluation process.

Design evaluation is insurance against making a fundamental design error and embedding this error so deeply in a system that it cannot later be changed for any reasonable cost. To support the requirement of confidentiality, the possible mechanisms are well enough understood that design evaluation may not be needed to ensure a good design. But for newer areas of functionality, such as supporting the requirement for integrity or secure distributed systems, there is less experience with design options.

This committee considers explicit design evaluation to be very important. There are many ways to obtain such review, and vendor prudence may be sufficient in some circumstances to ensure that this step is part of system design. However, in general, the committee endorses design evaluation by an independent team (involving personnel not employed by the vendor) as a standard part of secure system design and encourages that this step be undertaken whenever possible.

Implementation evaluation is also important, but generally is more difficult, more time consuming, and more costly. For the level of assurance generally required in the commercial market, it may be sufficient to carry out a minimal implementation evaluation (as part of overall system quality assurance procedures, including initial operational or Beta testing) prior to system release if a good design evaluation is performed. Moreover, if the incident reporting and tracking system proposed in Chapters 1 and 6 is instituted, implementation flaws can be identified and fixed in the normal course of system releases. (Of course, well-known systems with well-known design flaws continue to be used, and continue to be penetrated. But for systems with modest security pretensions, many attacks exploit implementation flaws that could be corrected through diligent incident reporting and fixing of reported flaws.) By contrast the current implementation evaluation process as practiced by NCSC is very time consuming, and because it must occur after implementation, it slows the delivery of evaluated systems to the marketplace.[2]

For systems attempting to conform to a baseline set of GSSP as recommended by the committee (see Chapter 1, "Overview and Recommendations," and Chapter 2, "Concepts of Information Security"), the committee recommends that in the short term a process of evaluating installed systems (field evaluation), rather than the a priori implementation evaluation now carried out by NCSC, be used to increase the level of implementation quality.

This process of field evaluation, while it shares the basic goal of the current NCSC process, differs from that process in several ways that the committee views as advantageous. First, because such field evaluation is less time consuming, it may be viewed as less onerous than the current method for implementation evaluation. It should also be less costly, which would increase its acceptability. One side effect is that the early customers of a system subject to field evaluation would not have the full benefit of evaluated security mechanisms, a situation that would prompt customers with relatively high concern for security to delay purchase. In exchange for this limitation for early customers, the system would reach the market promptly and then continue to improve as a result of field experience. This process would also accommodate new releases and revisions of a system more easily than the current NCSC procedure, the Rating Maintenance Phase (RAMP). New releases that revise the function of the system should receive an incremental design review. But revisions to fix bugs would naturally be covered by the normal process of field testing. Indeed, it would be hoped that revisions would follow naturally from the implementation evaluation.

This field evaluation process, if explicitly organized, can focus market forces in an effective way and lead to the recognition of outside evaluation as a valuable part of system assurance. The committee is concerned that, outside of the DOD, where the NCSC process is mandated, there is little appreciation of the importance of evaluation as an explicit step. Instead, the tendency initially is to accept security claims at face value, which can result in a later loss of credibility for a set of requirements. For example, customers have confused a bad implementation for a bad specification, and rejected a specification when one system implemented it badly. Thus the committee has linked its recommendation for the establishment of a broad set of criteria, GSSP, with a recommendation to establish methods, guidelines, and facilities for evaluating products with respect to GSSP.

The committee believes that the way to achieve a system evaluation process supported by vendors and users alike is to begin with a design evaluation, based on GSSP itself, and to follow up with an implementation evaluation, focusing on field experience and incident reporting and tracking. Incident reporting and tracking could have the added effect of documenting vendor attentiveness to security, educating customers, and even illuminating potential sources of legal liability. Over time, the following steps might be anticipated: If GSSP were instituted, prudent consumers would demand GSSP-conforming systems as a part of normal practice. GSSP would drive field evaluation. If vendors perceived field evaluation as helping them in the marketplace or reducing their liability, they would come to support the process, and perhaps even argue for a stronger implementation evaluation as a means to obtain a higher assurance rating for systems. Thus GSSP could combine with market forces to promote development of systems evaluated as having relatively high assurance (analogous to the higher levels of the current Orange Book), a level of assurance that today does not seem to be justified in the eyes of many vendors and consumers. For this chain of events to unfold, GSSP must be embraced by vendors and users. To stimulate the development of GSSP, the committee recommends basing the initial set of GSSP on the Orange Book (specifically, the committee recommends building from C2 and B1 criteria) and possibly making conformance to GSSP mandatory in some significant applications, such as medical equipment or other life-critical systems.

### Trade-offs in Grouping of Criteria

In developing product criteria, one of the primary trade-offs involves the extent to which security characteristics are grouped together. As noted above, aspects of security can be divided into two broad types: functionality and assurance. Some criteria, for example, the Orange Book and the TNI, tend to "bundle" together functionality and assurance characteristics to define a small set of system security ratings. Other criteria, for example, the proposed West German (ZSI) set, group characteristics of each type into evaluation classes but keep the two types independent, yielding a somewhat larger set of possible ratings. At the extreme, the originally proposed British (DTI) criteria (a new evaluation scheme for both government and commercial systems has since been developed (U.K. CESG/DTI, 1990)) are completely unbundled, defining security controls and security objectives and a language in which to formulate claims for how a system uses controls to achieve the objectives. Comparisons with the successor harmonized criteria, the ITSEC, which builds on both the ZSI and DTI schemes, are amplified in the section below titled "Comparing National Criteria Sets."

One argument in favor of bundling criteria is that it makes life easier for evaluators, users, and vendors. When a product is submitted for evaluation, a claim is made that it implements a set of security functions with the requisite level of assurance for a given rating. The job of an evaluator is made easier if the security functions and assurance techniques against which a product is evaluated have been bundled into a small number of ratings (e.g., six, as in the Orange Book). Because evaluators are likely to see many systems that have been submitted for the same rating, they gain experience that can be applied to later evaluations, thus reducing the time required to perform an evaluation.

When completely unbundled criteria are used (e.g., the proposed DTI set), the evaluators may have to examine anew the collection of security features claimed for each product, since there may not have been previously evaluated products with the same set of features. In this sense, evaluation associated with unbundled criteria would probably become more time consuming and more difficult (for a system with comparable functionality and assurance characteristics) than evaluation against bundled criteria.

Bundled criteria define what their authors believe are appropriate combinations of security functions and assurance techniques that will yield useful products. This signaling of appropriate combinations is an especially important activity if users and vendors are not competent to define such combinations on their own. Bundled criteria play a very powerful role in shaping the marketplace for secure systems, because they tend to dictate what mechanisms and assurances most users will specify in requests for proposals and what vendors will build (in order to match the ratings).

A small number of evaluation ratings helps channel user demands for security to systems that fall into one of a few rated slots. If user demands are not focused in this fashion, development and evaluation costs cannot be amortized over a large enough customer base. Vendors can then be faced with the prospect of building custom-designed secure systems products, which can be prohibitively expensive (and thus diminish demand). Bundled criteria enable a vendor to direct product development to a very small number of rating targets.

A concern often cited for unbundled criteria is that it is possible in principle to specify groupings of security features that might, in toto, yield "nonsecure" systems. For example, a system that includes sophisticated access control features but omits all audit facilities might represent an inappropriate combination of features. If vendors and users of secure systems were to become significantly more sophisticated, the need to impose such guidance through bundled criteria would become less crucial. However, there will always be users and vendors who lack the necessary knowledge and skills to understand how trustworthy a system may be. The question is whether it is wise to rely on vendors to select "good" combinations of security features for systems and to rely on users to be knowledgeable in requesting appropriate groupings if unbundled criteria are adopted.

While bundled criteria may protect the naive vendor, they may also limit the sophisticated vendor, because they do not reward the development of systems with security functionality or assurance outside of that prescribed by the ratings. For example, recent work on security models (Clark and Wilson, 1987) suggests that many security practices in the commercial sector are not well matched to the security models that underlie the Orange Book. A computer system designed expressly to support the Clark-Wilson model of security, and thus well suited to typical commercial security requirements, might not qualify under evaluation based on the Orange Book. A system that did qualify for an Orange Book rating and had added functions for integrity to support the Clark-Wilson model would receive no special recognition for the added functionality since that functionality, notably relating to integrity, is outside the scope of the Orange Book.[3]

The government-funded LOCK project (see Appendix B), for example, is one attempt to provide both security functionality and assurance beyond that called for by the highest rating (A1) of the Orange Book. But because this project's security characteristics exceed those specified in the ratings scale, LOCK (like other attempts to go beyond A1) cannot be "rewarded" for these capabilities within the rating scheme. It can be argued that if LOCK were not government funded it would not have been developed, since a vendor would have no means within the evaluation process of substantiating claims of superior security and users would have no means of specifying these capabilities (e.g., in requests for proposals) relative to the criteria (Orange Book).

Bundled criteria make it difficult to modify the criteria to adapt to changing technology or modes of use. Changing computer technology imposes the requirement that security criteria must evolve. The advent of networking represents a key example of this need. For example, as this report is prepared, none of the computers rated by the NCSC includes network interface software in the evaluated product, despite the fact that many of these systems will be connected to networks. This may be indicative, in part, of the greater complexity associated with securing a computer attached to a network, but it also illustrates how criteria can become disconnected from developments in the workplace. For some of these computers, the inclusion of network interface software will not only formally void the evaluation but will also introduce unevaluated, security-critical software. This experience argues strongly that evaluation criteria must be able to accommodate technological evolution so that fielded products remain true to their evaluations.

The discussion and examples given above demonstrate that constraints on the evolving marketplace can occur unless evaluation criteria can be extended to accommodate new paradigms in security functionality or assurance. Such problems could arise with unbundled criteria, but criteria like the Orange Book set seem especially vulnerable to paradigm shifts because their hierarchic, bundled nature makes them more difficult to extend.

Based on these considerations, the committee concludes that in the future a somewhat less bundled set of security criteria will best serve the needs of the user and vendor communities. It is essential to provide for evolution of the criteria to address new functions and new assurance techniques. The committee also believes that naive users are not well served by bundled criteria, but rather are misled to believe that complex security problems can be solved by merely selecting an appropriately rated product. If naive users or vendors need protection from the possibility of selecting incompatible features from the criteria, this can be made available by providing guidelines, which can suggest collections of features that, while useful, are not mandatory, as bundled criteria would be.

## Comparing National Criteria Sets

The Orange Book and its *Trusted Network Interpretation*, the Red Book, establish ratings that span four hierarchical divisions: D, C, B, and A, in ascending order. The "D" rating is given to products with negligible or no security; the "C," "B," and "A" ratings reflect specific, increasing provision of security. Each division includes one or more classes, numbered from 1 (that is, stronger ratings correlate with higher numbers), that provide finer-granularity ratings. Thus an evaluated system is assigned a digraph, for example, C2 or A1, that places it in a class in a division. At present, the following classes exist, in ascending order: C1, C2, B1, B2, B3, and A1. A summary of criteria for each class, reproduced from the Orange Book's Appendix C, can be found in Appendix A of this report. There are significant, security functionality distinctions between division-C and division-B systems. In particular, the C division provides for discretionary access control, while the B division adds mandatory access control. A1 systems, the only class today within the A division, add assurance, drawing on formal design specification and verification, but no functionality, to B3 systems. Assurance requirements increase from one division to the next and from one class to the next within a division. The Orange Book describes B2 systems as relatively resistant, and B3 as highly resistant, to penetration. The robustness of these and higher systems comes from their added requirements for functionality and/ or assurance, which in turn drive greater attention to security, beginning in the early stages of development. That is, more effort must be made to build security in, as opposed to adding it on, to achieve a B2 or higher rating.

In these U.S. criteria, both the language for expressing security characteristics and the basis for evaluation are thus embodied in the requirements for each division and class. This represents a highly "bundled" approach to criteria in that each rating, for example, B2, is a combination of a set of security functions and security assurance attributes.

The *Information Technology Security Evaluation Criteria* (ITSEC)—the harmonized criteria of France, Germany, the Netherlands, and the United Kingdom (Federal Republic of Germany, 1990)—represents an effort to establish a comprehensive set of security requirements for widespread international use. ITSEC is generally intended as a superset of TCSEC, with ITSEC ratings mappable onto the TCSEC evaluation classes (see below). Historically, ITSEC represents a remarkably easily attained evolutionary grafting together of evaluation classes of the German (light) Green Book (GISA, 1989) and the "claims language" of the British (dark) Green Books (U.K. DTI, 1989). ITSEC unbundles functional criteria (F1 to F10) and correctness criteria (E0 as the degenerate case, and E1 to E6), which are evaluated independently.

The functional criteria F1 to F5 are of generally increasing merit and correspond roughly to the functionality of TCSEC evaluation classes C1, C2, B1, B2, and B3, respectively. The remaining functionality criteria address data and program integrity (F6), system availability (F7), data integrity in communication (F8), data confidentiality in communication (F9), and network security, including confidentiality and integrity (F10). F6 to F10 may in principle be evaluated orthogonally to each other and to the chosen base level, F1, F2, F3, F4, or F5.

The correctness criteria are intended to provide increased assurance. To a first approximation, the correctness criteria cumulatively require testing (E1), configuration control and controlled distribution (E2), access to the detailed design and source code (E3), rigorous vulnerability analysis (E4), demonstrable correspondence between detailed design and source code (E5), and formal models, formal descriptions, and formal correspondences between them (E6). E2 through E6 correspond roughly to the assurance aspects of TCSEC evaluation classes C2, B1, B2, B3, and A1, respectively.

ITSEC's unbundling has advantages and disadvantages. On the whole it is a meritorious concept, as long as assurance does not become a victim of commercial expediency, and if the plethora of rating combinations does not cause confusion.

A particular concern with the ITSEC is that it does not mandate any particular modularity with respect to system architecture. In particular, it does not require that the security-relevant parts of the system be isolated into a trusted computing base, or TCB. It is of course possible to evaluate an entire system according to ITSEC without reference to its composability (e.g., as an application on top of a TCB), but this complicates the evaluation and fails to take advantage of other related product evaluations. The effectiveness of this approach remains to be seen.

The initial ITSEC draft was published and circulated for comment in 1990. Hundreds of comments were submitted by individuals and organizations from several countries, including the United States, and a special meeting of interested parties was held in Brussels in September 1990. In view of the volume and range of comments submitted, plus the introduction of a different proposal by EUROBIT, a European computer manufacturers' trade association, a revised draft is not expected before mid-1991.

The dynamic situation calls for vigilance and participation, to the extent possible, by U.S. interests. At present, the National Institute of Standards and Technology (NIST) is coordinating U.S. inputs, although corporations and individuals are also contributing directly. It is likely that the complete process of establishing harmonized criteria, associated evaluation mechanisms, and related standards will take some time and will, after establishment, continue to evolve. Because the European initiatives are based in part on a reaction to the narrowness of the TCSEC, and because NIST's resources are severely constrained, the committee recommends that GSSP and a new organization to spearhead GSSP, the Information Security Foundation, provide a focus for future U.S. participation in international criteria and evaluation initiatives.

## Reciprocity Among Criteria Sets

A question naturally arises with regard to comparability and reciprocity of the ratings of different systems. Even though ratings under one criteria set may be mappable to roughly comparable ratings under a different criteria set, the mapping is likely to be imprecise and not symmetric; for example, the mappings may be many-to-one. Even if there is a reasonable mapping between some ratings in different criteria, one country may refuse to recognize the results of an evaluation performed by an organization in another country, for political, as well as technical, reasons. The subjective nature of the ratings process makes it difficult, if not impossible, to ensure consistency among evaluations performed at different facilities, by different evaluators, in different countries, especially when one adds the differences in the criteria themselves. In such circumstances it is not hard to imagine how security evaluation criteria can become the basis for erecting barriers to international trade in computer systems, much as some have argued that international standards have become (Frenkel, 1990). Reciprocity has been a thorny problem in the comparatively simpler area of rating conformance to interoperability standards, where testing and certification are increasingly in demand, and there is every indication it will be a major problem for secure systems.

Multinational vendors of computer systems do not wish to incur the costs and delay to market associated with multiple evaluations under different national criteria sets. Equally important, they may not be willing to reveal to foreign evaluators details of their system design and their development process, which they may view as highly proprietary. The major U.S. computer system vendors derive a significant fraction of their revenue from foreign sales and thus are especially vulnerable to proliferating, foreign evaluation criteria. At the same time, the NCSC has interpreted its charter as not encompassing evaluation of systems submitted by foreign vendors. This has stimulated the development of foreign criteria and thus has contributed to the potential conflicts among criteria on an international scale.

Analyses indicate that one can map any of the Orange Book ratings onto an ITSEC rating. A reverse mapping (from ITSEC to Orange Book ratings) is also possible, although some combinations of assurance and functionality are not well represented, and thus the evaluated product may be "underrated." However, the ITSEC claims language may tend to complicate comparisons of ITSEC ratings with one another.

Products evaluated under the Orange Book could be granted ITSEC ratings and ratings under other criteria that are relatively unbundled. This should be good news for U.S. vendors, if rating reciprocity agreements are enacted between the United States and foreign governments. Of course, a U.S. vendor could not use reciprocity to achieve the full range of ratings available to vendors who undergo ITSEC evaluation directly.

Even when there are correspondences between ratings under different criteria, there is the question of confidence in the evaluation process as carried out in different countries.[4] Discussions with NCSC and NSA staff suggest that reciprocity may be feasible at lower levels of the Orange Book, perhaps B1 and below, but not at the higher levels (committee briefings; personal communications). In part this sort of limitation reflects the subjective nature of the evaluation process. It may also indicate a reluctance to rely on "outside" evaluation for systems that would be used to separate multiple levels of DOD classified data. If other countries were to take a similar approach for high assurance levels under their criteria, then reciprocity agreements would be of limited value over time (as more systems attain higher ratings). Another likely consequence would be a divergence between criteria and evaluations for systems intended for use in defense applications and those intended for use in commercial applications.

## SYSTEM CERTIFICATION VS. PRODUCT EVALUATION

The discussion above has addressed security evaluation criteria that focus on computer and network products. These criteria do not address all of the security concerns that arise when one actually deploys a system, whether it consists of a single computer or is composed of multiple computer and network products from different vendors. Procedural and physical safeguards, and others for personnel and emanations, enter into overall system security, and these are not addressed by product criteria. Overall system security is addressed by performing a thorough analysis of the system in question, taking into account not only the ratings of products that might be used to construct the system, but also the threats directed against the system and the concerns addressed by the other safeguards noted above, and producing a security architecture that address all of these security concerns.

The simple ratings scheme embodied in the Orange Book and the TNI have led many users to think in terms of product ratings for entire systems. Thus it is not uncommon to hear a user state that his system, which consists of numerous computers linked by various networks, all from different vendors, needs to be, for example, B1. This statement arises from a naive attempt to apply the environment guidelines developed for the Orange Book to entire systems of much greater complexity and diversity. It leads to discussions of whether a network connecting several computers with the same rating is itself rated at or below the level of the connected computers. Such discussions, by adopting designations developed for product evaluation, tend to obscure the complexity of characterizing the security requirements for real systems and the difficulty of designing system security solutions.

In fact, the term "evaluation" is often reserved for products, not deployed systems. Instead, at least in the DOD and intelligence communities, systems are certified for use in a particular environment with data of a specified sensitivity.[5] Unfortunately, the certification process tends to be more subjective and less technically rigorous than the product evaluation process. Certification of systems historically preceded Orange Book-style product evaluation, and certification criteria are typically less uniform, that is, varying from agency to agency.

Nonetheless, certification does attempt to take into account the full set of security disciplines noted above and thus is more an attempt at a systems approach to security than it is product evaluation.

Certified systems are not rated with concise designations, and standards for certification are less uniform than those for product evaluation, so that users cannot use the results of a certification applied to an existing system to simply specify security requirements for a new system. Unlike that from product evaluations, the experience gained from certifying systems is not so easily codified and transferred for use in certifying other systems. To approach the level of rigor and uniformity comparable to that involved in product evaluation, a system certifier would probably have to be more extensively trained than his counterpart who evaluates products. After all, certifiers must be competent in more security disciplines and be able to understand the security implications of combining various evaluated and unevaluated components to construct a system.

A user attempting to characterize the security requirements for a system he is to acquire will find applying system certification methodology a priori a much more complex process than specifying a concise product rating based on a reading of the TCSEC environment guidelines (Yellow Book; U.S. DOD, 1985b). Formulating the security architecture for a system and selecting products to realize that architecture are intrinsically complex tasks that require expertise most users do not possess. Rather than attempting to cast system security requirements in the very concise language of a product ratings scheme such as the Orange Book, users must accept the complexity associated with system security and accept that developing and specifying such requirements are nontrivial tasks best performed by highly trained security specialists.[6]

In large organizations the task of system certification may be handled by internal staff. Smaller organizations will probably need to enlist the services of external specialists to aid in the certification of systems, much as structural engineers are called in as consultants. In either case system certifiers will need to be better trained to deal with increasingly complex systems with increased rigor. A combination of formal training and real-world experience are appropriate prerequisites for certifiers, and licensing (including formal examination) of consulting certifiers may also be appropriate.

Increasingly, computers are becoming connected via networks and are being organized into distributed systems. In such environments a much more thorough system security analysis is required, and the product rating associated with each of the individual computers is in no way a sufficient basis for evaluating the security of the system as a whole. This suggests that it will become increasingly important to develop methodologies for ascertaining the security of networked systems, not just evaluations for individual computers. Product evaluations are not applicable to whole systems in general, and as "open systems" that can be interconnected relatively easily become more the rule, the need for system security evaluation, as distinct from product evaluation, will become even more critical.

Many of the complexities of system security become apparent in the context of networks, and the TNI (which is undergoing revision) actually incorporates several distinct criteria in its attempt to address these varied concerns. Part I of the TNI provides product evaluation criteria for networks, but since networks are seldom homogeneous products this portion of the TNI seems to have relatively little direct applicability to real networks. Part II and Appendix A of the TNI espouse an unbundled approach to evaluation of network components, something that seems especially appropriate for such devices and that is similar to the ITSEC F9 and F10 functionality classes. However, many of the ratings specified in Part II and Appendix A of the TNI are fairly crude; for example, for some features only "none" or "present" ratings may be granted. More precise ratings, accompanied by better characterizations of requirements for such ratings, must be provided for these portions of the TNI to become really useful. Appendix C of the TNI attempts to provide generic rules to guide users through the complex process of connecting rated products together to form trusted systems, but it has not proven to be very useful. This is clearly a topic suitable for further research (see Chapter 8).

## RECOMMENDATIONS FOR PRODUCT EVALUATION AND SYSTEM CERTIFICATION CRITERIA

The U.S. computer industry has made a significant investment in developing operating systems that comply with the Orange Book. This reality argues against any recommendation that would undercut that investment or undermine industry confidence in the stability of security evaluation criteria. Yet there are compelling arguments in favor of establishing less-bundled criteria to address some of the shortcomings cited above. This situation suggests a compromise approach in which elements from the Orange Book are retained but additional criteria, extensions of the TCSEC, are developed to address some of these arguments. This tack is consistent with the recommendations for GSSP made in Chapter 1, which would accommodate security facilities generally regarded as useful but outside the scope of the current criteria, for example, those supporting the model for Clark-Wilson integrity (Clark and Wilson, 1987).

The importance of maintaining the momentum generated by the Orange Book process and planning for some future reciprocity or harmonization of international criteria sets makes modernization of the Orange Book necessary, although the committee anticipates a convergence between this process and the process of developing GSSP. In both instances, the intent is to reward vendors who wish to provide additional security functionality and/or greater security assurance than is currently accommodated by the Orange Book criteria. The TNI should be restructured to be more analogous to the ITSEC (i.e., with less emphasis on Parts I and II and more on a refined Appendix A). The TNI is new enough so as not to have acquired a large industry investment, and it is now undergoing revision anyway. Thus it should be politically feasible to modify the TNI at this stage.

The ITSEC effort represents a serious attempt to transcend some of the limitations in the TCSEC, including the criteria for integrity and availability. However, it must be recognized that neither TCSEC nor ITSEC provides the ultimate answer, and thus ongoing efforts are vital. For example, a weakness of ITSEC is that its extended functional criteria F6 through F10 are independently assessable monolithic requirements. It might be more appropriate if integrity and availability criteria were graded similarly to criteria F1 through F5 for confidentiality, with their own hierarchies of ratings. (The draft Canadian criteria work in that direction.)

There is also a need to address broader system security concerns in a manner that recognizes the heterogeneity of integrated or conglomerate systems. This is a matter more akin to certification than to product evaluation.

To better address requirements for overall system security, it will be necessary to institute more objective, uniform, rigorous standards for system certification. The committee recommends that GSSP include relevant guidelines to illuminate such standards. To begin, a guide for system certification should be prepared, to provide a more uniform basis for certification. A committee should be established to examine existing system certification guidelines and related documentation—for example, password management standards—from government and industry as input to these guidelines. An attempt should be made to formalize the process of certifying a conglomerate system composed of evaluated systems, recognizing that this problem is very complex and may require a high degree of training and experience in the certifier. Development and evaluation of heterogeneous systems remain crucial research issues.

For systems where classified information must be protected, a further kind of criteria development is implied, notably development of an additional assurance class within the A division, for example, A2 (this is primarily for government, not commercial, users),[7] as well as functionality extensions for all divisions of the Orange Book.

The committee's conclusions and specific recommendations, which are restated in Chapter 1 under recommendation 1, are as follows:

1. A new generation of evaluation criteria is required and should be established, to deal with an expanded set of functional requirements for security and to respond to the evolution of computer technology, for example, networking. These criteria can incorporate the security functions of the existing TCSEC (at the C2 or B1 level) and thus preserve the present industry investment in Orange Book-rated systems. The committee's proposed GSSP are intended to meet this need.

2. The new generation of criteria should be somewhat unbundled, compared to the current TCSEC, both to permit the addition of new functions and to permit some flexibility in the assurance methodology used. Guidelines should be prepared to prevent naive users from specifying incompatible sets of requirements. The ITSEC represents a reasonable example of the desirable degree of unbundled specification.

3. Systems designed to conform to GSSP should undergo explicit evaluation for conformance to the GSSP criteria. Design evaluation should be performed by an independent team of evaluators. Implementation evaluation should include a combination of explicit system audit, field experience, and organized reporting of security faults. Such a process, which should be less costly and less onerous than the current NCSC process, is more likely to be cost-effective to the vendor and user, and is more likely to gain acceptance in the market.

4. Effort should be expended to develop and improve the organized methods and criteria for dealing with complete systems, as opposed to products. This applies particularly to distributed systems, in which various different products are connected by a network.

## NOTES

1. In the current environment, in which evaluations have been conducted by the NCSC, commercial system developers may face a greater challenge than those with defense contracting experience, who may have both cleared personnel and a working understanding of the documentation requirements. This practical problem underscores the need for a more effective interface between the commercial and the national security or classified worlds.

2. Based on information obtained in a briefing from NCSC officials, the NCSC evaluation process consists of five phases, including: (1) Pre-review Phase, (2) Vendor

Assistance Phase (VAP), (3) Design Analysis Phase, (4) Formal Evaluation Phase, and (5) Rating Maintenance Phase (RAMP).

In the Pre-review Phase vendors present the NCSC with a proposal defining the goals they expect to achieve and the basic technical approach being used. The pre-review proposal is used to determine the amount of NCSC resources needed to perform any subsequent evaluation. The Vendor Assistance Phase, which can begin at any stage of product development, consists primarily of monitoring and providing comments. During this phase, the NCSC makes a conscious effort not to "advise" the vendors (for legal reasons and because it is interested in evalution, not research and development). The Vendor Assistance Phase usually ends six to eight months before a product is released. The Design Analysis Phase takes an in-depth look at the design and implementation of a product using analytic tools. During this phase the Initial Product Analysis Report (IPAR) is produced, and the product is usually released for Beta testing. The Formal Evaluation Phase includes both performance and penetration testing of the actual product being produced. Products that pass these tests are added to the Evaluated Products List (EPL) at the appropriate level. Usually vendors begin shipping their product to normal customers during this phase. The Rating Maintenance Phase (RAMP), which takes place after products are shipped and pertains to enhancements (e.g., movement from one version of a product to another), is intended for C2 and B1 systems, to enable vendors to improve their product without undergoing a complete recertification.

3. The NCSC has argued that it is premature to adopt criteria that address security features that support Clark-Wilson integrity because formal models for such security policies do not yet exist. In this way they justify the present bundled structure of the TCSEC (committee briefing by NSA). The NCSC continues to view integrity and assured service as research topics, citing a lack of formal policy models for these security services. However, it is worth noting that the Orange Book does not require a system to demonstrate correspondence to a formal security policy model until class B2, and the preponderance of rated systems in use in the commercial sector are below this level, for example, at the C2 level. Thus the NCSC argument against unbundling the TCSEC to include integrity and availability requirements in the criteria, at least at these lower levels of assurance, does not appear to be consistent.

4. In the future software tools that capture key development steps may facilitate evaluation and cross-checks on evaluations by others.

5. In the DOD environment the term "accreditation" refers to formal approval to use a system in a specified environment as granted by a designated approval authority. The term "certification" refers to the technical process that underlies the formal accreditation.

6. The claims language of the ITSEC may be more amenable to system security specification. However, product evaluation and system certification are still different processes and should not be confused, even if the ratings terminology can be shared between the two.

7. Proposals for an A2 class have been made before with no results, but LOCK and other projects suggest that it may now be time to extend the criteria to provide a higher assurance class. This class could apply formal specification and verification technology to a greater degree, require more stringent control on the development process (compare to the ITSEC E6 and E7), and/or call for stronger security mechanisms (e.g., the LOCK SIDEARM and BED technology, described in Appendix B of this report). The choice of which additional assurance features might be included in A2 requires further study.

# 6
# Why the Security Market Has Not Worked Well

Currently available are a wide variety of goods and services intended to enhance computer and communications security. These range from accessory devices for physical security, identification, authentication, and encryption to insurance and disaster recovery services, which provide computer and communications centers as a backup to an organization's or individual's own equipment and facilities. This chapter focuses on the market for secure or trusted systems and related products, primarily software. It provides an overview of the market and its problems, outlines the influences of the federal government on this market, discusses the lack of consumer awareness and options for alleviating it, and assesses actual and potential government regulation of the secure system market. Additional details on the export control process and insurance are provided in two chapter appendixes.

## THE MARKET FOR TRUSTWORTHY SYSTEMS

Secure or trusted information systems are supplied by vendors of general- and special-purpose hardware and software. Overall, the market for these systems has developed slowly, although the pace is picking up somewhat now. Whereas the market in 1980 was dominated by commercial computer and communications systems with no security features, the market in 1990 includes a significant number of systems that offer discretionary access control and a growing number from both major and niche vendors with both discretionary and mandatory access control, which provides significant protections against breaches of confidentiality. Notable is the trend to produce systems rated at the Orange Book's B1 level (see Appendix A of this report), often by adapting products that had had fewer security features and less assurance.

According to vendors, consumers most frequently demand security in connection with networked systems, which serve multiple users. One market research firm (International Resource Development) has estimated that the market for local area network (LAN) security devices may grow up to sixfold by the mid-1990s; it also foresees significant growth in data and voice encryption devices, in part because their costs are declining (Brown, 1989a). Other factors cited for growth in the encryption market are requirements for control of fraud in financial services and elsewhere (Datapro Research, 1989a).

Prominent in the market has been host access control software for IBM mainframes, especially IBM's RACF and Computer Associates' ACF2 and Top Secret. This type of add-on software provides (but does not enforce) services, such as user identification, authentication, authorization, and audit trails, that the underlying operating systems lack. It was originally developed in the 1970s and early 1980s, driven by the spread of multiaccess applications (mainframe-based systems were not originally developed with security as a significant consideration). Both IBM and Computer Associates plan to make these products conform to Orange Book B1 criteria. Although IBM intends now to bring its major operating systems up to the B1 level, it is reluctant to undertake development to achieve higher levels of assurance (committee briefing by IBM). Moreover, the market for host access control systems is growing slowly because those who need them generally have them already.[1] One market analyst, Datapro, notes that sales come mostly from organizations required by federal or state regulations to implement security controls (Datapro Research, 1990a).

The most powerful alternatives to add-on software, of course, are systems with security and trust built in. In contrast to the mainframe environment, some vendors have been building more security features directly into midrange and open systems, possibly benefiting from the more rapid growth of this part of the market. Even in the personal computer market, newer operating systems (e.g., OS/2) offer more security than older ones (e.g., MS/DOS).

Multics, the first commercial operating system that was developed (by the Massachusetts Institute of Technology, General Electric, and AT&T Bell Laboratories) with security as a design goal, achieved a B2 rating in 1985. While Multics has a loyal following and is frequently cited as a prime exemplar of system security, its commercial history has not been encouraging. Its pending discontinuation by its vendor (now Bull, previously Honeywell, originally General Electric) apparently reflects a strategic commitment to other operating systems (Datapro Research, 1990b).

The history of Unix illustrates the variability of market forces during the lifetime of a single product. Originally Unix had security facilities superior to those in most commercial systems then in widespread use.[2] Unix was enthusiastically adopted by the academic computer science community because of its effectiveness for software development. This community, where security consciousness was not widespread, created new capabilities, especially to interface to DARPA-sponsored networking (e.g., remote log-in and remote command execution).[3] As Unix spread into the commercial marketplace, the new capabilities were demanded despite the fact that they undermined the ability to run a tight ship from the security standpoint. Subsequently, and largely spurred by the Orange Book, various efforts to strengthen the Unix system have been undertaken (including T-MACH, funded by DARPA; LOCK, funded by the National Security Agency; the IEEE POSIX 1003.6 standards proposal; and various manufacturers' projects). But the corrections will not be total: many customers still choose freedom over safety.

The slow growth of the market for secure software and systems feeds vendor perceptions that its profitability is limited. Both high development costs and a perceived small market have made secure software and system development appear as a significant risk to vendors. Moreover, a vendor that introduces a secure product before its competitors has only a year or two to charge a premium. After that, consumers come to expect that the new attributes will be part of the standard product offering. Thus the pace of change and competition in the overall market for computer technology may be inimical to security, subordinating security-relevant quality to creativity, functionality, and timely releases or upgrades. These other attributes are rewarded in the marketplace and more easily understood by consumers and even software developers.

While the overall market for computer technology is growing and broadening, the tremendous growth in retail distribution, as opposed to custom or low-volume/high-price sales, has helped to distance vendors from consumers and to diminish the voice of the growing body of computer users in vendor decision making. Although vendors have relatively direct communications with large-system customers—customers whom they know by name and with whom they have individualized contracts—they are relatively removed from buyers of personal computer products, who may be customers of a retail outlet rather than of the manufacturer itself. Retail distribution itself may constrain the marketing of security products. Vendors of encryption and access control products have indicated that some retailers may avoid offering security products because "the issue of security dampens enthusiasm," while some of these relatively small vendors avoid retail distribution because it requires more customer support than they can manage (Datapro Research, 1989a).

Many in the security field attribute the increased availability of more secure systems to government policies stimulating demand for secure systems (see "Federal Government Influence on the Market" below). Those policies have led to a two-tiered market: government agencies, especially those that process classified information, and their vendors, are likely to demand Orange Book-rated trusted systems; other agencies, commercial organizations, and individuals that process sensitive but unclassified information are more likely to use less sophisticated safeguards. This second market tier constitutes the bulk of the market for computer-based systems. The committee believes that, more often than not, consumers do not have enough or good enough safeguards, both because options on the market often appear to be ineffective or too expensive, and because the value of running a safe operation is often not fully appreciated. Since data describing the marketplace are limited and of questionable quality, the committee bases its judgment on members' experiences in major system user and vendor companies and consultancies. This judgment also reflects the committee's recognition that even systems conforming to relatively high Orange Book ratings have limitations, and do not adequately address consumer needs for integrity and availability safeguards.

## A SOFT MARKET: CONCERNS OF VENDORS

Vendors argue that a lack of broad-based consumer understanding of security risks and safeguard options results in relatively low levels of demand for computer and communications security. For example, one survey of network users found that only 17 percent of Fortune 1000 sites and 10 percent of other sites used network security systems (Network World, 1990). Thus, although market research may signal high growth rates in certain security markets, the absolute market volume is small. To gain insight into the current market climate for secure products, the committee interviewed several hardware and software vendors.

Vendors find security hard to sell, in part because consumers and vendors have very different perceptions of the security problem.[4] This situation calls for creative marketing: one vendor stresses functionality in marketing operating system software for single-user systems and security in marketing essentially the same software for multiuser local area networked systems. A commonly reported problem is limited willingness of management to pay for security, although the rise in expectations following publicity over major computer crimes suggests that at least at the technical level, consumers are ready for more security. From the consumer's perspective, it is easy to buy something that is cheap; buying something expensive requires risk assessment and an investment in persuading management of the need. Vendors observed that they hear about what consumers would like, but they do not hear consumers say that they will not buy products that lack certain security features.

Vendors differ in their attitudes toward the Orange Book as a stimulus to commercial product security. Some indicated that they saw the government as leading the market; others characterized the government as a force that motivates their customers but not them directly. Vendors familiar with the Orange Book find it offers little comfort in marketing. For example, one customer told a sales representative that he did not need the capabilities required by the Orange Book and then proceeded to list, in his own words, requirements for mandatory access control and complete auditing safeguards, which are covered extensively in the Orange Book. Overall, vendors maintained that the Orange Book has had limited appeal outside the government contracting market, in part because it is associated with the military and in part because it adds yet more jargon to an already technically complex subject. This sentiment echoes the findings of another study that gathered inputs from vendors (AFCEA, 1989). Vendors also indicated that marketing a product developed in the Orange Book environment to commercial clients required special tactics, extra work that most have been reluctant to undertake.

Vendors also complained that it is risky to develop products intended for government evaluation (associated with the Orange Book) because the evaluation process itself is expensive for vendors—it takes time and money to supply necessary information—and because of uncertainty that the desired rating will be awarded. Time is a key concern in the relatively fast-paced computer system market, and vendors complain about both the time to complete an evaluation and the timing of the evaluation relative to the product cycle. The vendor's product cycle is driven by many factors—competition, market demands for functionality, development costs, and compatibility and synchrony with other products—of which security is just one more factor, and a factor that is sometimes perceived as having a negative impact on some of the others. While vendors may have a product development-to-release cycle that takes about three to six years, the evaluations have tended to come late in the product cycle, often resulting in the issuing of ratings after a product has been superseded by newer technology.

The time to complete an evaluation has been a function of National Computer Security Center (NCSC) resources and practice. NCSC's schedule has been driven by its emphasis on security, the perceived needs of its principal clients in the national security community, and the (limited) availability of evaluation staff. By 1990, NCSC was completing evaluations at a rate of about five per year, although the shift from evaluating primarily C-level systems to primarily B-level systems was expected to extend the time required per evaluation (Anthes, 1989d; committee briefing by NSA). The time involved reflects the quality of the evaluation resources: individuals assigned to do evaluations have often had limited, if any, experience in developing or analyzing complex systems, a situation that extends the time needed to complete an evaluation; both vendors and NCSC management have recognized this. Further, as a member of the NCSC staff observed to the committee, "We don't speed things up." As of late October 1990, 1 system had obtained an A1 rating, none had been rated B3, 2 had been rated B2, 3 had been rated B1, 13 had been rated C2, and 1 had been rated C1 (personal communication, NSA, October 26, 1990). Prospects for future evaluations are uncertain, in view of the recent reorganization of the NCSC (see Chapter 7).

Vendors have little incentive to produce ratable systems when the absence of rated products has not detectably impaired sales. Customers, even government agencies that nominally require rated products, tend to buy whatever is available, functionally desirable, and or compatible with previously purchased technology. Customer willingness to buy unrated products that come only with vendor claims about their security properties suggests possibilities for false advertising and other risks to consumers.

Consider the multilevel secure database management system released by Sybase in February 1990 (Danca, 1990a). The Secure Server, as it is called, was designed and developed to meet B1-level requirements for mandatory access control as defined in the Orange Book. The development for that product began in 1985, with the initial operational (Beta) release in the spring of 1989. The Air Force adopted the Secure Server in its next version of the Global Decision Support System (GDSS), which is used by the Military Airlift Command to monitor and control worldwide airlift capabilities. However, at the time of its release, the Secure Server had not been evaluated against the Orange Book criteria because the relevant criteria, contained in the Trusted Database Interpretation (TDI), were still being reviewed. Although the TDI is expected to be released in late 1990 or early 1991, it will be at least six months (and probably nine months) before any official opinion is rendered by NCSC. In short, Sybase will be marketing a secure product that took five years to develop and the Air Force will be using that product for a full year before any evaluation information is released. Both the vendors and consumers have proceeded with some degree of risk.

## FEDERAL GOVERNMENT INFLUENCE ON THE MARKET

The federal government has tried to influence commercial-grade computer security through direct procurement, research support, and regulatory requirements placed on the handling of data in the private sector. That influence has been realized both directly through government actions (e.g., procurement and investment in research) and indirectly through regulations and policies that provide incentives or disincentives in the marketplace.[5] The influence of the Orange Book is discussed in Chapters 2 to 5 and in Appendix A. Procurement and strategic research programs are discussed briefly below.

### Procurement

The U.S. government has tried to suggest that a strong government and commercial market would exist for security products were such products available (EIA, 1987). Industry is skeptical of such promises, arguing that the government does not follow through in its procurement (AFCEA, 1989), even after sponsoring the development of special projects for military-critical technology. However, one step the government has taken that has apparently stimulated the market is known as "C2 by '92." A directive (NTISSP No. 200, issued on July 15, 1987) of the National Telecommunications and Information Systems Security Committee (NTISSC), the body that develops and issues national system security operating policies, required federal agencies and their contractors to install by 1992 discretionary access control and auditing at the Orange Book C2 level in multiuser computer systems containing classified or unclassified but sensitive information. This directive is widely believed to have stimulated the production of C2-level systems. However, its impact in the future is in question, given the divergence in programs for protecting classified and sensitive but unclassified information that has been reinforced by the Computer Security Act of 1987 and the revision of National Security Decision Directive 145 (see Chapter 7). The Computer Security Act itself has the potential for increasing the demand for trusted systems, but the security assessment and planning process it triggered fell short of expectations (GAO, 1990c).

Concern for security is not a consistent factor in government procurements. A small sample, compiled by the committee, of 30 recent

(1989) requests for proposal (RFPs), 10 of which were issued by DOD organizations and 20 of which were issued by the civil agencies, presents a picture of uneven concern for security: five RFPs had no stated security requirements. Five DOD and eight civil agency RFPs specified adherence to standards defined by the NCSC and the National Institute of Standards and Technology (NIST), although three of the DOD RFPs did not specify an Orange Book level. Two DOD and three civil agency RFPs indicated that unclassified but protectable data would be handled. None of the DOD RFPs specified encryption requirements; three civil agency RFPs required Data Encryption Standard (DES) encryption, and one required NSA-approved encryption technology. Access control features were required by 13 RFPs. Auditing features were required by six.

The procurement process itself provides vehicles for weakening the demand for security. Vendors occasionally challenge (through mechanisms for comment within the procurement process) strong security requirements in RFPs, on the grounds that such requirements limit competition. For example, a C2 requirement for personal computers was dropped from an RFP from the Air Force Computer Acquisition Command (AFCAC) because conforming systems were not available (Poos, 1990). Budgetary pressures may also contribute to weakening security requirements. Such pressures may, for example, result in the inclusion of security technology as a non-evaluated option, rather than as a requirement, leading to a vendor perception that the organization is only paying lip service to the need for security.

Interestingly, DOD itself is exploring novel ways to use the procurement process to stimulate the market beyond the Orange Book and military standards. In 1989 it launched the Protection of Logistics Unclassified/Sensitive Systems (PLUS) program to promote standards for secure data processing and data exchange among DOD and its suppliers. PLUS complements other DOD efforts to automate procurement procedures (e.g., electronic data interchange and Computer-aided Acquisition and Logistics Support (CALS) programs), helping to automate procurement (Kass, 1990). A subsidiary goal of PLUS is cheaper commercial security products (personal communication with PLUS staff).

## Strategic Federal Investments in Research and Development

The government, especially through DARPA funding, has contributed to computer technology through large-scale strategic research and development programs that supported the creation or enhancement of facilities such as the (recently decommissioned) Arpanet network serving researchers, Multics and ADEPT 50 (operating systems with security features), MACH (an extension of the Unix operating system that fully integrates network capabilities and that has been championed by the industry consortium Open Software Foundation), and the Connection Machine (an advanced parallel processor). Each of these projects—which were sponsored by DARPA—has moved the market into areas that are beneficial to both government and commercial computer users. The Arpanet and Multics experiences illustrate how very large scale, multifaceted, systems-oriented projects can catalyze substantial technological advances, expand the level of expertise in the research community, and spin off developments in a number of areas. Scale, complexity, and systems orientation are particularly important for progress in the computer and communications security arena, and the government is the largest supporter of these projects. Historically, security has been a secondary concern in such projects, although it is gaining more attention now. The widespread impact of these projects suggests that similar initiatives emphasizing security could pay off handsomely.

In the security field specifically, projects such as Multics and ADEPT 50 (which provided strong access control mechanisms), LOCK (hardware-based integrity and assurance), SeaView (a secure database management system), TMACH (a trusted or secure version of MACH), and the CCEP (Commercial COMSEC Endorsement Program for commercially produced encryption products) are intended to stimulate the market to develop enhanced security capabilities by reducing some of the development risks. The LOCK program, for example, was designed to make full documentation and background material available to major vendors so that they might profit from the LOCK experience; similar benefits are expected from the TMACH development program.

Another example is NSA's STU-III telephone project, which involved vendors in the design process. Five prospective vendors competed to develop designs; three went on to develop products. The interval from contract award to commercial product was less than three years, although years of research and development were necessary beforehand. The STU-III has decreased the price of secure voice and data communications from over $10,000 per unit to about $2,000 per unit, pleasing both government consumers and the commercial vendors. Moreover, in 1990 the DOD purchased several thousand STU-III terminals for use not only in DOD facilities but also for loan to qualified defense contractors; these firms will receive the majority of the purchased units. This program will help to overcome one obvious disincentive for commercial acquisition: to be of use, not only the party originating a call but also the receiver must have a STU-III.

For national security reasons, programs that are sponsored by NSA confine direct technology transfer to companies with U.S. majority ownership, thereby excluding companies with foreign ownership, control, or influence (FOCI). While the United States has legitimate national interests in maintaining technological advantage, the increasingly international nature of the computer business makes it difficult to even identify what is a U.S. company, much less target incentives (NRC, 1990). Another factor to consider in the realm of strategic research and development is the fact that, consistent with its primary mission, NSA's projects are relatively closed, whereas an agency like DARPA can more aggressively reach out to the computer science and technology community.

The proposed federal high-performance computing program (OSTP, 1989) could provide a vehicle for strategic research investment in system security technology; indeed, security is cited as a consideration in developing the component National Research and Education Network—and security would clearly be important to the success of the network. Agencies involved in generating technology through this program include DOD (with responsibility concentrated in DARPA), the National Science Foundation (NSF), the National Aeronautics and Space Administration (NASA), the Department of Energy (DOE), and NIST. However, funding uncertainty and delays associated with the high-performance computing program suggest both that security aspects could be compromised and that additional but more modest large-scale technology development projects that promote secure system development may be more feasible. Certainly, they would have substantial benefits in terms of advancing and commercializing trust technology. Other government-backed research programs that focus on physical, natural, or biomedical sciences (e.g., the anticipated database for the mapping and sequencing of the human genome, or remote-access earth sciences facilities) also have security considerations that could provide useful testbeds for innovative approaches or demonstrations of known technology.

## Export Controls as a Market Inhibitor

Vendors maintain that controls on exports inhibit the development of improved commercial computer and communications security products. Controls on the export of commercial computer security technology raise questions about the kind of technology transfer that should be controlled (and why), whether security technologies aimed at the civilian market should be considered to have military relevance (dual use), whether control should continue under the provisions aimed at munitions, and other considerations that affect how commercial and military perspectives should be weighed and balanced for these technologies. An overview of the export control process is provided in Chapter Appendix 6.1. The challenge for policymakers is to balance national security and economic security interests in drawing the line between technology that should be controlled, because it compromises national security (in this case by hampering intelligence gathering by government entities) and technology that need not be, and allowing that line to move over time.[6]

The committee considered controls on the export of trusted systems and on the export of commercial-grade cryptographic products. The current rules constraining the export of trusted (and cryptographic) systems were developed at a time when the U.S. position in this area of technology was predominant. As in other areas of technology, that position has changed, and it is time to review the nature of the controls and their application, to assure that whatever controls are in place balance all U.S. interests and thereby support national security in the fullest sense over the long term. The emergence of foreign criteria and evaluation schemes (see "Comparing National Criteria Sets" in Chapter 5) makes reconsideration of export controls on trusted systems especially timely.

Balancing the possible temporary military benefit against the long-run interests of both national security applications and commercial viability, the committee concludes that Orange Book ratings, per se, do not signify military-critical technology, even at the B3 and A1 levels. Of course, specific implementations of B3 and A1 systems may involve technology (e.g., certain forms of encryption) that does raise national security concerns, but such technology is not necessary for achieving those ratings. NSA officials who briefed the committee offered support for that conclusion, which is also supported by the fact that the criteria for achieving Orange Book ratings are published information. The committee urges clarifying just what aspects of a trusted system are to be controlled, independent of Orange Book levels, and targeting more precisely the technology that it is essential to control. It also urges reexamination of controls on implementations of the Data Encryption Standard (DES), which also derive from published information (the standard; NBS, 1977). Issues in both of these areas are discussed below.

*Technology Transfer: Rationale for Controlling Security Exports*

Currently, the military and intelligence communities provide the largest concentration of effort, expertise, and resources allocated to ensuring information security. Devoted to countering threats not likely to be experienced by industry, much of this effort and expertise gives rise to special, often classified, products that are not and should not be commercially available. However, a strong commercial security effort would make it possible for the defense sector to concentrate its development resources on military-critical technology. Then the flow of technology for dual-use systems could be substantially reversed, thus lessening concerns about the export of vital military technology.

Exports of dual-use computer technologies are controlled largely for defensive reasons, since those technologies can be used against U.S. national security—to design, build, or implement weaponry or military operations, for example. Computer security presents offensive and defensive concerns. Adversaries' uses of computer security technologies can hamper U.S. intelligence gathering for national security purposes (OTA, 1987b). As a result, DOD seeks to review sophisticated new technologies and products, to prevent potential adversaries of the United States from acquiring new capabilities, whether or not the DOD itself intends to use them. Another concern is that international availability exposes the technology to broader scrutiny, especially by potential adversaries, and thus increases the possibility of compromise of safeguards.

The need to minimize exposure of critical technology implies that certain military-critical computer security needs will continue to be met through separate rather than dual-use technology (see Appendix E, "High-grade Threats"). As noted in this report's "Overview" (Chapter 1), national security dictates that key insights not be shared openly, even though such secrecy may handicap the development process (see "Programming Methodology," Chapter 4). To maintain superiority, the export of such technology will always be restricted. Thus the discussion in this chapter focuses on dual-use technology.

## Export Control of Cryptographic Systems and Components

Historically, because of the importance of encryption to intelligence operations and the importance of secrecy to maintaining the effectiveness of a given encryption scheme, cryptographic algorithms and their implementations could not be exported at all, even to other countries that participate in the Coordinating Committee on Multilateral Export Controls (CoCom).

Restrictions on exports of DES have been contested by industry because of the growing use of DES. The restrictions were recently relaxed somewhat, allowing for export of confidentiality applications under the International Traffic in Arms Regulations (ITAR; Office of the Federal Register, 1990) to financial institutions or U.S.-company subsidiaries overseas. DES may also be exported for data integrity applications (NIST, 1990b). That is, DES may be used to compute integrity checks for information but may not be used to encrypt the information itself. Private (vendor-specific) algorithms are generally approved for export following review by NSA (although that review may result in changes in the algorithm to permit export). The Department of Commerce reviews export licenses for DES and other cryptographic products intended for authentication, access control, protection of proprietary software, and automatic teller devices.

Because of current controls, computer-based products aimed at the commercial market that incorporate encryption capabilities for confidentiality can only be exported for limited specific uses. (Ironically, encryption may even be unavailable as a method to assure safe delivery of other controlled products, including security products.) Affected products include Dbase-IV and other systems (including PC-oriented systems) with message and file security features. However, anecdotal evidence suggests that the regulations may not be applied consistently, making it difficult to assess their impact.

In some cases, the missing or disabled encryption function can be replaced overseas with a local product; indigenous DES implementations are available overseas. The local product may involve a different, locally developed algorithm. It is not clear, however, that modular replacement of encryption units will always be possible. The movement from auxiliary black-box units to integral systems suggests that it will become less feasible, and there is some question about whether modular replacement violates the spirit if not the letter of existing controls, which may discourage some vendors from even attempting this option. Vendors are most troubled by the prospect that the growing integration of encryption into general-purpose computing technology threatens the large export market for computer technology at a time when some 50 percent or more of vendors' revenues may come from overseas.

Much of the debate that led to the relaxation of export restrictions for DES centered on the fact that the design of DES is widely known, having been widely published for many years. Similarly, the RSA public-key algorithm (see "Selected Topics in Computer Security Technology," Appendix B) is well known and is, in fact, not patented outside the United States—because the basic principles were first published in an academic journal (Rivest et al., 1978). Consequently, there are implementations of DES and RSA that have been developed outside the United States and, as such, are not bound by U.S. restrictions.[7] However, they may be subject to foreign export control regimes. With

U.S. vendors enjoined from selling DES abroad, then foreign consumers and, more importantly, large multinational consumers will simply purchase equivalent systems from foreign manufacturers.

Recognizing the demand for a freely exportable confidentiality algorithm, NIST, in consultation with NSA, has announced plans to develop and certify a new algorithm for protecting sensitive but unclassified information, possibly drawing on a published public-key system. A joint NIST-NSA committee is working to develop a set of four cryptographic algorithms for use in the commercial environment. One algorithm would provide confidentiality and thus is a DES substitute. A public-key distribution algorithm would be used to distribute the keys used by the first algorithm. The last two algorithms would be used to provide digital signatures for messages: one would compute a one-way hash on a message and the other would digitally sign the hash. All of the algorithms would, by design, be exportable, thus addressing a major complaint about DES. However, this process has been delayed, apparently because of NSA's discomfort with NIST's reported preference for using RSA, which it perceives as almost a de facto standard (Zachary, 1990).

The announced development of one or more exportable algorithms has not satisfied vendors, who note that overseas competitors can offer local implementations of DES, which has become widely recognized as a standard. By contrast, the new algorithm, while promised to be at least as good as DES, may be difficult to sell as it will be incompatible with DES implementations in use and may be tainted as U.S.-government-developed. Under the circumstances, if national security objections to free DES export continue, they should at the least be explained to industry. Also, independent expert review of the new algorithm is desirable to elevate confidence to the level that DES has attained. Note that there are other (non-DES) commercially developed encryption algorithms that are licensed for export by the Department of State. The United States is typically involved in their development, and some 98 percent of the products implementing these algorithms are approved for export (committee briefing by NSA).

## Export Control of Trusted Systems

Trusted systems that have been evaluated at the Orange Book's levels B3 and above are subject to a case-by-case review, whether or not they incorporate cryptography or other technologies deemed military-critical.[8] That is, the government must approve the export of a given system to a given customer for a given application if it is, or could be, rated as B3 or above; products with lower ratings are not regarded as military-critical technology. The same rules extend to documentation and analysis (e.g., for a technical conference or journal) of affected products. An average of 15 such license applications per year (covering five to seven items) have been reviewed over the past three years, and all have been granted.[9] About half have involved U.S. vendors providing technical data to their subsidiaries. In the case of software verification tools, which are used to develop trusted systems, there is the added requirement that informal intergovernmental agreements exist to monitor the tools' installation and operation. This is somewhat less restrictive than the treatment for supercomputers.

Note that in some respects trusted systems technology is very difficult to control because it depends heavily on software, which is relatively easy to copy and transport (NRC, 1988a). As a result, such technology can never be the only line of defense for protection of sensitive information and systems.

## The Commercial Imperative

Because of the national security interests that dominate the ITAR, the current export control regime for high-level trusted systems and for most encryption products does not contain mechanisms for addressing vendor concerns about competitiveness. By contrast, commercial competitiveness concerns affect both the evolution of the Control List (CL) and the Commodity Control List (CCL) associated with the Export Administration Regulations (see Chapter Appendix 6.1) and the periodic reviews of dual-use technologies by the United States and other participants in CoCom. Under the terms of the Export Administration Act (50 U.S.C. APP. §§ 2401-2420, as amended), foreign availability may also justify the relaxation of controls for particular products, as it did for AT-class PCs in July 1989. Foreign availability is not, however, a factor in administering controls on military-critical technologies under the ITAR.

The discussions of controls on dual-use technology exports in general draw on a broader range of perspectives than do the discussions of technologies controlled under the ITAR, in part because there is generally no argument over whether a product is a munition or of fundamentally military value. As a result there is at least the potential for a greater balancing of policy interests in the making of control decisions affecting non-ITAR technologies. The complaints from industry surrounding controls on the export of DES and RSA, algorithms for encryption that fall in part under ITAR rules, signal a larger problem developing for exports of security technology. In today's global market for computer technology, commercial product line development, production economics, and competitive strategy lead producers to want to market products worldwide. Major vendors generally have a major share of business (often 50 percent or higher) from outside of the United States.

Industry has four key concerns: First, every sale is important for profitability in a small market, such as the current market for security-rated systems. This means that both actual disapproval of a given sale and the delay and uncertainty associated with the approval process are costly to vendors. (Supercomputers are an extreme case of this problem.) Second, the principal commercial customers today for trusted systems (and commercial-grade encryption) are multinational corporations. This means that if they cannot use a product in all of their locations around the world, they may not buy from a U.S. vendor even for their U.S. sites. Third, U.S. vendors have seen the beginnings of foreign competition in trust technology, competition that is being nurtured by foreign governments that have launched their own criteria and evaluation schemes to stimulate local industry (see "Comparing National Criteria Sets" in Chapter 5). These efforts may alter the terms of competition for U.S. vendors, stimulate new directions in international standards, and affect vendor decisions on where as well as in what to invest. Fourth, as security (and safety) technology becomes increasingly embedded in complex systems, system technology and users will come to depend on trust technology, and it will become more difficult to excise or modify in systems that are exportable. This last problem has been cited by vendors as a source of special concern; a related concern is providing interoperability if different standards are used in different countries or regions.

> The real difficulty arises if a vendor considers building security into a "mainstream" commercial product. In that event, the system's level of security, rather than its processing power, becomes its dominant attribute for determining exportability. A computer system that would export [sic] under a Commerce Department license with no delay or advance processing would become subject to the full State Department munitions licensing process. No vendor will consider subjecting a mainstream commercial product to such restrictions.[10]

The push by industry for expanded export flexibility for security-rated systems and low-grade encryption units highlights the tension between government encouragement of the supply of computer security technology, notably through the Orange Book evaluation of commercial products, and potential government restriction of the market for security products through export controls. The presence of an export control review threshold at B3, affecting B3 and A1 systems intended for other CoCom countries, has discouraged the enhancement of systems to these levels, for fear of making products more difficult, if not impossible, to export.

Since other factors, such as high development costs and softness of perceived demand, discourage development of highly rated systems, it is difficult to quantify the disincentive arising from export controls. However, the very real pressure to export DES and RSA does provide evidence of a developing international market for security technology beyond what may currently be exported. Those and similar or successor technologies are not the technologies that are used for defense purposes, and it may be time to endorse a national policy that separates but mutually respects both national security and commercial interests. Those interests may overlap in the long run: as long as policy encourages use of commercial off-the-shelf technology, a strong commercial technology base is essential for feeding military needs. Even specifically military systems profit from commercial experience. And the strength of the commercial technology base today depends on the breadth of the market, which has become thoroughly international.

## CONSUMER AWARENESS

Even the best product will not be sold if the consumer does not see a need for it. Consumer awareness and willingness to pay are limited because people simply do not know enough about the likelihood or the consequences of attacks on computer systems or about more benign factors that can result in system failure or compromise.[11] Consumer appreciation of system quality focuses on features that affect normal operations—speed, ease of use, functionality, and so on. This situation feeds a market for inappropriate or incomplete security solutions, such as antiviral software that is effective only against certain viruses but may be believed to provide broader protection, or password identification systems that are easily subverted in ordinary use.[12]

Further militating against consumer interest in newer, technical vulnerabilities and threats is the experience of most organizations with relatively unsophisticated abuses by individuals authorized to access a given system (often insiders), abuses that happen to have involved computers but that need not have. The bread-and-butter work of the corporate computer security investigator is mostly devoted to worrying about such incidents as the following:

1. Two members of management extract valuable proprietary data from a company's computer and attempt to sell the data to a competitor;

2. An employee of company A, working on a contract for company B, uses a computer of company B to send a bomb threat to company C;

3. An employee copies a backup tape containing confidential personnel information, which he then reveals to his friends;

4. An employee uses his access to company billing information on a computer to reduce the bills of certain customers, for which service he collects a fee; and

5. An employee uses company computer facilities to help him arrange illegal narcotics transactions.

All five of the above incidents are typical in a particular sense. In none of them did any single computer action of the perpetrator, as a computer action, extend beyond the person's legitimate authority to access, modify, transmit, and print data. There was no problem of password integrity, for example, or unauthorized access to data, or Trojan horses. Rather, it was the pattern of actions, their intent, and their cumulative effect that constituted the abuse.

The kinds of incidents listed above consume most of the security officer's time and shape his priorities for effective countermeasures. What the corporate computer and communications security specialist is most likely to want, beyond what he typically has, are better tools for monitoring and auditing the effects of collections of actions by authorized users: detailed logs, good monitoring tools, well-designed audit trails, and the easy ability to select and summarize from these in various ways depending on the circumstances he is facing.[13] This history in large measure accounts for the relatively low interest in the commercial sector in many of the security measures discussed in this report. Nevertheless, even attention to administrative and management controls, discussed in Chapter 2, is less than it could or should be.

Enhancing security requires changes in attitudes and behavior that are difficult because most people consider computer security to be abstract and concerned more with hypothetical rather than likely events. Very few individuals not professionally concerned with security, from top management through the lowest-level employee, have ever been directly involved in or affected by a computer security incident. Such incidents are reported infrequently, and then often in specialized media, and they are comprehensible only in broadest outline. Further, most people have difficulty relating to the intricacies of malicious computer actions. Yet it is understood that installing computer security safeguards has negative aspects such as added cost, diminished performance (e.g., slower response times), inconvenience in use, and the awkwardness of monitoring and enforcement, not to mention objections from the work force to any of the above. The Internet worm experience showed that even individuals and organizations that understand the threats may not act to protect against them.

The sensational treatment of computer crimes in the press and in movies about computer hijinks may obscure the growing role of computer technology in accomplishing more traditional and familiar crimes (e.g., fraud and embezzlement). In the public's eye, computer crimes are perpetrated by overzealous whiz-kids or spies, not disgruntled employees or professional criminals; prosecutors also complain that the media portray perpetrators as smarter than investigators and prosecutors (comments of federal prosecutor William Cook at the 1989 National Computer Security Conference). Public skepticism may be reinforced when, as in the case of recent investigations of the Legion of Doom and other alleged system abusers (Shatz, 1990), questions are raised about violation of First Amendment rights and the propriety of search and seizure techniques—issues of longstanding popular concern.[14]

Inevitably, resources are invested in safeguards only when there is a net payoff as measured against goals of the organization—whether such goals are chosen or imposed. It is notable that the banking industry's protection of computer and communications systems was stimulated by law and regulation. In the communications industry, lost revenues (e.g., through piracy of services) have been a major spur to tightening security.

### Insurance as a Market Lever

Insurance can offset the financial costs of a computer-related mishap. The development of the commercial market for computer insurance (described in Chapter Appendix 6.2) provides a window into the problems of achieving greater awareness and market response.[15]

The market for insurance against computer problems has grown slowly. Insurance industry representatives attribute the slow growth to low levels of awareness and concern on the part of organizations and individuals, plus uneven appreciation of the issues within the insurance industry, where underwriters and investigators may not fully understand the nature of the technology and its implications as used.[16] Insurance industry representatives also point to the reluctance of victims of computer mishaps to make their experiences public, even at the expense of not collecting on insurance.

The process of determining whether coverage will be provided involves assessing the controls provided by a prospect. Somewhat like auditors, underwriters and carriers evaluate security-related safeguards in place by focusing on physical and operational elements.

There is a concern for the whole control environment, including directly relevant controls and controls for other risks, which may indicate how well new risks may be controlled.

To the extent that premiums reflect preventive measures by an organization (e.g., off-site periodic backup copies of data, high-quality door locks, 24-hour guard coverage, and sprinkler or other fire control systems), insurance is a financial lever to encourage sound security, just as the Foreign Corrupt Practices Act (P.L. 95-215) and a variety of accounting principles and standards have encouraged stronger management controls in general (and, in some instances, stronger information security in particular (Snyders, 1983)).

### Education and Incident Tracking for Security Awareness

If some of the problems in the secure system marketplace are due to lack of awareness among consumers, options for raising consumer awareness of threats, vulnerabilities, and safeguards are obviously attractive. Two options are raised here as concepts—education and incident reporting and tracking. The committee's recommendation that incident tracking be undertaken by a new organization is discussed in Chapter 7.

#### Education

Society has often regulated itself by promoting certain behaviors, for example, taking care of library books. Societal care-taking norms must now be extended to information in electronic form and associated systems. The committee believes that elements of responsible use should be taught along with the basics of how to use computer and communication systems, much as people learn how to be responsible users of libraries. Building concern about security and responsible use into computing and general curricula (where computers are used) may be more constructive in the long run than focusing efforts on separate and isolated ethics units. This is not to discourage the many recent efforts among computer-related professional societies, schools, and companies to strengthen and discuss codes of ethics.[17] However, today much of the security training is funded by commercial companies and their employee students; that training, in turn, is focused on security officers and not end users. The committee underscores that the process becomes one to persuade, lead, and educate, and when possible, to make the unacceptability of not protecting computer systems outweigh the cost of taking appropriate action.

## Incident Reporting and Tracking

More extensive and systematic reporting and tracking of security and other system problems could help to persuade decisionmakers of their value and policymakers of related risks. For example, investigation and prosecution of computer crimes have proceeded slowly because of the uneven understanding within the legal community of the criminal potential as well as the relatively high costs involved in computer crimes (Conly, 1989; U.S. DOJ, 1989). At this time there is little statistical or organized knowledge about vulnerabilities, threats, risks, and failures. (Neumann and Parker (1989) represent one attempt to characterize vulnerabilities.) What is known about security breaches is largely anecdotal, as many security events happen off the record; one source of such information within the computer science and engineering community is the electronic forum or digest known as RISKS.[18] Estimates of aggregate losses vary widely, ranging from millions to billions of dollars, and estimates cited frequently in news reports are challenged by prosecutors (comments of federal prosecutor William Cook at the 1989 National Computer Security Conference). The European Community has begun to develop computer incident tracking capabilities; the British and the French both have new programs (Prefontaine, 1990). A reliable body of information could be used to make the public and the government more aware of the risks.

A means is needed for gathering information about incidents, vulnerabilities, and so forth in a controlled manner, whereby information would actually be available to those who need it—vendors, users, investigators, prosecutors, and researchers. There are a number of implementation issues that would have to be addressed, such as provision for a need-to-know compartment for unclassified information that is considered sensitive because of the potential implications of its widespread dissemination. It would also be necessary to couple reports with the caveat that yesterday's mode of attack may not necessarily be tomorrow's. The incident-reporting system associated with the National Transportation Safety Board illustrates one approach to data collection (although the handling, storage, and retrieval of the data are likely to be different—computer incident data are much more likely than transportation data to be exploited for copy-cat or derivative attacks).

Given the volume of transactions and activity that has occurred in the information systems of the private sector and occurs there each day, and given the decade or so during which numerous computer mishaps, intentional and accidental, have been documented and recorded, the validated evidence that has been accumulated remains minuscule by comparison to that of criminal incidents or accidents in other areas of business risk, for example, fire, embezzlement, and theft. This situation may reflect a relatively low incidence of problems to date, but there is strong evidence that available information is significantly underreported.[19] The effort begun by the DARPA Computer Emergency Response Team to develop a mechanism to track the emergency incidents to which it responds, and related plans at NIST, are a step in the right direction that could provide the impetus for a more comprehensive effort.[20] Such an effort is discussed in Chapter 7.

### Technical Tools to Compensate for Limited Consumer Awareness

Limited awareness of security needs or hazards can be offset in part by technical tools. Properly designed technical solutions may serve to reinforce safe behavior in a nonthreatening way, with little or no infringement of personal privacy or convenience. Impersonal, even-handed technical solutions may well be better received than nontechnical administrative enforcement. The key is to build in protections that preserve an organization's assets with the minimum possible infringement on personal privacy, convenience, and ease of use. As an explicit example, consider the ubiquitous password as a personal-identification safeguard. In response to complaints about forgetting passwords and about requirements to change them periodically, automated on-line prompting procedures can be introduced; a question-and-response process can be automatically triggered by elapsed calendar time since the last password change, and automated screening can be provided to deter a user from selecting an ill-conceived choice. Concerted vendor action, perhaps aided by trade associations, and consumer demand may be needed to get such tools offered and supported routinely by vendors.

Some issues pertaining to the proper use of such automated tools call for sensitivity and informed decision making by management. One concern is the potential for loss of community responsibility. Individual users no longer have the motivation, nor in many cases even the capability, to monitor the state of their system. Just as depersonalized "renewed" cities of high-rises and doormen sacrifice the safety provided by observant neighbors in earlier, apparently chaotic, gossip-ridden, ethnic neighborhoods (Jacobs, 1972), so a system that relies on carefully administered access controls and firewalls sacrifices the social pressure and community alertness that prevented severe malfeasance in older nonsecure systems. A perpetrator in a tightly controlled system knows better who to look out for than one in an open system. Furthermore, a tightly controlled system discourages, even punishes, the simple curiosity of ordinary users that can spot unusual acts. Wise management will avoid partitioning the community too finely lest the human component, on which all security ultimately rests, be lost. Simply put, technological tools are necessary but should not be overused.

## REGULATION AS A MARKET INFLUENCE: PRODUCT QUALITY AND LIABILITY

Regulation is a policy tool that can compensate for consumer inability to understand a complex product on which much may depend. Relatively little about computer systems is now regulated, aside from physical aspects of hardware.[21] Although software is a principal determinant of the trustworthiness of computer systems, software has generally not been subject to regulation. However, regulations such as those governing export of technology, the development of safety-critical systems (recently introduced in the United Kingdom), or the privacy of records about persons (as implemented in Scandinavia) do have an immediate bearing on computer security and assurance. The issue of privacy protection through regulation is discussed in Chapter 2, Appendix 2.1.

Like other industries, the computer industry is uncomfortable with regulation. Industry argues that regulations can discourage production, in part by making it more costly and financially risky. This is one of the criticisms directed against export controls. However, regulation can also open up markets, when market forces do not produce socially desirable outcomes, by requiring all manufacturers to provide capabilities that would otherwise be too risky for individual vendors to introduce. Vendors have often been put on an equal footing via regulation when public safety has been an issue (e.g., in the environmental, food, drug, and transportation arenas). In the market for trusted systems, the Orange Book and associated evaluations, playing the role of standards and certification, have helped to do the same—unfortunately, that market remains both small and uncertain.[22] As suggested above in "A Soft Market," individual vendors find adding trust technology into their systems financially risky because consumers are unable to evaluate security and trust and are therefore unwilling to pay for these qualities.[23]

Although in the United States regulation is currently a policy option of last resort, growing recognition of the security and safety ramifications of computer systems will focus attention on the question of whether regulation of computer and communications software and system developers is needed or appropriate, at least in specific situations (for example, where lives are at risk). The issue has already been broached in a recent congressional committee report (Paul, 1989). Although full treatment of that question is outside the scope of this report, the committee felt it necessary to lay out some of the relevant issues as a reminder that sometimes last resorts are used, and to provide reinforcement for its belief that some incentives for making GSSP truly generally accepted would be of value.

## Product Quality Regulations

System manufacturers generally have much greater technical expertise than system owners, who in acquiring and using a system must rely on the superior technical skill of the system vendor. The same observation, of course, applies to many regulated products on which the public depends, such as automobiles, pharmaceuticals, and transportation carriers. Similar motivations lie behind a variety of standards and certification programs, which may be either mandatory (effectively regulations) or voluntary (FTC, 1983). Whereas failure of an automobile can have severe, but localized, consequences, failure of an information system can adversely affect many users simultaneously—plus other individuals who may, for example, be connected to a given system or about whom information may be stored on a given system—and can even prevent efficient functioning of major societal institutions. This problem of interdependence was a concern in recent GAO inquiries into the security of government and financial systems (GAO, 1989e, 1990a,b). The widespread havoc that various computer viruses have wreaked amply demonstrates the damage that can occur when a weak spot in a single type of system is exploited. The accidental failure of an AT&T switching system, which blocked an estimated 40 million telephone calls over a nine-hour period on January 15, 1990, also illustrates the kind of disruption that is possible even under conditions of rigorous software and system testing. The public exposure and mutual interdependence of networked computer systems make trustworthiness as important for such systems as it is for systems where lives or large amounts of money are at stake, as in transportation or banking. Indeed, in settings as diverse as the testing of pharmaceuticals, the design of automobiles, or the creation of spreadsheet programs, results from programs and computers that are not directly involved in critical applications ultimately wind up in just such applications.

Goods and services that impinge on public health and safety have historically been regulated. Moreover, the direct risk to human life is a stronger and historically more successful motivation for regulation than the risk to economic well-being, except in the case of a few key industries (e.g., banks and insurance carriers). This situation suggests that regulation of safety aspects of computers, a process that has begun in the United Kingdom (U.K. Ministry of Defence, 1989a,b), has the best chance for success, especially with safety-critical industries such as medical devices and health care, or even transportation. It also suggests that the case for security-related regulation will be strongest where there are the greatest tie-ins to safety or other critical impacts. Thus computer systems used in applications for which some form of regulation may be warranted may themselves be subject to regulation, because of the nature of the application. This is the thinking behind, for example, the Food and Drug Administration's efforts to look at computer systems embedded in medical instruments and processes (Peterson, 1988). Note, however, that it is not always possible to tell when a general-purpose system may be used in a safety-critical application. Thus standardized ratings have been used in other settings.[24]

## Product Liability as a Market Influence

In addition to being directly regulated, the quality of software and systems and, in particular, their security and safety aspects, may be regulated implicitly if courts find vendors legally liable for safety- or security-relevant flaws. Those flaws could be a result of negligence or of misrepresentation; the law involved might involve contracts, torts, or consumer protection (e.g., warranties). At present, there is some indication from case law that vendors are more likely now than previously to be found liable for software or system flaws, and some legal analysts expect that trend to grow stronger (Agranoff, 1989; Nycum, 1989; Boss and Woodward, 1988). The committee applauds that trend, because it believes that security and trust have been overlooked or ignored in system development more often than not. Further, the committee believes that a recognized standard for system design and development, which could consist of GSSP, can provide a yardstick against which liability can be assessed.[25] Depending exclusively on legal liability as a mechanism to stimulate improvements in quality could backfire: it could inhibit innovation because of fears linking legal risks and the development of new products. GSSP could help allay such fears and curb capricious litigation by clarifying general expectations about what constitutes responsible design and development.

Software plays a critical role in assuring the trustworthiness of computer and communications systems. However, the risk that software may not function properly is borne largely by the consumer, especially for off-the-shelf software, which is typically obtained under licenses laden with disclaimers. Off-the-shelf applications programs and even operating systems are typically acquired by license with limited rights, under the terms specified by the manufacturer, as opposed to direct sale (which would imply that the vendor forfeits control over the terms and conditions of its use) (Davis, 1985). The purchaser typically has no bargaining power with respect to the terms and conditions of the license.[26] PC-based software licenses present the extreme case, since they are often sealed under shrink-wrap packaging whose opening signifies acceptance of the license. Typically, such licenses limit liability for damages to replacement of defective media or documentation, repair of substantial program errors, or refund of the license fee. From the vendor's perspective, this is not surprising: the revenue from an individual "sale" of PC software is very small, in the tens or hundreds of dollars; from the consumer's perspective, the absence of additional protections contributes to relatively low prices for packaged software. By contrast, customized applications systems, which may well be purchased rather than licensed, are developed in response to the specifically stated requirements of the client. The terms and conditions are those negotiated between the parties, the buyer has some real bargaining power, and the contract will reflect the intent and objectives of both parties.

Some consumer protection may come from the Uniform Commercial Code (UCC). Consumer protection may also come from the Magnuson-Moss Warranty Act (15 USC § 2301 et seq. (1982)), which provides standards for full warranties, permits limited warranties, and requires that warranties be expressed in understandable language and be available at the point of sale.

The UCC is a uniform law, drafted by the National Conference of Commissioners on Uniform State Laws and adopted as law by 49 states, that governs commercial transactions, including the sale of goods. While there is no law requiring express warranties in software licenses, the UCC addresses what constitutes an express warranty where provided, how it is to be enforced, and how to disclaim implied warranties.[27] The acquisition of a good by license is a "transaction" in goods and is generally covered by Article 2 of the UCC, although some provisions of the code refer specifically to "sale" and may not be applicable to licensed goods. The National Conference of Commissioners is expected to clarify the issue of whether software is a "good" (and therefore covered by the UCC) by including software within the definition of a "good." In any case, the state courts are quite familiar with the UCC and tend to apply its principles to software license transactions. Note that a proposed extension to the UCC, Section 4A, would impose liability on banks for errors in electronic funds transfers under certain conditions. This provision is already seen as motivating greater wire transfer network security among banks (Datapro Research, 1989b).

The UCC provides a number of protections for the buyer of goods. In every sale of a product by a seller that deals in goods of the kind sold, there is an implied warranty that the product is merchantable. The usual test for merchantability is whether the product is fit for the ordinary purposes for which such products are used. The buyer can recover damages whether or not the seller knew of a defect, or whether or not the seller could have discovered such a defect. The UCC also provides an implied warranty of fitness for a particular purpose. This warranty provides damages where any seller, whether a dealer in goods of the kind sold or not, has any reason to know the specific use to which the product will be put, and knows that the buyer is relying on the seller's superior expertise to select a suitable product. These warranties may be, and almost always are, disclaimed as part of PC software shrink-wrap licenses, often by conspicuously including such words as "as is" or "with all faults."

The UCC does permit the vendor to limit or exclude consequential and incidental damages, unless such limitation is unconscionable (e.g., because it is overly one-sided). Consequential damages are compensation for an injury that does not flow immediately and directly from the action, but only from the consequences or results of the action. For example, damages from a computer break-in that exploited a flawed password mechanism would be deemed consequential to the extent that the supplier of the password mechanism was held responsible. Recovery from suppliers can take other less far-reaching (and more plausible) forms, such as incidental damages. Incidental damages include commercially reasonable charges incurred incident to a breach, such as costs incurred to mitigate the damage.

While disclaimers and standard-form contracts or licenses are legal and help to keep prices down, as applied to software they raise questions about whether consumers understand what is happening and what popular licensing practices may mean. These questions were noted in a recent review of computer contract cases:

> Since purchasers generally base their selection of equipment and software on the sellers' representations as to the technical performance capabilities and reliability of equipment, the buyers often ignore the generally broad disclaimers of express and implied warranties in standard vendor contracts. When they become disappointed and discover that disclaimers foreclose their contract remedies, they turn to the law of misrepresentation for relief.

Misrepresentation cases will continue to proliferate until the industry more closely aligns its express warranties with the reasonable expectations of its customers, who assume that the hardware and software they buy will perform as described by the sellers' representatives who sold them the product. (Boss and Woodward, 1988, p. 1533)

The vulnerability of consumers and the mismatch of expectations even where individualized contracts are involved have been underscored by a few recent incidents involving vendor disabling of installed software in the course of disputes with customers.[28]

### Software and Systems Present Special Problems

It is clear from the foregoing discussion that a buyer of off-the-shelf software has extremely limited recourse should the licensed software not perform as expected. The major motivation for the vendor to produce trustworthy software is the desire to remain competitive. In the process, however, features for which customer demand is not high may receive inadequate attention. For example, restraints to protect passengers and emission controls to protect the public at large are now universally installed in automobiles because they have been mandated by government action. Although public interest groups helped spur government action, few individual consumers demanded these features, perhaps because of the increased cost or the perception of reduced performance or the inability of an individual to bargain for them effectively. Yet few would argue that these impositions are not in the public interest; what does stimulate argument is the stringency of the safeguard required.

Unsafe or nonsecure software poses analogous risks to users and to others exposed to it (see Chapter 2's "Risks and Vulnerabilities"). More trustworthy software may, like safer and cleaner automobiles, carry a higher product price tag and may also suffer from a perception of reduced performance. In the absence of general consumer demand for more trustworthy software, should manufacturers of off-the-shelf software be subjected to governmental action? In particular, should the government act to reduce a software vendor's ability to disclaim warranties and to limit damages?

The software industry and software itself exhibit some characteristics that limit the scope for governmental action. On the one hand, complex software will inevitably contain errors; no human being can guarantee that it will be free of errors. Imposition of strict liability (without a finding of malice or negligence) for any error would clearly not be equitable, since the exercise of even an exceptionally high degree of care in software production would not guarantee an error-free product. On the other hand, tools and testing methods to reduce the probability of errors are available. Systematic use of such tools and methods prior to software release reduces the frequency and severity of errors in the fielded product. The committee believes that these tools and methods are not now in wide use both because they are not well known (e.g., the forefront technology of automated protocol analysis, which can dramatically shorten the development cycle) or because, given the evolution of products and practices in the industry, they appear to have been ignored by vendors (e.g., as has been the case for strongly type-checked link editors).

Of course, licensees must accept many risks in using software. Users must train themselves sufficiently in the proper operation of a computer system and software before relying on them. A software vendor should not be held liable for damage caused by users' gross ignorance.[29]   At the same time, the software vendor must bear a degree of responsibility in helping to properly train the user through adequate and clear documentation describing proper use of the product, and its limitations, including their bearing on security and safety. The superior knowledge and skill of the software vendor itself should impose a duty of care on that vendor toward the unskilled licensee, who in purchasing the product must rely on the vendor's representations, skill, and knowledge.[30]  At the same time, any imposition of liability on the vendor must imply a concomitant imposition of responsibility on the user to make a reasonable effort to learn how to use the software properly.

Perhaps the most compelling argument against increasing product liability for software and systems vendors is the potential for adverse impacts on the dynamic software industry, where products come quickly to the market and advances are continually made—both of which are major consumer benefits. Innovation is frequently supported by venture capital, and imposition of heavy warranty liability can chill the flow of capital and restrict the introduction of new products or the proliferation of new ventures. Even when raising capital is not an issue, risk aversion itself can discourage innovation. In either case, the increased business risk to the vendor is reflected in higher product prices to the consumer, which in turn may mean that fewer consumers benefit from a given piece of software.

## Toward Equitable Allocation of Liability

The possible adverse consequences of holding software and system vendors to a higher standard of care must be carefully weighed against the potential benefits.  As more powerful and more highly interconnected systems become more widespread, there will be increasing concern that the current allocation of the risk of software failure is too one-sided for an information society, at least for off-the-shelf software. The industry is sufficiently mature and verification tools and methodologies are sufficiently well understood today that total insulation of the industry from the consequences of software failure can no longer be justified. Operating system software and the major off-the-shelf applications software packages are produced by companies with a business base substantial enough to support quality assurance programs that would yield safer and more secure software; such programs could also reduce any liability risk to manageable proportions. As it is, vendors have already begun programs to make sure that their own development and production efforts are free of contamination from viruses. IBM, for example, set up its High-Integrity Computing Laboratory for this purpose (Smith, 1989; committee briefing by IBM), and ADAPSO, a trade association, has been promoting such efforts for its constituent software and services companies (Landry, 1990). Similarly, vendors do, to varying degrees, notify users of security-related flaws. For example, Sun Microsystems recently announced the Customer Warning System for handling security incidents[31] (Ulbrich and Collins, 1990).

Shifting more (not all) risk to the vendors would result in greater care being taken in the production and testing of software. The British move to require greater testing of safety-relevant software illustrates that these concerns are not just local, but are in fact relevant to a worldwide marketplace. The resulting increased use of verification techniques would not only improve the level of software trustworthiness in the most general sense, but would also necessarily improve the level of trust in the specific information security context. (See Chapter 4's "Relating Specifications to Programs" and "Formal Specification and Verification.")

The national interest in the trustworthiness of software is sufficiently strong that Congress should review this question to determine (1) whether federal law is required (or whether state efforts are adequate) and (2) to what extent risks that can be averted through safer software should be shifted from user to vendor. Equitable risk allocation, which reasonably balances vendor and user interests, is achievable and will advance the national interest.

The development of GSSP, as recommended in Chapters 1 and 2, would provide a positive force to balance and complement the negative force of product liability. GSSP would provide a clear foundation of expectation that customers may count on as standards of performance and vendors may regard as standards of adequacy, against which legal claims could be judged. Interestingly, a similar notion was expressed by insurance industry representatives interviewed for this study, who suggested that some form of standard that could be harmonized with accounting standards would be a potent mechanism to improve security controls in the business community. Their rationale was that such standards would raise the profile of the issue with corporate directors and officers, who are liable to owners (stockholders, partners, and so on).[32]

The committee recognizes that security is not the only property involved in the issue of product liability; safety is obviously another such property. However, as security is a subliminal property of software, it is here that the gap between unspoken customer expectations and unarticulated vendor intentions looms largest. Advances in articulating GSSP would go far toward clarifying the entire field. Both customers and vendors stand to gain.

## APPENDIX 6.1—EXPORT CONTROL PROCESS

National security export controls (hereafter, "export controls") limit access in other countries to technologies and products that could be valuable for military purposes. The control process, which varies by type of product, involves a list of controlled items and an administrative structure for enforcing controls on the export of listed items. Controlled exports do not mean no exports. Rather, these exports are controlled in terms of destination and, in some cases, volume or end use, with restrictions specified as part of the export license. It should be noted that even the tightest export controls do not totally block access to protected technology.

Four organizations have been the principal influences on the export control policy and process of the United States, namely the Coordinating Committee for Multilateral Export Control (CoCom), in which the United States participates, and the U.S. Departments of State, Commerce, and Defense. Each of these organizations has its own policies and jurisdictions for export control, but all the organizations interact heavily with regard to common pursuits (NAS, 1987).

CoCom, a multilateral effort to curb the flow of technology from the West to the Soviet Union and what have been its allies in the East Bloc, has included representatives from Japan, Australia, and all NATO countries except Iceland. Products controlled by CoCom are listed on the Industrial List (IL). The Department of State administers the International Traffic in Arms Regulations (ITAR; 22 CFR, Parts 120-130) through its Center for Defense Trade (formerly the Office of Munitions Control) in consultation with the Department of Defense.

That office maintains the U.S. Munitions Control List, which includes technologies and products representing an obvious military threat, such as weaponry. Finally, the Department of Commerce administers the Export Administration Regulations (EAR; CFR Parts 368-399), in consultation with the Department of Defense. Commerce maintains the Control List (CL), which has classified elements, and the Commodity Control List (CCL), which is not classified. Both of these lists contain dual-use technologies and products, which have both military and civilian/commercial value, and military-critical technologies that may be treated specially.

Recent developments in Eastern Europe have placed pressure on CoCom as an institution and on the United States, which is generally more conservative than other CoCom nations about controlling exports of dual-use technology. Even the topic of trade with other CoCom countries has stirred substantial debate within the U.S. government, some centering on how products are labeled (the most publicized controversy pertains to defining what is a supercomputer) and where they are listed, and much on whether a product should be listed at all.

Exports of general- and special-purpose computer systems are controlled if the systems offer one or more of three qualities: high performance (potentially useful in such strategic applications as nuclear bomb development or war gaming), specific military-critical functionality (e.g., radiation hardening and ruggedness or applications like on-board fire control), or the capability to produce high-performance or military-critical computer systems (e.g., sophisticated computer-aided design and manufacturing systems). Exports of supercomputers to countries other than Canada and Japan are subject to case-by-case review, which can take months, and require special conditions associated with the sale, installation, and operation of the supercomputer, so-called supercomputer safeguard plans.

### APPENDIX 6.2—INSURANCE

Insurance is a means for sharing a risk. The insured pays the insurer (up front, through a premium, and/or when receiving reimbursement, through a deductible or other copayment) to share his risks; if an adverse event takes place, the insurance policy provides for payment to compensate for the damage or loss incurred. The business community already buys insurance for risks ranging from fire to theft as well as for protection against employee dishonesty (bonding).

To be insurable requires the following:

- A volume base for risk spreading (insurance on communication satellites has a very small volume, something that contributes to its cost);
- An establishable proof of loss;
- A quantifiable loss (e.g., the value of mailing lists and research data cannot be consistently and objectively quantified, according to insurance representatives);
- An ability to tie a loss to a time frame of occurrence;
- An ability to credit responsibility for the loss; and
- A knowable loss base.

With these elements, a purchaser of insurance can effectively transfer risk to a carrier and prove a loss. Risks that do not satisfy these elements include inherent business risks.

Another factor to consider is the nature of the consequences, which influences the liability base: a computer-aided manufacturing program controlling a robot may put lives at risk, whereas a number-crunching general ledger program will not.

The earliest insurance offerings covering computer environments were directed at third-party providers of computer services (e.g., service bureaus) concerned about direct and contingent liability associated with losses to their customers. Also leading the computer insurance market were banks—driven by state and federal auditors' concerns—and electronic funds transfer (EFT) systems, ranging from those established by the Federal Reserve (e.g., Fedwire) to the automated clearinghouses, for which there was legislative impetus behind the establishment and use of insurance coverage. This governmental urging of provisions for insurance against computer system risks was initially resisted by the insurance industry, which claimed not to understand the risks.

Insurance for banks and other financial services institutions is relatively well developed, reflecting both the size of the potential loss, the ease with which the risk can be underwritten, and regulations requiring such protection. Much computer-related insurance for the banking industry, for example, builds on a historic base in bonds that protect against employee dishonesty, since most crimes against banks are perpetrated on the inside or with insider participation.

Outside of financial services, the insurance picture is mixed and less mature. There is some coverage against computer system mishaps available through employee bonding and property and casualty coverage. It is easiest to insure the tangible elements of a computer system. By contrast, coverage may be available for restoring a database, but not for reconstructing it from scratch. Another basis for insurance is found in business interruption coverage. Thus recovery of costs for system downtime is available. A new development in the

1980s was the introduction of limited coverage against external intrusions and associated offenses, including tampering, extortion, and others. Although the insurance described above protects the system-using organization, insurance representatives suggest there is a growing potential for coverage of errors and omissions on the part of the vendor, arising from the development of hardware, firmware, and software, to protect the vendor against liability claims. Such coverage appears targeted to developers of such complex products as engineering design software.

## NOTES

1. Note that add-on controls are futile unless the user has full control over all the software on a machine.

2. A glaring example of a facility that can compromise security is "object reuse," which never was an issue in Unix, because it could not happen. Today's non-Unix systems from Digital Equipment Corporation and IBM still allow object reuse.

3. As noted by one analyst, Unix was originally designed by programmers for use by other programmers in an environment fostering open cooperation rather than privacy (Curry, 1990).

4. The fact that consumers are preoccupied with threats posed by insiders and have problems today that could benefit from better procedures and physical security measures, let alone technical measures, is discussed in the section titled "Consumer Awareness."

5. For example, the most recent of a series of intra-governmental advisories is the Office of Management and Budget's (OMB's) *Guidance for Preparation of Security Plans for Federal Computer Systems that Contain Sensitive Information* (OMB, 1990). This bulletin addresses the security planning process required by the Computer Security Act of 1987 (P.L. 100-235). It is expected to be superseded by a revision to OMB Circular Number A-130 and incorporated into future standards or guidelines from the National Institute of Standards and Technology.

6. An examination of this challenge for computing technologies generally can be found in a previous Computer Science and Technology Board report, *Global Trends in Computer Technology and Their Impact on Export Control* (NRC, 1988a).

7. There may also have been instances in which software implementations of DES or RSA were sent abroad by oversight or because the transmitter of the implementation was unaware of the law. The physical portability of software makes such slips almost inevitable.

8. Note that the United Kingdom and Australia set the threshold at B2 or the equivalent.

9. Note that in this time period only one A1 product has been on the evaluated product list. The information on approval rates came from NSA briefings for the committee.

10. This point was made by Digital Equipment Corporation in July 1990 testimony before the House Subcommittee on Transportation, Aviation, and Materials.

11. For example, observers of the market for disaster recovery services have noted that until a 1986 fire in Montreal, a principal marketing tool was a 1978 study assessing how long businesses could survive without their data processing operations; more recent fires (affecting the Hinsdale, Ill., central office for telephone service and lower

Manhattan's business district) have also provided dramatic evidence of the consequences of system mishaps (Datamation, 1987).

12. This situation and a variant, in which bad products effectively drive out good ones, is not unique (see Akerlof, 1970).

13. A security officer may even occasionally need to decrypt an encrypted file that was encrypted by a suspect using a key known only to the suspect; the security officer may have very mixed feelings about the optimum strength of an encryption method that is available for routine use in protecting the company's data.

14. These issues have been actively discussed on electronic bulletin boards and forums (e.g., RISKS, CuD, the Well) and in the general and business press with the publicized launch of the Electronic Frontiers Foundation in response to recent investigations and prosecutions.

15. "Insurance as a Market Lever" and Chapter Appendix 6.2 draw on discussions with insurance industry representatives, including carrier and agent personnel.

16. Insurance industry representatives voice concern about technology outpacing underwriting: if a policy is written at one point in time, will the language and exclusions prove appropriate when a claim is filed later, after new technology has been developed and introduced?

17. Indeed, there is some evidence that universities should do even more. For example, based on a recent survey, John Higgins observed the following:

> It seems evident that a substantial majority of current university graduates in computer science have no formal introduction to the issues of information security as a result of their university training. . . . While it is unlikely that every institution would develop a variety of courses in security, it is important that some institutions do. It establishes and helps to maintain the credibility of the subject and provides a nucleus of students interested in security topics. The most favorable interpretation of the survey seems to suggest that at present there are at best only two or three such universities in the nation. (Higgins, 1989, p. 556)

18. RISKS, formally known as the Forum on Risks to the Public in the Use of Computers and Related Systems, was established in August 1985 by Peter G. Neumann as chair of the Association for Computing Machinery's (ACM) Committee on Computers and Public Policy. It is an electronic forum for discussing issues relating to the use and misuse of computers in applications affecting our lives. Involving many thousands of people around the world, RISKS has become a repository for anecdotes, news items, and assorted comments thereon. The most interesting cases discussed are included in the regular issues of ACM's *Software Engineering Notes* (See Neumann, 1989). An updated index to about a thousand cases is under development.

19. The relative reluctance of victims to report computer crimes was noted to the committee by prosecutors and insurance representatives.

20. Experience shows that many users do not repair flaws or install patches (software to correct a flaw) even given notification. Since penetrators have demonstrated the ability to "reverse engineer" patches (and other remedies) and go looking for systems that lack the necessary corrections, the proper strategy for handling discovered flaws is not easy to devise.

21. Computer hardware, for example, must meet the Federal Communications Commission's regulations for electronic emanations, and European regulations on ergonomic and safety qualities of computer screens and keyboards have affected the appearance and operation of systems worldwide.

22. This point was made by Digital Equipment Corporation in July 1990 testimony before the House Subcommittee on Transportation, Aviation, and Materials.

23. Vendors also argue that some consumers may prefer products with little security, but the prevalent lack of consumer understanding of the choices casts doubt on this explanation for the weak market.

24. For example, rope manufacturers use a system of standardized strength ratings, since one cannot tell at the point of manufacture whether a rope will be used to tie packages or to suspend objects, for example. Of course, some highly specialized rope, such as climbing lines, carries extra assurance, which comes with added cost.

25. Michael Agranoff observes, "Such standards would not eliminate computer abuse, especially by 'insiders'; they would not eliminate computer-related negligence. They would, however, provide a 'curb on technology,' a baseline from which to judge both compensation for victims of computer abuse and the efficacy of measures to combat computer crime" (Agranoff, 1989, p. 275).

26. The terms and conditions governing the acquisition of operating-system and off-the-shelf software have many of the attributes of an adhesion contract (although whether there is a contract at all is open to debate). An adhesion contract is a standardized contract form offered on a "take-it-or-leave-it" basis, with no opportunity to bargain. The prospective buyer can acquire the item only under the stated terms and conditions. Of course, the "buyer" has the option of not acquiring the software, or of acquiring a competing program that is most likely subject to the same or a similar set of terms and conditions, but often the entire industry offers the item only under a similar set of terms and conditions.

27. The UCC upholds express warranties in Section 2-313. An express warranty is created when the seller affirms a "fact or promise, describes the product, and provides a sample or model, and the buyer relies on the affirmation, description, sample, or model as part of the basis of the bargain." By their very nature, express warranties cannot be disclaimed. The UCC will not allow a vendor to make an express promise that is then disclaimed. Language that cannot be reasonably reconciled is resolved in favor of the buyer.

28. Most recently, Logisticon, Inc., apparently gained telephone access to Revlon, Inc.'s computers and disabled software it supplied. Revlon, claiming dissatisfaction with the software, had suspended payments. While Logisticon argued it was repossessing its property, Revlon suffered a significant interruption in business operations and filed suit (Pollack, 1990).

29. Although it would be inequitable to impose liability for clearly unintended uses in unintended operating environments, a vendor should not escape all liability for breach of warranty simply because a product can be used across a wide spectrum of applications or operating environments.

30. That superior knowledge is an argument for promoting the technical steps discussed in the section titled "Consumer Awareness," such as shipping systems with security features turned on.

31. The Customer Warning System involves a point of contact for reporting security problems; proactive alerts to customers of worms, viruses, or other security holes; and distribution of fixes.

32. The Foreign Corrupt Practices Act is one step toward linking accounting and information security practices; it requires accounting and other management controls that security experts interpret as including computer security controls (Snyders, 1983). Also, note that an effort is under way on the part of a group of security practitioners to address the affirmative obligations of corporate officers and directors to safeguard information assets (personal communication from Sandra Lambert, July 1990).

# 7
# The Need to Establish an
# Information Security Foundation

In the preceding chapters, this report identifies factors contributing to low levels of computer security in commercial or nonmilitary systems, and it recommends a variety of actions intended to promote security in the design, selection, and use of computer systems. This chapter argues that a new organization should carry out many of those actions. In the discussion below, the proposed organization is called the Information Security Foundation, or ISF. Mindful that U.S. efforts have been fragmented and inadequate whereas efforts in Europe are gaining momentum and cohesion, this recommendation is intended to fill a troubling void. After reviewing the requirements and options for such an organization, the committee concluded that the ISF should essentially be a private, not-for-profit organization, largely outside the government once it is launched. It would need the highest level of support from government as well as industry; the strongest expression of such support would be a congressional charter.

## ACTIONS NEEDED TO IMPROVE COMPUTER SECURITY

As documented in other chapters, several actions are necessary to improve computer security. These actions form the basis for the mission of the ISF:

• Defining requirements and evaluation criteria for users of commercial systems, including private sector users and government processors of sensitive but unclassified information. A major part of this effort is the development and promulgation of the Generally Accepted

System Security Principles (GSSP), which would provide a set of requirements guidelines for trustworthy computer and communications system design and use.

• Conducting research and development, especially into criteria and evaluation procedures, in support of the above.

• Evaluating the quality of security measures in industry-developed products during their development and throughout their life cycle, and publishing evaluation results. In particular, evaluating products for conformance to GSSP. Eventually evaluations should also consider other aspects of system trustworthiness, such as safety. (See "Assurance Evaluation" in Chapter 5.)

• Developing and maintaining a system for tracking and reporting security and safety incidents, threats, and vulnerabilities.

• Promoting effective use of security and safety tools, techniques, and management practices through education for commercial organizations and users.

• Brokering and enhancing communications between industry and government where commercial and national security interests may conflict.

• Focusing efforts to achieve standardization and harmonization of commercial security practice and system safety in the U.S. and internationally.

These actions are complementary and would be pursued most effectively and economically by a single organization. At present, some of these actions are attempted by the National Security Agency (NSA), the National Institute of Standards and Technology (NIST), and other organizations. However, current efforts fall short of what is needed to accomplish the tasks at hand, and the dominant missions of existing agencies and organizations limit the scope of their involvement in addressing the issues of computer security and trustworthiness. In particular, relevant government agencies are poorly suited to represent the needs of nongovernmental system users (although they may take some input from major system users and generate publications of interest to users).

## ATTRIBUTES AND FUNCTIONS OF
## THE PROPOSED NEW INSTITUTION

The ISF should have the following attributes and functions:

• It should be free from control by the computer and communication vendors, but it must communicate and work effectively with them. This quality is important to prevent the appearance or reality of bias or conflict of interest. Vendors can be expected to be responsive to consistent and credible user demand, but they have not shown (and cannot be expected to show) leadership in defining and bringing to market systems with enhanced security. Thus trade associations and conventional industry consortia are not credible vehicles for the needed activities, although they would be a valuable conduit for inputs and for dissemination of outputs such as GSSP.

• It should have a strong user presence, through membership and participation in its governance.

• It must have defined relationships to existing governmental organizations, particularly NIST and NSA, but also other organizations relevant to its missions, such as the Defense Advanced Research Projects Agency (DARPA) and the National Science Foundation (NSF). By charter and by action, it must command the respect of both government and industry and must seek open personal and institutional communications with both. It must have ready access to technical assistance from government agencies. Most importantly, because of existing agency activities there would have to be a delineation of where the ISF would have lead responsibility in the above areas. Industry, for example, would not tolerate a situation calling for evaluations by both NSA and a new entity—but it should find tolerable a situation involving NSA evaluations for military-critical systems and ISF evaluations for other, GSSP-compliant systems, with coordination between ISF and NSA to minimize any duplication of effort.

• It must serve more than just a single industry or just the governmental sector, to ensure the broad relevance of GSSP and of the evaluations that would be performed to ensure conformance to GSSP.

• It must strive to be at the forefront of the computer security field, attracting top-notch people to enable it to lead the field. Staffing would take time, but the opportunity to do research is necessary to attract the most talented candidates.

• It should address the broader problem of how to make computer systems trustworthy, integrating security with related requirements such as reliability and safety. Implementing these related requirements can benefit from similar techniques and mechanisms in many instances. While the ISF should focus initially on security, it should consider related areas such as safety and reliability from the start. Although a security constituency seems to be emerging outside of government, there is nothing analogous for computer system reliability and safety. The ISF could lead in helping to establish a constituency for system trustworthiness.

• It should have a strong, diversified funding base. In particular, it must not depend on government funding, although federal seed money would be appropriate. Although government has much in common with the rest of the economy in terms of the kinds of computer systems and applications it chooses, governmental priorities in system design, use, and management may differ from those found elsewhere, even for systems processing sensitive but unclassified information. Perhaps most importantly, government funding is unlikely to reach the levels or have the stability necessary to sustain the ISF. Finally, policy independence may be necessary in some cases, such as when the ISF is called on to seek a middle ground between commercial and defense perspectives.

The development and dissemination of GSSP would be central functions of the ISF. These activities would build on research and on consensus across a variety of stakeholding communities (vendors, commercial users, the general public, and government). The goal is to achieve universal recognition along the lines that the Financial Accounting Standards Board (FASB) has for what have been called Generally Accepted Accounting Principles (GAAP). Although the analogy to FASB is not perfect, it presents some notable parallels:

> The FASB plays a unique role in our society. It is a [de facto] regulator that is not a government agency. It is an independent private foundation financed by contributions and by revenues from the sale of its publications. Contributions are primarily from corporations and public accounting firms, but the FASB is independent of the contributors by virtue of a carefully drawn charter. By the same token, the FASB is independent of both the American Institute of CPAs and the Securities and Exchange Commission, even though its "clout" comes from the fact that both institutions accept FASB pronouncements as the prime authority for purposes of preparing financial statements in accordance with generally accepted accounting principles. . . .
>
> The FASB is the latest in a line of accounting standard-setting bodies that go back to the stock market crash of 1929 and the consequent Securities Acts of 1933 and 1934. The stock market crash drove home the point that the U.S. economy depends greatly on a smoothly functioning capital market. . . . (Mosso, 1987)

While FASB's GAAP are intended to assure fair disclosure by companies to investors and creditors, GSSP are intended to protect companies and individuals both inside and outside a computer-system-using entity. However, similar motivations inform the proposed ISF and FASB. If industry does not pursue such an effort to protect itself and the public, there is a possibility of greater government regulation (see "Regulation as a Market Influence" in Chapter 6).

## OTHER ORGANIZATIONS CANNOT
## FULFILL ISF'S MISSION

### Government Organizations

As noted above, the beginnings of the ISF's mission can be found in government. The history of government involvement in computer and communications security is outlined in Chapter Appendix 7.1. The forebear closest to the proposed ISF is the National Computer Security Center (NCSC), which has supported the development of the Orange Book and performed evaluations of products against its criteria (see Appendix A of this report). As is discussed in preceding chapters, the Orange Book criteria and the associated evaluation process fall short of what vendors, users, and a wide range of security experts consider necessary. Perhaps most important, the NCSC has undergone a reorganization and downsizing that may severely limit its ability to meet its old mission, let alone an expanded mission.

A number of significant events have shaped the role of the NCSC in civilian computing. The promulgation of National Security Decision Directive (NSDD) 145 in 1984 expanded the NCSC's scope to include civilian government and some aspects of the private sector's concerns for protection of sensitive unclassified information. Subsequent passage of the Computer Security Act of 1987 (P.L. 100-235) and the July 1990 issuance of NSD 42, revising NSDD 145, substantially limited that scope to classified, national-security-related activities. As a result, the NCSC's influence on commercial and civilian government use of computers has been greatly reduced.

Starting in 1985, internal reorganizations within the NSA have merged the separate and distinct charter of the NCSC with NSA's traditional communications security role. Most recently, the NCSC was reduced to a small organization to provide an external interface to product developers. The actual evaluations will be performed by NSA staff, sometimes assisted by specific outsiders (e.g., MITRE Corporation and Aerospace Corporation), in direct response to requirements of the national security community. Although outsourcing evaluation work is a practical solution to NSA's limited resources, it raises questions about the accountability of and incentives facing the evaluators. These questions are of great concern to industry, which has complained about the duration of evaluations and the lateness within the product cycle of the evaluation process. Another issue raised by the reorganization is the extent to which NSA will remain concerned with evaluation of systems at the lower levels of the Orange Book, such as C2.[1]

The other major government player in this area is NIST, which through the National Computer Systems Laboratory (NCSL) is concerned with computer and communications security. At present NIST lacks the technical and financial resources to execute the agenda defined here for ISF, and it also lacks the necessary charter and organizational support. The recent move by NIST to coordinate a clearinghouse with industry focused on protections against viruses illustrates NIST's opportunities for expansion, but it also illustrates NIST's limited resources—this is a small-scale limited-focus effort (Danca, 1990e).

In the computer security arena, NIST has traditionally focused on supporting technical standards (e.g., those related to Open Systems Interconnection (OSI) and Integrated Services Digital Networking) and developing guidelines for system management and use. These activities are more straightforward than articulating GSSP and developing guidelines for associated evaluations. Evaluating the security functionality and assurance of a computer system, for example, is more difficult than evaluating conformance to interoperability standards. Although NIST has been involved with standards conformance testing (and has begun a program to establish testing for conformance to certain DES standards), it has so far not undertaken either to specify evaluation criteria for the civil government or to evaluate commercial products against any criteria, or to offer guidelines for system-level evaluation.[2] Such guidelines would have to describe how to judge the effectiveness of security safeguards against an anticipated threat.

Finally, its relations with NSA, on which it relies for technical assistance and with which it has an agreement not to compete with the Orange Book process, have not given NIST the scope to act with substantial independence. The committee has doubts that NIST's National Computer Systems Laboratory could play the role that is required, given its present charter and in particular the difficulty it has in achieving satisfactory and consistent funding.

## Private Organizations

As banks, insurance companies, and business in general have become increasingly interested in computer security, these organizations have found that their interests are not well served by the present activities of NCSC or NIST. This situation is evidenced by either ignorance of or resistance to the Orange Book (see Chapter 6) and by observations on the inadequate budget and program of NIST.

But existing private organizations are also poorly suited to undertake the actions needed to improve computer security. Currently, much activity in the private sector is driven by vendors, regulated industries, and large computer and communications system users. They affect the overall state of commercial security through the marketplace, trade associations, and relevant standards-setting ventures. As discussed in Chapter 6, the influence is uneven and tends to be reactive rather than proactive.

Largely (but not exclusively) in the private sector are security specialists or practitioners and their relatively new professional societies (discussed in Chapter Appendix 7.2). Security practitioners are the principal force promoting computer and system security within organizations, but they operate under a variety of constraints. In particular, the voluntary nature of professional societies for security practitioners limits their reach. Also, professional societies tend to focus exclusively on security and show no signs of addressing broader issues of system trustworthiness (in particular, safety).

## WHY ISF'S MISSION SHOULD BE PURSUED OUTSIDE OF THE GOVERNMENT

Apart from the specific limitations of NIST and the NCSC, there are more general concerns about a governmental basis for the ISF.

• The government has difficulty attracting and keeping skilled computer professionals. The NCSC, for example, appears to have been largely staffed by young, recently graduated computer scientists who have little practical experience in developing complex computer systems. Issues that constrain federal hiring include salary ceilings and limitations on the capitalization available to technical personnel.

• The defense budget is shrinking. Department of Defense resources have supported the activities in the NCSC and relevant activities elsewhere in NSA, DARPA, and research units of the armed services (e.g., the Naval Research Laboratory). As noted in Chapter 8, defense resources will continue to be valuable for supporting relevant research and development.

• The international standards arena may become a forum for the negotiation of standards for security and safety and for evaluation criteria. The American National Standards Institute (ANSI) and other private U.S. standards organizations depend on voluntary contributions of time and talent, and the role that NIST and other agencies can play in contributing to international efforts is limited. The United States needs a strong presence in these commercial standards-setting processes, complementing the existing military standards process that to date has been a major impetus to development of trusted systems.

• Government's necessary concern for national security sometimes obscures legitimate commercial interests, occasionally handicapping technology and market development that may be in the country's long-term economic security interests.

The realities of the government environment suggest that accelerating the development and deployment of computer and communications security requires a greater role for the commercial sector.[3]

## A NEW NOT-FOR-PROFIT ORGANIZATION

Given the limitations of private and public organizations, the committee concludes that the proposed Information Security Foundation will be most likely to succeed as a private not-for-profit organization. To assure that its viability would not depend on special-interest funding, multiple sources are necessary.

The ISF would need the highest level of governmental support, and the strongest expression of such support would be a congressional charter that would define its scope and, in particular, set parameters that would permit it to work with NSA, NIST, and other agencies as appropriate. There are general precedents for government establishment of organizations acting in the public interest, including organizations that perform tasks previously performed by public or private entities.[4] In all of these organizations, effective working relationships with government and operational flexibility, which would be critical for the ISF, have been key.

Good working relationships with relevant agencies would be necessary so that ISF could contribute to satisfying government needs, especially in developing GSSP and associated evaluations, and to avoid unnecessary duplication of effort. For example, as noted above, there should be one recognized source of evaluations for a given type of system. Government recognition of evaluations conducted by the ISF would also be necessary to support international reciprocity in handling the results of evaluations in different countries (see Chapter 5).

One relatively new government initiative in computer security, the establishment of Computer Emergency Response Teams (CERTs) to deal with threatened or actual attacks in networks and systems, presents a specific opportunity for coordination between agencies and the ISF. The ISF could, building from the base already provided by DARPA, provide a common point for collecting reports of security problems in vendor products and passing these back to the vendor in a coordinated way. This function could be a part of the larger action of providing an incident database (which would not be limited to emergency situations in large networked systems); the ISF should be able to devote more resources to this important activity than does DARPA or NIST, although DARPA-funded CERT activities could be an input into the ISF.

Success for the ISF would depend on strong participation by users and vendors. The appeal to users is that ISF would provide, through the GSSP and related evaluation processes, a mechanism for making vendors more responsive to users' needs for systems that are more trustworthy and a forum designed to identify and alleviate user problems. Vendors would get a more responsive evaluation mechanism and broader guidance for developing trusted systems than they have had in the NCSC. Both vendors and users would gain from having a single, well-endowed focal point for system security and trustworthiness.

## Critical Aspects of an ISF Charter

If the concept of establishing the ISF is accepted, the details of the ISF's form and function will be discussed extensively. This report cannot offer too detailed a vision of the ISF, lest it prematurely over-constrain the approach. However, certain aspects of the ISF seem critical. Summarized here, they should be reflected in any legislation that might bring the ISF into existence.

• The board of directors of the ISF must include government, vendor, and user representatives.

• The ISF must be permitted to receive private funds as its major source of income. As discussed below, such funds would most likely be in the form of subscription fees and in charges to vendors for product evaluations.

• The ISF must not have the salary levels of its employees tied to government scales but must be able to pay competitive rates. The nature of its work means that its most significant asset and the largest source of expense will be technical personnel.

• The ISF must be able to solicit support from the government for specific activities, such as research. It should be able to regrant such funds, under appropriate controls.

• The legal liability that the ISF might incur by performing an evaluation must be recognized and managed, given the necessarily subjective nature of evaluations. The goal is to facilitate evaluations to protect users and vendors; of course, the ISF must be accountable in the event of negligence. This problem, which has been addressed for product-testing organizations, might in ISF's case best be handled by careful explanation of what an evaluation does and does not signify; for example, it might signify a given probability of resistance to certain types of attack, although no amount of testing and evaluation can ever guarantee that a system will be impervious to all attacks. It might be necessary for the ISF to set up operating procedures to resolve disputes arising from evaluations; one option would be arbitration, which, unlike litigation, would avoid introducing details of product design and strategy into the public record.

## Start-up Considerations

The NCSC experience shows how difficult it can be to launch an effective evaluation program, in which success includes widespread industry awareness and support as well as reasonable cost and time for evaluation. Consequently, the committee believes it might take longer to inaugurate an effective ISF evaluation program than to undertake other ISF activities. The committee believes that GSSP is a vital foundation for increasing customer awareness and vendor accountability, and by extension for building an effective evaluation program. A critical pacing factor would be vendor demand for evaluations. This might be a function of true general acceptance for GSSP, coupled with case law trends that might increase vendors' perceived liability for software and system defects. If prudent customers were to specify GSSP, and vendors then used compliance with GSSP in marketing, independent evaluation of GSSP compliance would protect both vendors and users. Evaluation provides for truth in advertising from the customer's point of view, and it provides a mechanism for the vendor to demonstrate good faith. Note as a precedent that recently proposed legislation would ease the liability burden for vendors of products evaluated by the Food and Drug Administration (FDA) and the Federal Aviation Administration (Crenshaw, 1990).

Selection of an appropriate initial leader for the organization would be a critical step; that person's job would involve not only developing a business plan but also securing commitment from key stakeholders and recruiting a strong core staff. A parent organization should be designated to shelter the ISF during this first stage. Although using a government agency would expose the ISF to government politics during this first critical period, no obvious private group could play this role. A suitable "launch site" would have to be sought while the details of a charter, operating plan, and budget were being developed.

## Funding the ISF

This committee recommends a not-for-profit consortium funded by consumers and procurers of secure systems and functioning as a foundation. The most difficult aspect is to establish stable long-term funding to ensure the ISF's effectiveness, enabling such a foundation to be a credible source for requirements and evaluation and to attract and keep a first-class staff. The committee suggests that funding be derived from two sources: basic subscription fees, and usage fees from the computer manufacturers and commercial users.[5] Also, the committee urges that the federal government provide seed money to launch the operation and sustain it in the early stages. The overall budget for this kind of organization would likely be about $15 million to $20 million. This assumes a budget devoted largely to costs for technical personnel, plus essential plant, equipment, and software tools. While evaluations, which are labor-intensive, might be the most expensive activity, they would be paid for by vendors.

Membership fees paid by private sector consumers of computer security products should be the basic source of funds, since consumers rather then vendors would be the main beneficiaries and would need a guarantee that their interests are paramount. For example, the first increment of funds could derive from basic subscription fees paid by all members. This funding would be used to establish the base of research and criteria development needed for the foundation to function efficiently. Note that subscription fees for Fortune 500 companies of, for example, $50,000 per year per company would generate $10 million annually if 200 participated. This seems to be a modest amount for a $5 billion organization to spend. Successful fund-raising would likely hinge on obtaining commitments from industry clusters (i.e., multiple organizations in each industry); this pattern has been observed in other consortia.

System manufacturers might be asked to pay a subscription fee ranging from $50,000 to $500,000 based on their overall revenue. Twenty vendors contributing an average of $250,000 each would generate an additional $5 million for the base fund. The basic subscription would entitle an organization to participate in the foundation's research, evaluation, and education programs. As a reference point, note that membership in the Corporation for Open Systems, which promotes development of systems that comply with open systems standards and conducts or supplies tools for conformance testing, costs $200,000 for vendors and $25,000 for users.

Contributions that range into six figures are difficult to obtain, especially at a time when computer-related research and standards consortia have proliferated (e.g., Open Software Foundation, Corporation for Open Systems, Microelectronics and Computer Technology Corporation, Sematech, X/Open) and when competitive considerations and the prospect of a recession prompt budget cutting. The mission of the proposed ISF differs from that of any other entity, but the combination of a government charter and an assured role in product evaluations will be central for gaining the necessary corporate commitments. As noted above, the impact of GAAP comes not merely because a FASB exists but because the government, through the Securities and Exchange Commission and other vehicles, has endorsed GAAP (while industry has a strong voice in GAAP development).

The second source of funds could be fees for the evaluation of industry-developed products. This is analogous to other kinds of product testing, from drug testing (for which producers incur costs directly) to testing requested by vendors but carried out by independent laboratories (e.g., Underwriters Laboratories, Inc.). The actual cost incurred by the foundation for each evaluation would be billed to the vendor. Because the base of research and criteria development activities would be funded by subscription fees, the foundation could maintain a core staff to conduct evaluations and thus could establish its independence from vendors. The special nature of the ISF would eliminate any prospect of competition with vendors and would be consistent with the necessary protection of proprietary information. Furthermore, the stability of the foundation would mean that evaluation fees could be held to a minimum. Without the pool of subscription funds as general base funding, the cost of an evaluation might be prohibitive.

It is critical that the evaluations be charged to the producer of the product. Although it would be nice to imagine the government paying for this service, the committee concludes that this option (which is provided by the NCSC today) is unrealistic. If the government pays, there is no way to adjust the level of effort to meet vendor demands. If the vendor were to pay, the ISF could allocate funds to meet the product cycle of the vendor, and in this way the evaluation process could be more responsive to vendor needs. Vendor funding would permit the organization to respond quickly with appropriate levels of qualified individuals and would provide a critical incentive to complete the evaluation process expeditiously yet thoroughly by working with vendors throughout the entire development process. The evaluations could be completed and available as the products enter the marketplace (instead of years later). The government could use the results of the ISF directly in its own evaluation of particular systems.

## ALTERNATIVES TO THE ISF

A number of alternatives to the ISF, ranging from government centers to industry facilities, must at least be considered. The base against which alternatives should be measured is the present situation wherein the NCSC does detailed technical evaluations for the classified national security community and NIST serves in a limited advisory role to the civilian government. The limitations of this situation have been discussed.

One alternative is that NIST develop its own computer security evaluation facility comparable to the NCSC. The current NIST course of (at least limited) endorsement of the Orange Book plus no direct involvement in actual evaluations argues against this alternative. Without a significant change in operational orientation and funding for NIST, successfully implementing this alternative is highly unlikely.

An alternative considered in 1980, prior to the formation of the NCSC, was the establishment of a single federal computer security evaluation center for all of government, separate from the NSA but involving NSA, NIST, and other personnel representing other parts of government. The 1980 proposal would have been funded jointly by the Department of Defense (DOD) and the Department of Commerce (DOC), and it would have resulted in a center located at the National Bureau of Standards (now NIST) and thus capable of operating in an open, unclassified environment, but with the ability to deal with highly sensitive or classified issues as necessary.

Taking such an approach now would require major changes in management philosophy and funding by DOD and DOC and would most certainly require legislative action crossing many firmly established jurisdictional boundaries. For these reasons and because this alternative echoes the weaknesses of the NIST alternative, the second alternative described is unlikely to succeed. However, if industry were to resist a nongovernmental entity, then a single federal computer security evaluation organization would offer improvements over what is currently available, and it could fulfill the additional missions (development of GSSP or broader educational efforts) proposed above.

A third alternative that might avoid the staffing problems faced by government agencies would be an independent laboratory involved in computer security technology development and funded by the government at a federally funded research and development center (FFRDC) such as MITRE Corporation, Aerospace Corporation, or the Institute for Defense Analysis. Such organizations already participate in NCSC evaluations on a limited basis and can pay higher salaries and retain a core of knowledgeable experts, perhaps even rotating experts from industry. Unfortunately, the experience gained to date with these organizations assisting the NCSC and the nature of the contractual arrangement between them and NCSC have not provided opportunities for improving the existing process or for conducting research and development on the process of evaluation. Also, the involvement of these groups in developing systems for the government might cause vendors to perceive them as potential or actual competitors, thereby inspiring reluctance to divulge the proprietary information essential for thorough evaluation. This concern has been raised by U.S. vendors in response to the U.K. plans to establish commercial licensed evaluation facilities (CLEFs).

Another approach is that taken by the FDA, a government organization that reviews testing done in-house by the producer of the product. In the case of computer and communications systems, for which evaluation is of necessity rather subjective and the quality of assessments not easily quantified, it seems unreasonable to expect that using vendor staff as evaluators could yield an unbiased result. There is no effective way for a government agency to control the process of evaluating computers and systems if it is limited to review of the results of a vendor's evaluation.

Finally, note that the mission envisioned for the ISF is not one that current independent testing laboratories can fill. Evaluating trusted systems is much more difficult and time-consuming than evaluating the performance of various forms of hardware or conformance to existing technical standards.

## APPENDIX 7.1—A HISTORY OF GOVERNMENT INVOLVEMENT

The dominant public institutions affecting computer and communications security in the United States are government agencies—in particular, but far from exclusively, agencies within the Department of Defense (DOD). Driven by national security concerns, the U.S. government has actively supported and directed the advance of computer security since the dawn of computer development; its involvement with communications security dates back to the Revolutionary War. The government's long history of involvement in computer and communications security illustrates how public institutions can nurture new technology and stimulate associated markets; it also shows where work remains to be done.

### The National Security Agency and the DOD Perspective

The government's involvement with computer security grew out of the evolving field of communications security in the early 1950s, when it was deemed necessary in the United States to establish a single organization, the then very secret National Security Agency (NSA), to deal with communication security and related matters (e.g., signals intelligence) (Kahn, 1967).  The historical role of the DOD and, in particular, of the NSA, has been responsible for a longstanding tension between the DOD, which seeks to fulfill its mission of protecting national security, and civilian agencies concerned with computer security, notably the National Institute of Standards and Technology, together with the general vendor community.

The overall policy responsibility for communications security matters was originally assigned to the U.S. Communications Security (COMSEC) Board, consisting of cabinet-level officials from all branches of the government, that dealt with classified government information. This structure and NSA's highly classified responsibilities under that board existed from the early 1950s until the mid-1970s, when the issue of using encryption to protect other than classified information caused a division within the government.  The publication of the Data Encryption Standard (DES) in 1977 (NBS, 1977) (see discussion below) was a major triumph for both the civilian government and commercial communities (IBM contributed substantially to the development of DES) but has been regarded by some in the national security community as a major disaster.[6]  Up to that time, cryptography had remained largely a dark science, hidden in government secrecy.  Encryption systems were designed by and for the government and were built and distributed under strict and highly classified government control.  There had also been some open research, particularly in public-key cryptography.

Computer security does not have as extensive a history as does communications security.  It has been recognized as a difficult issue needing attention for at least the past two decades.  In the early 1970s, the DOD funded research into how to build computer systems that could be relied on to separate access to sensitive information in accordance with a set of rules.  In the mid-1970s, several research projects (e.g., secure Multics) were initiated to demonstrate such systems, and in 1978, the DOD Computer Security Initiative was formed both to promote the development of such systems by industry and to explore how to evaluate them so that they could become widely available for both government and commercial use.  Perhaps the most important result of the work during the 1970s was the formulation of a computer-relevant model of multilevel security, known as the Bell and La Padula Model (Bell and La Padula, 1976), which became the focal point of DOD computer security research and development. That model (discussed in Chapter 3) formalized decades of DOD policies regarding how information could be accessed, and by whom, in manual paper-based systems.

In 1981, the DOD Computer Security Evaluation Center was established at NSA as an entity separate from the communications security structure already in place. The reasons for this separation included the recognition that while communications security had been largely a government-owned function in which NSA developed encryption algorithms, contracted for their production, and fully controlled their distribution and use throughout the government, computers were far more widely deployed even in the early 1980s and could not be developed, produced, and controlled in the same way as encryption systems. A separate organization capable of working with industry, instead of directing it through procurement contracts, was needed.

The DOD Computer Security Center, as it came to be called, published the *Trusted Computer System Evaluation Criteria* (TCSEC, or Orange Book) in 1983 (superseded in 1985 by DOD 5200.28-STD; U.S. DOD, 1985d) and began working with industry to evaluate how well their products met the various levels of those criteria. It should be noted that the establishment of the Computer Security Center as a separate function at NSA was opposed both within and outside the agency at the time. The internal opposition stemmed from the perception that computer security was merely a subset of communications security and should be handled in the same way by the same organization. The opposite view was that communications security was becoming increasingly dependent on computers, computer networks, and network protocols, and required a new technology base managed by a new organization. The external opposition derived from the negative concerns of many in the defense community, including other parts of DOD and defense contractors, that NSA's slowness to respond and dictatorial authority in the communications security arena would hamper the development of products needed to solve today's problems. These two opposing forces both within and outside NSA continue today to influence the evolution of both computer security and communications security.

Up until the establishment of the Computer Security Center, the preceding U.S. COMSEC Board and another key policy group, the National Communications Security Committee, largely ignored the computer security problem, lumping it, if considering it at all, into the communications security arena. The 1977 Presidential Directive 24 (PD 24), which created the National Communications Security Committee, split the responsibility for communications security, giving NSA authority over the protection of classified and national security-related information and the National Telecommunications and Information Administration, a part of the Department of Commerce not related to the National Bureau of Standards (NBS), responsibility for protecting unclassified and non-national security information. This split in responsibility resulted in much confusion and was opposed by many in the national security community.

Growing controversy over computer security led to intense pressure during the early days of the Reagan Administration to correct the situation. Those efforts resulted in the publication in September 1984 of National Security Decision Directive 145 (NSDD 145), the National Policy on Telecommunications and Automated Information Systems Security, which expanded NSA's role in both communications and computer security and extended its influence to the national level, to the civilian government, and to a limited extent, to the commercial world. NSDD 145 required federal agencies to establish policies, procedures, and practices to protect both classified and unclassified information in computer systems. It established the National Telecommunications and Information Systems Security Committee (NTISSC) to develop and issue national system security operating policies.

When NSDD 145 was emerging in 1983-1984, computer security had come into its own with a separate organization at NSA. NSDD 145 swept the two forces together and elevated the DOD Computer Security Center to the National Computer Security Center (NCSC), giving it and the NSA's COMSEC Board roles in the civilian government as well as in the commercial world.

In late 1985 a reorganization at NSA created the Deputy Directorate for Information Security, merging the COMSEC and Computer Security functions and encompassing the NCSC. Since it was becoming clear that the technologies needed to develop communications security systems and computer security systems were becoming inextricably linked, this merger was viewed by many as a positive force. Others, however, viewed the expansion of NSA's role beyond the defense and intelligence communities in a highly negative way, and efforts began in Congress to redefine roles and limit the scope of NSA to its traditional communities of interest. The Computer Security Act of 1987 (U.S. Congress, 1987, P.L. 100-235) defined the role of NBS (now NIST) in protecting sensitive information (see below), and limited NSA to its traditional responsibilities for the protection of classified information.

Two recent developments have continued the withdrawal of NSA from direct and active involvement in the nondefense marketplace and its refocusing on the defense community and the protection of classified information and systems generally. First, in mid-1990, NCSC research and evaluation functions were integrated with the NSA's communications security functions. Officially, however, the restructuring was done to more effectively address network and system security issues and was prompted by "increasing recognition that current user applications virtually eliminate traditional distinctions between telecommunications and information systems" (NSA, 1990a). Second, NSDD 145 was revised in July 1990, resulting in NSD 42, so that NSA no longer had responsibility for sensitive but unclassified information. In compliance with the Computer Security Act of 1987, that responsibility was assigned solely to NIST, and all references to the private sector were removed. The NTISSC became the National Security Telecommunications and Information Systems Security Committee (NSTISSC), under the new National Security Council Policy Coordinating Committee for National Security Telecommunications and Information Systems.

## The National Institute of Standards and Technology

The other government agency with a longstanding interest in enhancing computer and communications security is the National Institute of Standards and Technology (NIST; formerly the National Bureau of Standards, (NBS)), which serves all government unclassified, non-Warner Amendment interests. Involvement in computer and communication security began in the late 1970s and early 1980s at NIST in what is now known as the National Computer Systems Laboratory (NCSL) (formerly the Institute for Computer Sciences and Technology).

The National Institute of Standards and Technology's involvement in computer security has most often resulted in the publication of federal standards or guidelines on topics such as password protection, audit, risk analysis, and others that are important to the use of computers but do not necessarily relate to the technical aspects of protection within computer systems. These documents, formally known as Federal Information Processing Standards (FIPS) publications, are widely used within the civilian government as the basis for computer processing and computer system procurement. NIST has also issued other, tutorial publications to enhance awareness in government, in particular, of issues such as computer viruses. The FIPS publications provide valuable information to government computer managers who have little time to study the detailed technical issues concerning computer systems, but who are responsible for their proper use. FIPS publications may also be valuable to industry, but they are not widely known outside the government (although they are recognized by many security practitioners).

In 1972-1973 interest in the establishment of an encryption algorithm suitable for use by the nonclassified portions of the government and, potentially, the private sector, led to the DES project at NBS. The issue of what constitutes "information related to national security" arose, perhaps not for the first time and definitely not for the last time, during this period.  The DES controversy triggered the first in a series of actions intended to ensure that public policy addressed the broader public interest in computer and communications security, not just the military interest.  In particular, it helped to motivate PD 24, discussed above.  It is worth noting here that the number of people involved in cryptography and its related activities at NBS during this time frame never approached 1 percent of the number involved at NSA, and NBS's activities were substantially influenced on a continuous basis by the constraints of NSA.  NBS got by with few resources by leveraging investments by IBM, which was responsible for the technical development of the cryptographic algorithm that became the DES.

As noted above, the implementation of PD 24 contributed to the issuance of NSDD 145, and concern about the associated expansion of NSA's role led to the passage of the Computer Security Act of 1987 (P.L. 100-235), which defined specific information-protection roles for NBS and thereby limited NSA's responsibilities.  Shortly thereafter, NBS was renamed the National Institute of Standards and Technology (NIST).  Although the renamed organization has yet to be funded at a level commensurate with its current or anticipated mission, the intent was to strengthen the organization as a vehicle for stimulating nondefense technology development.  Under P.L. 100-235, NIST is primarily responsible for establishment and dissemination of standards and guidelines for federal computer systems, including those needed "to assure the cost-effective security and privacy of sensitive information in federal computer systems."  NIST is also involved with other objectives of P.L. 100-235 intended to raise security awareness in the federal computing community:  the establishment of security plans by operators of federal computer systems containing sensitive information, and training of all persons associated with such systems.

The complementary nature of the respective computer security missions of NSA and NIST as well as NSA's larger role in its national security arena necessitates cooperation between the two.  That cooperation has recently been shaped by a Memorandum of Understanding (MOU) developed to help implement P.L. 100-235 and to assure national security review of areas of mutual interest (NIST/NSA, 1989).  The Computer Security Act of 1987 calls for NIST to draw on NSA for technical assistance (e.g., research, development, evaluation, or endorsement) in certain areas.  The MOU calls for NIST to draw on NSA's expertise and products "to the greatest extent possible" in developing telecommunications security standards for protecting sensitive but unclassified computer data, and to draw on NSA's guidelines for computer system security to the extent that they are "consistent with the requirements for protecting sensitive information in federal computer systems." Under the MOU, a joint NSA-NIST technical working group was established "to review and analyze issues of mutual interest" regarding the protection of systems processing sensitive information, especially those issues relating to cryptography.

The National Security Agency as well as NIST personnel are also involved with the NIST Computer and Telecommunications Security Council and with the Computer Systems Security and Advisory Board organized by NIST under P.L. 100-235.

According to the MOU, NIST is prevented from developing a competing set of ratings for security product evaluation.[7] It plans instead to issue a management guide, aimed at civilian government, that will explain what trusted and evaluated systems are, and will point agencies toward evaluated systems as appropriate (this topic has already been treated in an *NCSL Bulletin*). Although NIST does not give specific product ratings or endorsements, it is involved with developing tests of products for conformance to its standards, and it has plans to accredit other organizations to validate products for conformance to certain FIPS. NIST does not appear likely to follow the NSA in publishing lists of evaluated products such as NCSC's Evaluated Products List.

Unlike the NSA, NIST has had only a small program in security-related research. In particular, it has sponsored none of the fundamental operating system research needed to develop or evaluate trusted computer systems, although NBS monitored the research and development activities of the 1970s and held an invitational Rancho Santa Fe Access Control workshop in 1972. NIST continues to participate in the DOD Computer Security Initiative through joint sponsorship of the "NBS" (now National) Computer Security Conference, and NIST has recently held a series of workshops aimed at generating guidelines for integrity.

Observers suggest that NSA continues to have a substantial, although not always direct, influence on NIST's activities, drawing on NSA's national security mission. While NIST's computer security responsibilities grew as a result of P.L. 100-235, it was denied several budget increases requested by the Administration, and it remains funded in this area at the level (i.e., taking into account growth in expenses like salaries) in place prior to the passage of the law. Out of an appropriated NIST budget of approximately $160 million (a level almost matched by externally sponsored research), the appropriated FY 1990 NIST security program was $2.5 million; the NSA budget, the details of which are classified, is on the order of $10 billion (Lardner, 1990b). Accordingly, the number of people involved in computer security at NBS/NIST has always been relatively small compared with the number at NSA.

## Other Government Agency Involvement

The historic emphasis on the roles of NSA and NIST makes it easy to overlook the fact that other government agencies and groups are also involved in promoting computer and communications security. As discussed in Chapter 8, other DOD agencies and the Department of Energy engage in security-related research and development, although, with the exception of DARPA, much of this work is tied to the operating mission of the relevant organization; the National Science Foundation (NSF) funds basic research in mathematics and computer science that is relevant to the development of secure and trusted systems. Note that while the DOD's research and procurement have emphasized a specific area of computer security—namely access control, which has a long-established basis in manual systems—it took almost two decades to transform research concepts into commercially produced, government-evaluated products, which are only now beginning to satisfy DOD application needs. This lengthy gestation reflected the need to develop, and achieve some consensus on, complex technology and an associated vocabulary.

As recognized by P.L. 100-235, the computerization of government activities creates a need for computer and communications security in all government agencies and organizations. For example, in an informal committee survey of 1989 government requests for proposals (RFPs), some of the highest computer security requirements were stipulated for systems being procured by the Treasury Department, the Federal Aviation Administration, and the Senate. Across the government, security is one of many concerns captured in Federal Information Resources Management Regulations (President's Council on Integrity and Efficiency, 1988; GSA, 1988), and P.L. 100-235 mandates computer security planning and precautions for federal organizations. However, merely having a plan on paper is no guarantee that sound or effective precautions have been taken. The GAO has repeatedly raised this concern in connection with government computer systems (GAO, 1990c).

Two agencies, the General Services Administration (GSA; which coordinates government procurement) and the Office of Management and Budget (OMB; which influences government procurement and has a general interest in the efficient use of information and systems), set the operating climate for computer and communications security within civil government through circulars (e.g., A-130) and other directives. Despite this nominal breadth, defense agencies, which operate under a security-oriented culture and with a strong system of information classification, have been more active than most civilian agencies in seeking greater security. They have a relatively high degree of concern about unauthorized disclosure and access control, and they have been prodded by military standards (e.g., the Orange Book, which was made into a military standard) and by procurement requirements for specific types of systems in certain applications (e.g., Tempest units that have shielding to minimize electronic emanations).

Federal concerns regarding protection of unclassified systems and data include protection against improper disclosure of personal data, as required by the Privacy Act of 1974 (P.L. 93-579), protection against fraud, and protection of the availability and integrity of government systems (on which millions depend for a variety of payments and other services).

Although the scale of and public interest in government systems may be unique, the government shares many of the same problems found in commercial and other organizations, including inadequate awareness and inadequate precautions. Because of these commonalities, many of NIST's activities, while nominally aimed at meeting civilian government needs, are relevant to industry.

A third group of government entities involved with computer and communications security are the investigating and prosecuting agencies, including the Federal Bureau of Investigation (responsible for major federal law enforcement and also for counterintelligence), the Secret Service (responsible for investigating computer crimes involving finance and communications fraud), the Department of Justice and the U.S. Attorneys (both responsible for prosecuting federal cases), agencies with specialized law enforcement responsibilities (e.g., U.S. Customs Service), and state and local law enforcement entities (Conly, 1989; Cook, 1989). These agencies are concerned with deterring and prosecuting computer crimes, which may result from inadequate computer and communications security. Among the challenges they have faced are encouraging the development of laws that fit emerging and anticipated patterns of crime, and applying laws developed under different technological regimes (e.g., laws against wire fraud) to computer crimes. (See Box 7.1 for a list of relevant laws.) These agencies report difficulties in achieving support from the public (computer-related crimes often go unreported), difficulties in obtaining the necessary technical expertise, and difficulties in obtaining management support for investigations of crimes that, compared to others, require a relatively large expenditure of resources for investigation relative to the nominal losses[8] involved (Conly, 1989; Cook, 1989).

---

### BOX 7.1  LEGISLATIVE TOOLS

Congress has responded to the computer and telecommunication threat by providing federal investigators and prosecutors with impressive tools.

18 U.S.C. §1029: Prohibits fraudulent activity in connection with using access devices in interstate commerce, including computer passwords, telephone access codes, and credit cards.

18 U.S.C. §1030: Prohibits remote access with intent to defraud in connection with federal interest computers and/or government-owned computers and prohibits unauthorized computer access by company employees.

18 U.S.C. §1343: Prohibits the use of interstate communications systems to further a scheme to defraud.

18 U.S.C. §2512: Prohibits making, distributing, possessing, and advertising communication interception devices and equipment.

18 U.S.C. §2314: Prohibits interstate transportation of stolen property valued at over $5,000.

17 U.S.C. §506: Prohibits copyright infringement violations—but only if the copyright is actually on file.

22 U.S.C. §2778: Prohibits illegal export of Department of Defense-controlled software and data.

50 USCA p. 2510: Prohibits illegal export of Department of Commerce-controlled software and data.

18 U.S.C. §793: Prohibits espionage—including obtaining (and/or copying) information concerning telegraph, wireless, or signal station, building, office, research laboratory, or station—for a foreign government, or to injure the United States.

18 U.S.C. §2701: Prohibits unlawful access to electronically stored information.

18 U.S.C. §1962: Prohibits racketeering, which is in turn defined as two or more violations of specific crimes, including 18 U.S.C. §1029, §1343, and §2314.

SOURCE: Cook (1989).

---

### APPENDIX 7.2—SECURITY PRACTITIONERS

Many organizations rely on a security specialist or practitioner for guidance on computer and communications security problems and practices. Most such individuals are associated with information systems planning and operation units; others may be involved with the security of larger corporate functions (including physical facilities security as well as computer system concerns), with internal or external auditing responsibilities, or with an internal or external consulting service. As this range of roles suggests, security practitioners have a variety of backgrounds and tend to be in staff positions. Informal communication with such individuals revealed a shared perception among security practitioners that their job is often made difficult by management's resistance to recommendations for greater security-related controls. Nevertheless, while much of the debate about technology development has been dominated by technical (research, development, and evaluation) experts, security practitioners are a more prominent influence on the ever-growing system-using community. These are the individuals responsible for selecting, recommending, and implementing security technology and procedures.

Several professional societies provide guidelines, continuing education, and other tools and techniques to computer and communications security practitioners. They include, for example, the Information Systems Security Association (ISSA), the Computer Security Institute (CSI), the Special Interest Group for Computer Security (SIG-CS) of the Data Processing Management Association (DPMA), the American Society for Industrial Security (ASIS), and the EDP Auditors Association. Another such group has been organized by SRI International, which offers a "continuing multiclient service" called the International Information Integrity Institute (I-4). The membership of I-4 is limited, by membership decision, to approximately 50 firms that are typically represented by security practitioners (SRI International, 1989). Other groups include large-scale users groups like Guide and Share for IBM system users and industry-specific associations like the Bank Administration Institute.

The need for professional certification has been a growing concern among security practitioners. By the mid-1980s professional societies recognized that certification programs attesting to the qualifications of information security officers would enhance the credibility of the computer security profession. After attempting without success to associate with existing accredited certification programs, the Information Systems Security Association (ISSA) decided to develop its own. Committees were formed to develop the common body of knowledge, criteria for grandfathering (to accommodate the transition to the new regime of certification), and test questions. The common body of knowledge refers to the knowledge deemed necessary to accomplish the tasks or activities performed by members in the field.

Elements of the common body of knowledge identified by a committee of a new consortium of professional societies described below include the following:

• Access control—capabilities used by system management to achieve the desired levels of integrity and confidentiality by preventing unauthorized access to system resources.

• Cryptography—use of encryption techniques to achieve data confidentiality.

• Risk management—minimizing the effects of threats and exposures through the use of assessment or analysis, implementation of cost-effective countermeasures, risk acceptance and assignment, and so on.

• Business continuity planning—preparation for actions to ensure that programs critical to preserving a business are run.

• Data classification—implementation of rules for handling data in accordance with its sensitivity or importance.

• Security awareness—consciousness of the reality and significance of threats and risks to information resources.

• Computer and systems security—understanding computers, systems, and security architectures so as to be able to determine the appropriate type and amount of security appropriate for the operation.

• Telecommunications security—protection of information in transit via telecommunications media and control of the use of telecommunications resources.

• Organization architecture—structure for organization of employees to achieve information security goals.

• Legal/regulatory expertise—knowledge of applicable laws and regulations relative to the security of information resources.

• Investigation—collection of evidence related to information security incidents while maintaining the integrity of evidence for legal action.

• Application program security—the controls contained in application programs to protect the integrity and confidentiality of application data and programs.

• Systems program security—those mechanisms that maintain the security of a system's programs.

• Physical security—methods of providing a safe facility to support data processing operations, including provision to limit (physical) access to authorized personnel.

• Operations security—the controls over hardware, media, and the operators with access privileges to the hardware and media.

• Information ethics—the elements of socially acceptable conduct with respect to information resources.

• Security policy development—methods of advising employees of management's intentions with respect to the use and protection of information resources.

In November 1988 a consortium of organizations interested in the certification of information security practitioners began to forge a joint certification program. In mid-1989, the International Information Systems Security Certification Consortium or (ISC)2 was established as a nonprofit corporation (under the provisions of the General Laws, Chapter 180, of the Commonwealth of Massachusetts) to develop a certification program for information systems security practitioners. Participating organizations include the Information Systems Security Association (ISSA), the Computer Security Institute (CSI), the Special Interest Group for Computer Security (SIG-CS) of the Data Processing Management Association (DPMA), the Canadian Information Processing Society (CIPS), the International Federation of Information Processing, agencies of the U.S. and Canadian governments, and Idaho State University (which has developed computer security education modules). Committees of volunteers from the various founding organizations are currently developing the products needed to implement the certification program, such as a code of ethics, the common body of knowledge, an RFP for obtaining a testing service, a marketing brochure for fund raising, and preliminary grandfathering criteria. Funds are being sought from major computer-using and computer-producing organizations.

According to (ISC)2 literature, certification will be open to all who "qualify ethically" and pass the examination—no particular affiliation with any professional organization is a prerequisite for taking the test. The examination will be a measure of professional competence and may be a useful element in the selection process when personnel are being considered for the information security function.[9] Recertification requirements will be established to ensure that individual certifications remain current in this field that is changing rapidly as technological advancements make certain measures obsolete and provide more effective solutions to security problems.

The growth of security practitioner groups and activities is a positive force, one that can help to stimulate demand for trust technology. Because this profession is new, still evolving, and diverse in composition, it is not clear that it can have the impact on security that, say, certified public accountants have on accounting. That assumption is based in part on the absence to date of generally accepted computer and communications security principles and mature standards of practice in this arena, as well as the absence of the kind of legal accountability that other professions have achieved.

## NOTES

1. The concerns discussed focus on the NCSC's ability to reach out into the commercial world and influence the marketplace. The substantive thrust of the reorganized NCSC—a new emphasis on heterogeneous, networked systems—should generate valuable insights and techniques, although who will benefit from them outside the government is not at all clear.

2. In September 1990, the Computer System Security and Privacy Advisory Board established under the Computer Security Act of 1987 proposed that NIST issue guidelines on civilian agency computer security analogous to the Rainbow Series and published as Federal Information Processing Standards. However, it is not clear how or by whom such a document would be developed, in part because NIST lacks relevant funding (Danca, 1990e).

3. Ironically, it was a similar recognition that led to the launch of the NCSC in the first place.

4. Note that the federal government already has a number of vehicles for action that do not involve direct administration by federal employees, such as nonprofit federally funded research and development centers (FFRDCs), government-owned/contractor-operated (GOCO) industrial plants, and specially chartered quasi-public organizations such as federally sponsored financing agencies that conduct activities formerly conducted by the private sector. Comsat is perhaps the most widely recognized example; it was specially chartered by Congress, but it is profit making and is funded by selling shares. More relevant is the FFRDC concept, also involving congressional charters, which in general does not, however, permit the flexibility in funding or in mission envisioned for the ISF (Musolf, 1983).

5. Another source of funds might eventually be sales of publications. Such sales provide about $10 million in revenue for FASB, for example (FASB, 1990).

6. The emergence of DES in the 1970s, its promotion by the then Institute for Computer Sciences and Technology (ICST) of the then National Bureau of Standards (NBS), and the role of the NSA in that evolution, have been well publicized (OTA, 1987b).

7. The MOU states that NIST will "recognize the NSA-certified rating of evaluated trusted systems under the Trusted Computer Security Evaluation Criteria Program without requiring additional evaluation," and it also makes many references to coordination with NSA to avoid duplication of effort or conflict with existing technical standards aimed at protecting classified information.

8. The nominal losses in a specific case are misleading. They signal a potential for greater loss through repetitions of undetected abuse.

9. Note that the movement toward certification among security practitioners contrasts with the ongoing heated debate among systems developers and software engineers over certification.

# 8

# Research Topics and Funding

Earlier chapters of this report included discussions of the state of the art in computer security that also addressed a variety of research activities. This chapter addresses the broader issue of the state and structure of the research community and also outlines some areas of research where the current level of effort seems insufficient. In addition, the committee also addresses directions for federally funded extramural research programs.

The committee believes that there is a pressing need for a stronger program of university-based research in computer security. Such a program should have two explicit goals: addressing important technical problems and increasing the number of qualified people in the field. This program should be strongly interconnected with other fields of computer science and cognizant of trends in both theory and uses of computer systems.

In the 1970s the Department of Defense (DOD) aggressively funded an external research program that yielded many fundamental results in the security area, such as the reference monitor and the Bell and La Padula model (Bell and La Padula, 1976). But with the establishment of the National Computer Security Center (NCSC) in the early 1980s, the DOD shifted its emphasis from basic research to the development and application of evaluation criteria and the development of applications that meet mission needs. The specific focus of most DOD funding for basic research has been related to nondisclosure of information. Furthermore, relatively little of the DOD-funded research on computer security is currently being done at universities.

The committee reviewed (unclassified) research on information security conducted by the National Security Agency (NSA), and the

NCSC in particular. Now the research activities of the two are combined, owing to NCSC's recent reorganization, and the committee is not in a position to comment on the newly structured program. Although NSA supports active research at several private centers (e.g., SRI International and MITRE Corporation), its support for academic research in computer security appears to have been quite limited in scope and level. That support cannot be tracked straightforwardly, because some of it is passed through other agencies and some recipients have been asked not to divulge NSA's support. NSA has provided some funding for programs, such as the outside cryptographic research program (OCREAE) and DOD's University Research Initiative (URI), that seek to increase the pool of appropriately trained American graduates. In late August 1990, NSA announced a new Computer Security University Research Program, a modest effort aimed at supporting university summer study projects (which are inherently limited in scope and scale).

At the same time, the other agencies with significant agendas related to research in computer security, such as the Department of Energy (DOE), the Navy's Office of Naval Research (ONR), and the National Institute of Standards and Technology (NIST), have had limited programs in funded external research.[1] In the area of information integrity, NIST has attempted to establish a role for itself by holding a series of workshops, but no significant research funding has resulted.[2]

Not-for-profit and vendor laboratories are pursuing a variety of projects, many of which are discussed elsewhere in this report (e.g., see Chapter 4). However, support for these activities fluctuates with both government interest in security and short-term business needs. Although many of the topics proposed below are relevant to industrial research conducted independently or in collaboration with universities, the committee focused on the need to stimulate academic research.

University-based research in computer security is at a dangerously low level.[3] Whereas considerable research is being done on theoretical issues related to security—for example, number theory, cryptology, and zero-knowledge proofs—few research projects directly address the problem of achieving system security. This lack of direct attention to system security is particularly serious given the ongoing dramatic changes in the technology of computing (e.g., the emergence of distributed systems and networks) that make it necessary to rethink some of the current approaches to security. High-risk and long-term research, a traditional strength of universities, is essential. Furthermore, the small number of academicians with research interests in the area of computer security makes it impossible to train a sufficient number of qualified experts capable of participating in commercial research and development projects.

Various issues contribute to the lack of academic research in the computer security field. One is the occasional need for secrecy, which conflicts with the tradition of open publication of research results. Another is the holistic nature of security. There is a risk in studying one aspect of security in isolation; the results may be irrelevant because of changes or advances in some other part of the computer field. In many academic environments, it is difficult to do the large demonstration projects that provide worked examples (proofs of concepts) of total security solutions.

Meanwhile, evidence suggests a growing European research and development effort tied to national and regional efforts to develop the European industrial base. Although not focused specifically on security, several of these projects are developing advanced assurance techniques (e.g., formal methods and safety analysis). The Portable Common Tool Environment (PCTE) consortium of vendors and universities has proposed extensions to PCTE that allow programming tools to utilize common security functions, modeled after but more general than those outlined in the Orange Book (IEPG, 1989; European Commission, 1989a, p. 8). On another front, Esprit funding is establishing a pattern of collaboration that could pay off significantly in systems-oriented fields such as security and safety, as researchers learn to work effectively in relatively large academic and industrial teams.[4] Although MITI in Japan is conducting a study of security problems in networks, the committee has found no widespread Japanese interest in developing indigenous security technology at this time.


## A PROPOSED AGENDA FOR RESEARCH TO
## ENHANCE COMPUTER SECURITY

The committee identified several specific technical issues currently ripe for research. It is expected that the issues described will have aspects that are best addressed variously by universities, contractors, nonprofit research laboratories, government laboratories, and vendor laboratories. The key is to develop a broad range of system security expertise, combining the knowledge gained in both academic and industrial environments. The list that follows is by no means complete (rather, a research agenda must always reflect an openness to new ideas) but is provided to show the scope and importance of relevant research topics and to underscore the need to cultivate progress in areas that have received insufficient attention.

• *Security modularity:* How can a set of system components with known security properties be combined or composed to form a larger system with known security properties?

• *Security models:* The disclosure control problem has benefited from a formal model, the Bell and La Padula model, which captures some of the desired functionality in an abstract manner. Other security requirements, such as integrity, availability, and distributed authentication and authorization, do not have such clean models. Lacking a clean model, it is difficult to describe what a system does or to confirm that it does so. For example, models are needed that deal with separation of duty and with belief and trust in situations of incomplete knowledge.

Efforts should be directed at establishing a sound foundation for security models. The models that have been used in the past lack, for the most part, any formal foundation. The Franconia workshops (IEEE, 1988-1990) have addressed this issue, but more work is necessary. Security models should be integrated with other systems models, such as those related to reliability and safety.

• *Cost/benefit models for security:* How much does security really cost, and what are its real benefits? Both the cost of production and the cost of use should be addressed. Benefit analysis must be based on careful risk analysis. This is particularly difficult for computer security because accurate information on penetrations and loss of assets is often not available, and analyses must depend on expert opinion. The recommended reporting and tracking function envisioned for the Information Security Foundation proposed in Chapter 7 would facilitate model generation and validation.

• *New security mechanisms:* As new requirements are proposed, as new threats are considered, and as new technologies become prevalent, new mechanisms will be required to maintain security effectively. Recent examples of such mechanisms are the challenge-response devices developed for user authentication. Among the mechanisms currently needed are those to support critical aspects of integrity (e.g., separation of duty), distributed key management on low-security systems, multiway and transitive authentication (involving multiple systems and/or users), availability (especially in distributed systems and networks), privacy assurance, and limitations on access in networks, to permit interconnection of mutually suspicious organizations.

• *Assurance techniques:* The assurance techniques that can be applied to secure systems range from the impractical extremes of exhaustive testing to proofs of all functions and properties at all levels of a system. It would be beneficial to know the complete spectrum of assurance techniques, the practicality of their application, and to what aspects of security they best apply. For instance, formal specification and verification techniques can be applied to some encryption protocols but may be more useful for testing formal specifications in an effort to discover design weaknesses (Millen et al., 1987; Kemmerer, 1989a). Also, formally specifying and verifying an entire operating system may not be cost-effective, yet it may be reasonable to thoroughly analyze a particular aspect of the system using formal specification and verification techniques. (This is one of the reasons for grouping the security-relevant aspects of a secure operating system into a security kernel that is small enough to be thoroughly analyzed.) Identifying effective and easily usable combinations of techniques, particularly ones that can be applied early in software production, is a current area of interest in the field of testing, analysis, and verification. In addition, attention must be given to modernizing the existing technology base of verification and testing tools, which are used to implement the techniques, to keep pace with new technology.

• *Alternative representations and presentations:* New representations of security properties may yield new analysis techniques. For example, graphics tools that allow system operators to set, explore, and analyze proposed policies (who should get access to what) and system configurations (who has access to what) may help identify weaknesses or unwanted restrictions as policies are instituted and deployed systems are used.

• *Automated security procedures:* A practical observation is that many, if not most, actual system penetrations involve faults in operational procedures, not system architecture. For example, poor choice of passwords or failure to change default passwords is a common failure documented by Stoll (1989). Research is needed in automating critical aspects of system operation, to assist system managers in avoiding security faults in this area. Examples include tools to check the security state of a system (Baldwin, 1988), models of operational requirements and desired controls, and threat assessment aids. Fault-tree analysis can be used to identify and assess system vulnerabilities, and intrusion detection (Lunt, 1988) through anomaly analysis can warn system administrators of possible security problems.

• *Mechanisms to support nonrepudiation:* To protect proprietary rights it may be necessary to record user actions so as to bar a user from later repudiating these actions. Research into methods of recording user actions in a way that respects the privacy of users is difficult.

• *Control of computing resources:* Resource control is associated with the prevention of unauthorized use and piracy of proprietary software or databases owned or licensed by one party and legitimately installed in a computing system belonging to another. It has attracted little research and implementation effort, but it poses some difficult technical problems and possibly privacy problems as well, and it is, therefore, an area that warrants further research.

• *Systems with security perimeters:* Most network protocol design efforts have tended to assume that networks will provide general interconnection. However, as observed in Chapter 3, a common practical approach to achieving security in a distributed system is to partition the system into regions that are separated by a security perimeter. This is not easy to do. If, for example, a network permits mail but not directory services (because of security concerns about directory searches), the mail may not be deliverable due to the inability to look up the address of a recipient. To address this problem, research is needed in the area of network protocols that will allow partitioning for security purposes without sacrificing the advantages of general connectivity.

## DIRECTIONS FOR FUNDING SECURITY RESEARCH

There are several strategic issues basic to broadening computer security research and integrating it with the rest of computer science: funding agencies' policies, cross-field fertilization, and the kinds of projects to be undertaken. The areas of study sketched above are suitable for funding by any agency with a charter to address technical research topics.

The committee recommends that the relevant agencies of the federal government (e.g., DARPA and NSF) undertake funded programs of technology development and research in computer security. These programs should foster integration of security research with other related research areas, such as promoting common techniques for the analysis of security, safety, and reliability properties. The committee recommends that NIST, in recognition of its interest in computer security (and its charter to enhance security for sensitive but unclassified data and systems), work to assure funding for research in areas of key concern to it, either internally or in collaboration with other agencies more traditionally associated with research. NIST may be particularly effective, under its current regime, at organizing workshops that bring together researchers and practitioners and then widely disseminating the resulting workshop reports.

Although federal agencies have traditionally been viewed as the primary source of funding for computer science research, many states, such as Texas, Virginia, and California, have substantial funding programs geared toward regional industry and academic needs. The proposed research agenda should be brought to the attention of state funding agencies, especially in those states where industrial support and interaction are likely.

Both the Defense Advanced Research Projects Agency (DARPA) and the National Science Foundation (NSF) should proceed to justify a program in extramural computer security research. However, because of differences in the traditional roles of DARPA and NSF, this committee has identified specific activities that it recommends to each.

## Funding by the Defense Advanced Research Projects Agency

The Defense Advanced Research Projects Agency has traditionally been willing to fund significant system-development projects. The committee believes that this class of activity would be highly beneficial for security research. Security is a hands-on field in which mechanisms should be evaluated by deploying them in real systems. Some examples of suitable projects are the following:

• Use of state-of-the-art software development techniques and tools to produce a secure system. The explicit goal of this effort should be to evaluate the development process and to assess the expected gain in system quality.

• Development of distributed systems with a variety of security properties. A project now under way, and funded by DARPA, is aimed at developing encryption-based private electronic mail. Another candidate for study is decentralized, peer-connected name servers.

• Development of a system supporting an approach to ensuring the integrity of data. There are now some proposed models for integrity, but without worked examples it will be impossible to validate them. This represents an opportunity for a cooperative effort by DARPA and NIST.

## Funding by the National Science Foundation

The National Science Foundation has tended to fund smaller, less development-oriented projects. A key role for NSF (and for DARPA, as well), beyond specific funding of relevant projects, is to facilitate increased interaction between security specialists and specialists in related fields (such as distributed computing, safety, and fault-tolerant computing). Examples of areas in which creative collaboration might advance computer security include:

• *Safety:* Concern about the safety-related aspects of computer processing is growing both in the United States and internationally. Great Britain has already formulated a policy that requires the use of stringent assurance techniques in the development of computer systems that affect the safety of humans (U.K. Ministry of Defence, 1989a,b). Unfortunately, safety and related issues pertaining to computer systems—unlike security—have no constituency in the United States.

• *Fault-tolerant computing:* Over the years a great deal of research has been directed at the problem of fault-tolerant computing. Most of this work has addressed problems related to availability and integrity; little attention has been directed to the problems of malicious surreptitious attacks. An attempt should also be made to extend this work to other aspects of security.

• *Code analysis:* Researchers working on optimizing and parallelizing compilers have extensive experience in analyzing both source and object code for a variety of properties. Some of their techniques have been used for covert channel analysis (Haigh et al., 1987; Young and McHugh, 1987). An attempt should be made to use similar techniques to analyze code for other properties related to security.

• *Security interfaces:* People experienced at writing careful specifications of interfaces and verifying high-level properties from these specifications should be encouraged to specify standardized interfaces to security services and to apply their techniques to the specification and analysis of high-level security properties.

• *Theoretical research:* Theoretical work needs to be properly integrated in actual systems. Often both theoreticians and system practitioners misunderstand the system aspects of security or the theoretical limitations of secure algorithms. Practitioners and theoreticians should be encouraged to work together.

## Promoting Needed Collaboration

Both DARPA and NSF have a tradition of working with the broad science community and should initiate programs to facilitate collaboration. Some suggestions for specific actions are the following:

• Start a program aimed specifically at bringing together people with different backgrounds and skills, for example, by providing grants to support visiting researchers for a period of one to two years.

• Show a willingness to support research in computer security by people with complementary expertise (in accounting or distributed systems, for example), although they may have no track record in the security area.

• Run a series of one- or two-week-long workshops for graduate students who are interested in doing research on problems related to computer security. Prior experience in security should be secondary to interest and evidence of accomplishment in related fields. Workshops should, where possible, include laboratory experience with security products and assurance technology.

Traditionally, computer security research has been performed in computer science and engineering departments. However, another research approach that seems relevant is the methodology of the business school. Although business schools have in the past shown little interest in security research, obvious study topics include:

- *Value of security:* A current research topic in business schools is assessing information technology's actual value to an organization. As a part of these studies, it might be possible to develop models for the value of the security aspects of information technology from a business perspective, for example, drawing on the value of a corporate information base to be protected.
- *Privacy in information systems:* The use of a computer system in the corporate environment will be influenced by the degree to which the users perceive the information in the system as public or private. The sociological aspects of privacy may have a strong impact on the effective use of information technology. A valuable contribution would be case studies leading to a working model that relates perceived protection of privacy to an application's effectiveness. Those involved in the emerging field of computer-supported cooperative work (also known as collaboration technology or groupware) should be made aware of (1) the need for security mechanisms when information is shared and (2) the influence of requirements for privacy on the processes being automated or coordinated. In general, any study of information flow in an organization should also note and assess the security and privacy aspects of that information flow.

## NOTES

1. The Office of Naval Research, however, has an ongoing internal program (at the Naval Research Laboratory) in applied security research that includes such projects as methodologies for secure system developers and tools for secure software development. The lack of appropriately trained individuals has been cited by ONR as a major impediment to expanding their research efforts.

The Department of Energy has responded to the recent spate of computer security breaches with an effort centered at their Lawrence Livermore National Laboratory to develop tools, techniques, and guidelines for securing computer systems. Areas currently under investigation include viruses, intrusion detection systems, and security maintenance software tools. The DOE also created a Computer Incident Advisory Capability (CIAC) similar to DARPA's Internet CERT, but specifically to support DOE. Further effort is being expended on developing guidelines for system security testing, incident handling, and others. DOE is also supporting efforts to develop a university-based research capability.

2. A limited computer security budget has hampered even internal NIST efforts to date, although several programs are under development that would group funds from private industry or other federal agencies to address mutual security concerns (see Chapter 7 for a more complete discussion of NIST activities).

3. Consider, for example, the following indicators of low academic participation in the field of computer security. At the January 1989 NIST integrity workshop, of the 66 listed attendees, only 6 were from U.S. academic institutions. At the 1988 Institute of Electrical and Electronics Engineers Symposium on Security and Privacy, a more general security conference with considerable attention to DOD interests, less than 6 percent were academic attendees out of an approximate total of 316. In contrast, at a broad conference on computer systems, the 1989 Association of Computing Machinery Symposium on Operating System Principles, approximately 36 percent of the attendees were from U.S. academic institutions.

4. Examples include provably correct systems (ProCoS), a result of basic research oriented toward language design, compiler systems, and so on, appropriate for safety-critical systems; Software Certification On Programs in Europe (SCOPE), which will define, experiment with, and validate an economic European software certification procedure applicable to all types of software and acceptable and legally recognized throughout Europe; and Demonstration of Advanced Reliability Techniques for Safety-related computer systems (DARTS), whose aim is to facilitate the selection of reliable systems for safety-critical applications (European Commission, 1989a, pp. 27 and 55; 1989b).

# Bibliography

Adams, E. 1984. "Optimizing preventative service of software products," *IBM Journal of R&D*, Vol. 28, No. 1.

Adrion, W. R. 1989. *Testing Techniques for Concurrent and Real-time Systems*, University of Massachusetts, Amherst.

Agranoff, Michael H. 1989. "Curb on technology: Liability for failure to protect computerized data against unauthorized access," *Computer and High Technology Law Journal*, Vol. 5, pp. 265-320.

Akerlof, George A. 1970. "The market for 'lemons': Quality uncertainty and the market mechanism," *Quarterly Journal of Economics*, 87, pp. 488-500.

Alexander, Michael. 1989a. "Computer crime fight stymied," *Federal Computer Week*, October 23, pp. 43-45.

Alexander, Michael. 1989b. "Business foots hackers' bill," *Computerworld*, December 11.

Alexander, Michael. 1989c. "Trojan horse sneaks in with AIDS program," *Computerworld*, December 18, p. 4.

Alexander, Michael. 1990a. "Biometric system use widening—security devices measure physical-based traits to restrict access to sensitive areas," *Computerworld*, January 8, p. 16.

Alexander, Michael. 1990b. "High-tech boom opens security gaps," *Computerworld*, April 2, pp. 1, 119.

Allen, Michael. 1990. "Identity crisis: To repair bad credit, advisers give clients someone else's data," *Wall Street Journal*, August 14, p. A1.

Allen-Tonar, Larry. 1989. "Networked computers attract security problems abuse," *Networking Management*, December, p. 48.

American Bar Association. 1984. *Report on Computer Crime*, Task Force on Computer Crime, Section on Criminal Justice, Chicago, Ill., June.

American Institute of Certified Public Accountants (AICPA). 1984. *Report on the Study of EDP-Related Fraud in the Banking and Insurance Industries*, EDP Fraud Review Task Force, AICPA, New York.

Anderson, J. P. 1972. *Computer Security Technology Planning Study*, ESD-TR-73-51, Vol. I, AD-758 206, ESD/AFSC, Hanscom AFB, Bedford, Mass., October.

Anderson, J. P. 1980. *Computer Security Threat Monitoring and Surveillance*, James P. Anderson Co., Fort Washington, Pa., April.

Anthes, Gary, H. 1989a. "ACC tunes in to illicit hacking activity—firm ferrets out threats," *Federal Computer Week*, September 18, pp. 1, 53.

Anthes Gary, H. 1989b. "U.S. software experts track British standards," *Federal Computer Week*, September 18, pp. 3, 8.

Anthes, Gary H. 1989c. "DARPA response team spawns private spinoffs," *Federal Computer Week*, December 11.

Anthes, Gary H. 1989d. "Vendors skirt NCSC evaluations: Security system testing faulted for length and cost in process," *Federal Computer Week*, December 11, p. 4.

Anthes, Gary H. 1990a. "NIST combats confusion on encryption standard," *Federal Computer Week*, January 29, p. 7.

Anthes, Gary H. 1990b. "Oracle, AF to build secure data base system: Project will build operational relational DBMS to meet A1 trust," *Federal Computer Week*, March 12.

Armed Forces Communications and Electronics Association (AFCEA). 1989. *Information Security Study*, Fairfax, Va., April.

Bailey, David. 1984. "Attacks on computers: Congressional hearings and pending legislation," *Proceedings of the 1984 IEEE Symposium on Security and Privacy*, IEEE Computer Society, Oakland, Calif., April 29-May 2, pp. 180-186.

Baldwin, Robert W. 1988. *Rule Based Analysis of Computer Security*, Technical Report 401, Massachusetts Institute of Technology, Laboratory for Computer Science, Cambridge, Mass., March.

Beatson, Jim. 1989. "Is America ready to 'fly by wire'?" *Washington Post*, April 2, p. C3.

Becker, L. G. 1987. *An Assessment of Resource Centers and Future Requirements for Information Security Technology*, prepared for the National Security Agency, Fort Meade, Md., September.

Bell, Elliott D. 1983. "Secure computer systems: A retrospective," *Proceedings of the 1983 IEEE Symposium on Security and Privacy*, IEEE Computer Society, Oakland, Calif., April 25-27, pp. 161-162.

Bell, Elliot D. 1988. "Concerning modeling of computer security," *Proceedings of the 1988 IEEE Symposium on Security and Privacy*, IEEE Computer Society, Oakland, Calif., April 18-21, pp. 8-13.

Bell, Elliott D. and L. J. La Padula. 1976. *Secure Computer System: Unified Exposition and Multics Interpretation*, ESD-TR-75-306, MITRE Corp., Bedford, Mass., March.

Beresford, Dennis R., et al. 1988. "What is the FASB's role, and how well is it performing?" *Financial Executive*, September/October, pp. 20-26.

Berman, Jerry and Janlori Goldman. 1989. *A Federal Right of Information Privacy: The Need for Reform*, American Civil Liberties Union/Computer Professionals for Social Responsibility, Washington, D.C.

Berton, Lee. 1989. "Audit firms are hit by more investor suits for not finding fraud," *The Wall Street Journal*, January 24, pp. A1, A12.

Betts, Mitch. 1989. "Senate takes tentative look at virus legislation," *Computerworld*, May 22.

Biba, K. J. 1975. *Integrity Considerations for Secure Computer Systems*, Report MTR 3153, MITRE Corp., Bedford, Mass., June.

Birrell, Andrew D., B. W. Lampson, R. M. Needham, and M. D. Schroeder. 1986. "A global authentication service without global trust," *Proceedings of the 1986 IEEE Symposium on Security and Privacy*, IEEE Computer Society, Oakland, Calif., April 7-9, pp. 223-230.

BloomBecker, Jay, Esq. (Ed). 1988. *Introduction To Computer Crime*, 2nd ed., National Center for Computer Crime Data, Los Angeles, Calif.

Bloomfield, R. E. 1990. *SafeIT: The Safety of Programmable Electronic Systems*, a government consultation document on activities to promote the safety of computer controlled systems, *Volume 1: Overall Approach* and *Volume 2: A Framework for Safety Standards*, ICSE Secretariat, Department of Trade and Industry, London, United Kingdom, June.

Boebert, E. 1985. "A practical alternative to hierarchical integrity policies," *Proceedings of the 8th National Computer Security Conference*, September 30, NIST, Gaithersburg, Md.

Boebert, W. E., R. Y. Kain, W. D. Young, and S. A. Hansohn. 1985. "Secure ADA target: Issues, system design, and verification," *Proceedings of the 1985 IEEE Symposium on Security and Privacy*, IEEE Computer Society, Oakland, Calif., April 22-24, pp. 176-183.

Boss, A. H. and W. J. Woodward. 1988. "Scope of the uniform commercial code; survey of computer contracting cases," *The Business Lawyer* 43, August, pp. 1513-1554.

Bozman, Jean S. 1989. "Runaway program gores sabre," *Computerworld*, May 22.

Brand, Russell L. 1989. *Coping with the Threat of Computer Security Incidents: A Primer from Prevention through Recovery*, July. Available from the Defense Advanced Research Projects Agency, Arlington, Va., or at the following address: 1862 Euclid, Department 136, Berkeley, CA 94709.

Branstad, D. 1973. "Security aspects of computer networks," *Proceedings of the AIAA Computer Network Systems Conference*, Paper 73-427, Huntsville, Ala., April, American Institute of Aeronautics and Astronautics (AIAA), Washington, D.C.

Branstad, Dennis K. and Miles E. Smid. 1982. "Integrity and security standard based on cryptography," *Computers & Security*, Vol. 1, pp. 225-260.

Brewer, D. F. C. 1985. *Software Integrity: (Verification, Validation, and Certification)*, Admiral Computing Limited, Camberley, Surrey, England, January, pp. 111-124.

Brown, Bob. 1989a. "Security risks boost encryption outlays," *Network World*, January 9, pp. 11-12.

Brown, Bob. 1989b. "CO fire, virus attack raise awareness, not preparation," *Network World*, July 3, p. 1.

Browne, Malcolm W. 1988. "Most ferocious math problem is tamed," *New York Times*, October 12, p. A1.

Buckley, T. F. and J. W. Wise. 1989. "Tutorial: A guide to the VIPER microprocessor," *Proceedings: COMPASS '89 (Computer Assurance)*, IEEE Computer Society, New York, June 23.

Burgess, John. 1989. "Computer virus sparks a user scare," *Washington Post*, September 17, p. H3.

Burgess, John. 1990. "Hacker's case may shape computer security law," *Washington Post*, January 9, p. A4.

Burrows, M., M. Abadi, and R. Needham. 1989. *A Logic of Authentication*, Digital Systems Research Center, Palo Alto, Calif., February.

*Business Week*. 1988. "Is your computer secure," (cover story), August 1, pp. 64-72.

California, State of. 1985. *Informational Hearing: Computers and Warranty Protection for Consumers*, Sacramento, Calif., October.

Canadian Government, System Security Centre, Communications Security Establishment. 1989. *Canadian Trusted Computer Product Evaluation Criteria*, Version 1.0, draft, Ottawa, Canada, May.

Carnevale, Mary Lu and Julie Amparano Lopez. 1989. "Making a phone call might mean telling the world about you," *Wall Street Journal*, November 28, pp. A1, A8.

Casatelli, Christine. 1989a. "Smart signatures at FED," *Federal Computer Week*, May 22.

Casatelli, Christine. 1989b. "Disaster recovery," *Federal Computer Week*, December 11, pp. 28-29, 33.

Casey, Peter. 1980. "Proposals to curb computer misuse," *JFIT News*, No. 8, November, p. 2.

Chalmers, Leslie S. 1986. "An analysis of the differences between the computer security practices in the military and private sectors," *Proceedings of the 1986 IEEE Symposium on Security and Privacy,* IEEE Computer Society, Oakland, Calif., April 7-9, pp. 71-74.

Chandler, James P. 1977. "Computer transactions: Potential liability of computer users and vendors," *Washington University Law Quarterly,* Vol. 1977, No. 3, pp. 405-443.

Chaum, David (Ed.). 1983. *Advances in Cryptology: Proceedings of Crypto 83,* Plenum, New York.

Chor, Ben-Zion. 1986. *Two Issues in Public-Key Cryptography: RSA Bit Security and a New Knapsack Type System,* MIT Press, Cambridge, Mass.

*Christian Science Monitor.* 1989. "Computer and spy: Worrisome mix," March 7, p. 4.

*Chronicle of Higher Education.* 1988a. "'Virus' destroys campus computer data," February 3.

*Chronicle of Higher Education.* 1988b. "Worries over computer 'viruses' lead campuses to issue guidelines," March 2.

Clark, D. D. and D. R. Wilson. 1987. "A comparison of commercial and military computer security policies," *Proceedings of the 1987 IEEE Symposium on Security and Privacy,* IEEE Computer Society, Oakland, Calif., April 27-29, pp. 184-194.

Cohen, Fred. 1984. "Computer viruses: Theory and experiments," Seventh DOD/NBS Conference on Computer Security, Gaithersburg, Md.

Cole, Patrick and Johathan B. Levine. 1989. "Are ATMs easy targets for crooks?" *Business Week,* March 6, p. 30.

Comer, Douglas. 1988. *Internetworking with TCP/IP Principles, Protocols, and Architectures,* Prentice-Hall, Englewood Cliffs, N.J.

*Communications Week.* 1990a. "Hack it through packet," April 16, p. 10.

*Communications Week.* 1990b. "What's in the mail?" editorial, July 16, p. 20.

Computer and Business Equipment Manufacturers Association (CBEMA). 1989a. Statement to U.S. Congress (101st), Senate, Subcommittee on Technology and the Law, Hearing on Computer Viruses, May 19.

Computer and Business Equipment Manufacturers Association (CBEMA). 1989b. Statement to U.S. Congress (101st), House of Representatives, Committee on the Judiciary, Subcommittee on Criminal Justice, Hearing on Computer Virus Legislation, November 8.

*Computer Crime Law Reporter.* 1989. "Computer crime statutes at the state level," August 21 update based on the "State-Net" database and compiled and distributed by the National Center for Computer Crime Data, 2700 N. Cahuenga Blvd., Los Angeles, CA 90068.

*Computer Fraud & Security Bulletin.* 1989-1990. Elsevier Science Publishing Co., Oxford, United Kingdom.

Computer Law Associates Annual Meeting. 1978. Unpublished proceedings: Brooks, Daniel J., "Natures of liabilities of software program suppliers"; DeRensis, Paul R., "Impact of computer systems on the liabilities of various types of professionals"; Hutcheon, Peter D., "Computer system as means for avoidance of liability"; Jenkins, Martha M., "Effects of computer-system records on liabilities of suppliers, users, and others"; Freed, Roy N., "How to handle exposures to, and impacts of, liability arising from computer use." Washington, D.C., Computer Law Association, Fairfax, Va., March 6.

*Computer Security Journal.* 1986-1988. Computer Security Institute, 500 Howard Street, San Francisco, CA 94105.

*Computers & Security.* 1988. "Special supplement: Computer viruses," Vol. 7, No. 2, Elsevier Advanced Technology Publications, Oxford, United Kingdom, April.

*Computers & Security.* 1988-1990. Elsevier Advanced Technology Publications, Oxford, United Kingdom.

*Computerworld.* 1988a. "OSI security system revealed," October 5, pp. 53, 58.

*Computerworld.* 1988b. "Virus ravages thousands of systems," November 7, pp. 1, 157.

Conly, Catherine H. 1989. *Organizing for Computer Crime Investigation and Prosecution,* U.S. Department of Justice, National Institute of Justice, Washington, D.C., July.

Consultative Committee on International Telephony and Telegraphy (CCITT). 1989a. *Data Communication Networks Message Handling Systems,* Vol. VIII, Fascicle VIII.7, Recommendations X.400-X.420, CCITT, Geneva, p. 272.

Consultative Committee on International Telephony and Telegraphy (CCITT). 1989b. *Data Communications Networks Directory,* Vol. VIII, Fascicle VIII.8, Recommendations X.500-X.521, CCITT, Geneva.

Cook, William J. 1989. "Access to the access codes '88-'89: A prosecutor's perspective," *Proceedings of the 12th National Computer Security Conference,* National Institute of Standards and Technology/National Computer Security Center, Baltimore, Md., October 10-13.

Cooper, James Arlin. 1989. *Computer & Communications Security—Strategies for the 1990s,* McGraw-Hill Communications Series, McGraw-Hill, New York.

Cornell University. 1989. *The Computer Worm. A Report to the Provost from the Commission of Preliminary Enquiry,* Ithaca, N.Y., February 6.

Cowan, Alison Leigh. 1990. "The $290,000 job nobody wants," *New York Times,* October 11, D1, D9.

Craigen, D. and K. Summerskill (Eds.). 1990. *Formal Methods for Trustworthy Computer Systems (FM '89), a Workshop on the Assessment of Formal Methods for Trustworthy Computer Systems,* Springer-Verlag, New York.

Crawford, Diane. 1989. "Two bills equal forewarning," *Communications of the ACM,* Vol. 32, No. 7, July.

Crenshaw, Albert B. 1990. "Senate panel approves liability bill," *Washington Post,* May 23.

Cullyer, W. 1989. "Implementing high integrity systems: The Viper microprocessor," *IEEE AES Magazine,* May 13.

Curry, David A. 1990. *Improving the Security of Your UNIX System,* ITSTD-721-FR-90-21, Information and Telecommunications Sciences and Technology Division, SRI International, Menlo Park, Calif., April.

Cutler, Ken and Fred Jones. 1990. "Commercial international security requirements," unpublished draft paper, American Express Travel Related Services Company, Inc., Phoenix, Ariz., August 3.

Danca, Richard A. 1989. "LAN group helps managers handle security risks," *Federal Computer Week,* July 10.

Danca, Richard A. 1990a. "Sybase unveils multilevel secure DBMS," *Network World,* February 19, pp. 1, 37.

Danca, Richard A. 1990b. "NCSC decimated, security role weakened," *Federal Computer Week,* July 16, pp. 1, 6.

Danca, Richard A. 1990c. "Bush revises NSDD 145," *Federal Computer Week,* July 16, pp. 6, 41.

Danca, Richard A. 1990d. "NCSC affirms shakeup in its structure," *Federal Computer Week,* August 27, pp. 1, 4.

Danca, Richard A. 1990e. "NIST may issue civilian computer security guide: Proposed document could become federal information processing standard," *Federal Computer Week,* September 17, p. 60.

Danca, Richard A. 1990f. "NIST, industry team up for anti-virus consortium," *Federal Computer Week,* October 8, p. 2.

Danca, Richard A. 1990g. "Torricelli charges NIST with foot-dragging on security," *Federal Computer Week,* October 8, p. 9.

*Datamation.* 1987. "Disaster recovery: Who's worried?" February 1, pp. 60-64.

Datapro Research. 1989a. "All about data encryption devices," *Datapro Reports: Information Security*, Report no. IS37-001, McGraw-Hill, Delran, N.J., pp. 101-109.

Datapro Research. 1989b. "All about microcomputer encryption and access control," *Datapro Reports: Information Security*, Report no. IS31-001, McGraw-Hill, Delran, N.J., pp. 101-108.

Datapro Research. 1989c. *Security Issues of 1988: A Retrospective*, McGraw-Hill, Delran, N.J., March.

Datapro Research. 1990a. "Host access control software: Market overview," *Datapro Reports: Information Security*, Report no. IS52-001, McGraw-Hill, Delran, N.J., pp. 101-104.

Datapro Research. 1990b. "Bull security capabilities of Multics," *Datapro Reports: Information Security*, Report no. IS56-115, McGraw-Hill, Delran, N.J., pp. 101-106.

Daunt, Robert T. 1985. "Warranties and mass distributed software," *Computers and High-Technology Law Journal*, Vol. 1, pp. 255-307.

Davies, D. and W. Price. 1984. *Security for Computer Networks: An Introduction to Data Security in Teleprocessing and Electronic Funds Transfers*, Wiley, New York.

Davis, Bob. 1988. "A supersecret agency finds selling secrecy to others isn't easy," *Wall Street Journal*, March 28, p. A1.

Davis, Bob. 1989. "NASA discloses computer virus infected network," *Wall Street Journal*, October 18, p. B4.

Davis, G. Gervaise, III. 1985. *Software Protection: Practical and Legal Steps to Protect and Market Computer Programs*, Van Nostrand Reinhold, New York.

Davis, Otto A. and Morton I. Kamien. 1969. "Externalities, information, and alternative collective action," *The Analysis and Evaluation of Public Expenditures: The PPB System*, compendium of papers submitted to the Subcommittee on Economy in Government of the Joint Economic Committee of the U.S. Congress, Washington, D.C., U.S. GPO, pp. 67-86.

Davis, Ruth M. 1989. "CALS Data Protection—Computer-aided Acquisition and Logistic Support, Data Protection and Security Policy Statement," The Pymatuning Group, Arlington, Va., January.

Defense Communications Agency (DCA). 1989. "DDN Security Coordination Center operational," *Defense Data Network Security Bulletin*, DDN Security Coordination Center, DCA DDN Defense Communications System, September 22.

Denning, D. E. 1987. "An intrusion-detection model," *Proceedings of the 1986 Symposium on Security and Privacy*, National Bureau of Standards, Gaithersburg, Md., September.

Denning, D. E., T. F. Lunt, R. R. Schell, W. R. Shockley, and M. Heckman. 1988. "The SeaView security model," *Proceedings of the 1988 IEEE Symposium on Security and Privacy*, IEEE Computer Society, Oakland, Calif., April 18-21, pp. 218-233.

Denning, Dorothy. 1976. "A lattice model of secure information flow," *Communications of the ACM*, Vol. 19.

Denning, Dorothy E., Peter G. Neumann, and Donn B. Parker. 1987. "Social aspects of computer security," *Proceedings of the 10th National Computer Security Conference*, National Bureau of Standards/National Computer Security Center, Baltimore, Md., September 21-24, pp. 320-325.

Dewdney, A. K. 1989. "Of worms, viruses, and core war," *Scientific American*, March, pp. 110-113.

Dickman, Steven. 1989. "Hackers revealed as spies," *Nature*, March 9, p. 108.

DiDio, Laura. 1989. "Rash of viruses puts spotlight on security," *Network World*, October 30, p. 19.

DiDio, Laura. 1990. "Virus threat obscured by slow growth in early stages," *Network World*, April 23, p. 23.

Diffie, W. and M. Hellman. 1976. "New directions in cryptography," *IEEE Transactions on Information Theory*, IT-22, November 16, pp. 644-654.

Dillon, Laura K. 1989. *Research on Validation of Concurrent and Real-time Software Systems,*" University of California, Santa Barbara.

Dobson, J. E. and B. Randell. 1986. "Building reliable secure computing systems out of unreliable insecure components," *Proceedings of the 1986 IEEE Symposium on Security and Privacy,* IEEE Computer Society, Oakland, Calif., April 7-9, pp. 187-193.

Early, Peter. 1988. *Family of Spies: Inside the John Walker Spy Ring,* Bantam Books, New York.

Eason, Tom S., Susan Higley Russell, and Brian Ruder. 1977. *Systems Auditability and Control Study: Data Processing Control Practices Report,* Vol. 1 of 3 volumes, Institute of Internal Auditors, Altamonte Springs, Fla.

*Economist.* 1988. "Keeping out the Kaos Club," Science and Technology Section, July 9, pp. 77-78.

Electronic Industries Association (EIA). 1987. *Proceedings: Communications & Computer Security (COMSEC & COMPUSEC): Requirements, Opportunities and Issues,* EIA, Washington, D.C., January 14.

Emergency Care Research Institute (ECRI). 1985. "Unauthorized use of computers: An often-neglected security problem," *Issues in Health Care Technology,* ECRI, Plymouth Meeting, Pa., July, pp. 1-6.

Emergency Care Research Institute (ECRI). 1988a. "Legal implications of computerized patient care," *Health Technology,* Vol. 2, No. 3, May/June, pp. 86-95, ECRI, Plymouth Meeting, Pa.

Emergency Care Research Institute (ECRI). 1988b. *An Election Administrator's Guide to Computerized Voting Systems,* Vol. 1 and 2, ECRI, Plymouth Meeting, Pa.

Ernst & Young. 1989. *Computer Security Survey: A Report,* Cleveland, Ohio.

Estrin, D. and G. Tsudik. 1987. "VISA scheme for inter-organization network security," *Proceedings of the 1987 IEEE Symposium on Security and Privacy,* IEEE Computer Society, Oakland, Calif., April 27-29, pp. 174-183.

European Commission. 1989a. Basis for a Portable Common Tool Environment (PCTE), Esprit Project Number 32, *Esprit, The Project Synopses, Information Processing Systems,* Vol. 3 of a series of 8, September.

European Commission. 1989b. Basis for a Portable Common Tool Environment (PCTE), Esprit Project Number 32, *Basic Research Actions and Working Groups,* Vol. 8 of a series of 8, September.

European Computer Manufacturers Association (ECMA). 1989. *Standard ECMA-XXX Security in Open Systems: Data Elements and Service Definitions,* ECMA, Geneva.

Falk, David. 1975. "Building codes in a nutshell," *Real Estate Review,* Vol. 5, No. 3, Fall, pp. 82-91.

*Federal Computer Week.* 1988. "Analysis, task forces work to keep Internet safe," November 14, pp. 1, 49.

*Federal Computer Week.* 1989. "Selling viruses," November 27, p. 25.

Federal Republic of Germany, Ministry of Interior. 1990. *Information Technology Security Evaluation Criteria (ITSEC),* the harmonized criteria of France, Germany, the Netherlands, and the United Kingdom, draft version 1, May 2, Bonn, Federal Republic of Germany.

Federal Trade Commission (FTC). 1983. *Standards and Certification,* final staff report, Bureau of Consumer Protection, Washington, D.C., April.

Fetzer, James H. 1988. "Program verification: The very idea," *Communications of the ACM,* Vol. 31, No. 9, September, pp. 1048-1063.

Financial Accounting Foundation (FAF) (n.d.). "Establishing standards for financial reporting," FASB, Norwalk, Conn. [undated pamphlet]

Financial Accounting Foundation (FAF). 1990. *Financial Accounting Foundation Annual Report 1989,* FAF, Norwalk, Conn.

Financial Accounting Standards Board (FASB). 1990. "Facts about FASB," FASB, Norwalk, Conn.

Fitzgerald, Karen. 1989. "The quest for intruder-proof computer systems," *IEEE Spectrum*, August, pp. 22-26.

Flaherty, David. 1990. *Protecting Privacy in Surveillance Societies*, The University of North Carolina Press, Chapel Hill.

Florida State Legislature. 1984. *Overview of Computer Security*, a report of the Joint Committee on Information Technology Resources, Jacksonville, Fla., January.

Forcht, Karen A. 1985. "Computer security: The growing need for concern," *The Journal of Computer Information Systems*, Fall.

Francett, Barbara. 1989. "Can you loosen the bolts without disarming the locks?" (Executive Report: Security in Open Times), *ComputerWorld*, October 23.

Frenkel, Karen A. 1990. "The politics of standards and the EC," *Communications of the ACM*, Vol. 33, No. 7, pp. 41-51.

Galen, Michele and Jeffrey Rothfeder. 1989. "Is nothing private?" *Business Week*, September 4, pp. 74-77, 80-82.

Gasser, Morrie. 1988. *Building a Secure Computer System*, Van Nostrand Reinhold, New York.

Gasser, Morrie, A. Goldstein, C. Kaufman, and B. Lampson. 1989. "The Digital distributed system security architecture," *Proceedings of the 12th National Computer Security Conference*, National Institute of Standards and Technology/National Computer Security Center, Baltimore, Md., October 10-13, pp. 305-319.

Gemignani, Michael C. 1982. "Product liability and software," *Rutgers Journal of Computers, Technology and Law*, Vol. 8, p. 173.

General Accounting Office. 1980. *Increasing Use of Data Telecommunications Calls for Stronger Protection and Improved Economies*, Washington, D.C.

General Accounting Office (GAO). 1987. *Space Operations: NASA's Use of Information Technology*, GAO/IMTEC-87-20, Washington, D.C., April.

General Accounting Office (GAO). 1988a. *Information Systems: Agencies Overlook Security Controls During Development*, GAO/IMTEC-88-11, Washington, D.C., May.

General Accounting Office (GAO). 1988b. *Information Systems: Agencies Overlook Security Controls During Development*, GAO/IMTEC-88-11S, Washington, D.C., May.

General Accounting Office (GAO). 1988c. *Satellite Data Archiving: U.S. and Foreign Activities and Plans for Environmental Information*, GAO/RCED-88-201, Washington, D.C., September.

General Accounting Office (GAO). 1989a. *Federal ADP Personnel: Recruitment and Retention*, GAO/IMTEC-89-12BR, Washington, D.C., February.

General Accounting Office (GAO). 1989b. *Electronic Funds: Information on Three Critical Banking Systems*, Washington, D.C., February.

General Accounting Office (GAO). 1989c. *Computer Security: Compliance With Training Requirements of the Computer Security Act of 1987*, GAO/IMTEC-89-16BR, Washington, D.C., February.

General Accounting Office (GAO). 1989d. *Computer Security: Virus Highlights Need for Improved Internet Management*, GAO/IMTEC-89-57, Washington, D.C., June.

General Accounting Office (GAO). 1989e. *Computer Security: Unauthorized Access to a NASA Scientific Network*, GAO/IMTEC-90-2, Washington, D.C., November.

General Accounting Office (GAO). 1990a. *Electronic Funds Transfer: Oversight of Critical Banking Systems Should Be Strengthened*, Washington, D.C., January.

General Accounting Office (GAO). 1990b. *Financial Markets: Tighter Computer Security Needed*, GAO/IMTEC-90-15, Washington, D.C., January.

General Accounting Office (GAO). 1990c. *Computer Security: Government Planning Process Had Limited Impact*, GAO/IMTEC-90-48, Washington, D.C., May.

General Accounting Office (GAO). 1990d. *Justice Automation: Tighter Computer Security Needed*, GAO/IMTEC-90-69, Washington, D.C., July.

General Accounting Office (GAO). 1990e. *Computers and Privacy: How the Government Obtains, Verifies, Uses, and Protects Personal Data*, GAO/IMTEC-90-70BR, Washington, D.C., August.

General Services Administration (GSA). 1988. *Information Technology Installation Security*, Office of Technical Assistance, Federal Systems Integration and Management Center, Falls Church, Va., December.

German Information Security Agency (GISA). 1989. *IT Security Criteria: Criteria for the Evaluation of Trustworthiness of Information Technology (IT) Systems*, 1st version, Koln, Federal Republic of Germany.

Gilbert, Dennis M. and Bruce K. Rosen. 1989. *Computer Security Issues in the Application of New and Emerging Information Technologies*, a white paper, National Institute of Standards and Technology, Gaithersburg, Md., March.

Godes, James N. 1987. "Developing a new set of liability rules for a new generation of technology: Assessing liability for computer-related injuries in the health care field," *Computer Law Journal*, Vol. VII, pp. 517-534.

*Government Computer News*. 1986. "DP courses don't include ethics study," July 4.

*Government Computer News*. 1988. "GCN spotlight: Security," April 29, pp. 35-54.

Gray, J. 1987. "Why do computers stop and what can we do about it?" *6th International Conference on Reliability and Distributed Databases*, IEEE Computer Society, Engineering Societies Library, New York.

Green, Virginia D. 1989a. "Overview of federal statutes pertaining to computer-related crime," (memorandum), Reed, Smith, Shaw, and McClay, Washington, D.C., July 7.

Green, Virginia D. 1989b. "State computer crime statutes and the use of traditional doctrines to prosecute the computer criminal," (memorandum), Reed, Smith, Shaw, and McClay, Washington, D.C., July 7.

Greenberg, Ross M. 1988. "A form of protection for you and your computer," *2600 Magazine*, Summer.

Greenhouse, Steven. 1990. "India crash revives French dispute over safety of Airbus jet," *New York Times*, February 24.

Gregg, Robert E. and Thomas R. Folk. 1986. "Liability for substantive errors in computer software," *Computer Law Reporter* (Washington D.C.), Vol. 5, No. 1, July, pp. 18-26.

Grimm, Vanessa Jo. 1989. "Hill halves NIST budget for security," *Government Computer News*, Vol. 8, No. 22, October 30.

Gruman, Galen. 1989a. "Software safety focus of new British standard," *IEEE Software*, May.

Gruman, Galen. 1989b. "Major changes in federal software policy urged," *IEEE Software*, November, pp. 78-80.

Haigh, J., R. A. Kemmerer, J. McHugh, and B. Young. 1987. "An experience using two covert channel analysis techniques on a real system design," *IEEE Transactions on Software Engineering*, Vol. SE-13, No. 2, February.

Hamlet, Richard. 1988. "Special section on software testing," *Communications of the ACM*, Vol. 31, No. 6, June.

Hanna, Keith, Neil Daeche, and Mark Longley. 1989. *VERITAS+: A Specification Language Based on Type Theory*, Technical Report, Faculty of Information Technology, University of Kent, Canterbury, United Kingdom, May.

Harrison, Warren. 1988. "Using software metrics to allocate testing resources," *Journal of Management Systems*, Vol. 4, Spring.

Helfant, Robert and Glenn J. McLoughlin. 1988. *Computer Viruses: Technical Overview and Policy Considerations*, Science Policy Research Division, Congressional Research Service, Washington, D.C., August 15.

Hellman, M. 1979. "The mathematics of public-key cryptography," *Scientific American*, 241(2):146-157.

Henderson, Nell. 1989. "Programming flaw, keyboard cited in airline delays twice in 2 weeks," *Washington Post*, November 18, p. B4.

Higgins, John C. 1989. "Information security as a topic in undergraduate education of computer scientists," *Proceedings of the 12th National Computer Security Conference*, National Institute of Standards and Technology/National Computer Security Center, Baltimore, Md., October 10-13.

Hilts, Philip J. 1988. "Computers face epidemic of 'information diseases,'" *Washington Post*, May 8, p. A3.

Hoffman, Lance J. 1988. *Making Every Vote Count: Security and Reliability of Computerized Vote-counting Systems*, George Washington University, School of Engineering and Applied Science, Department of Electrical Engineering and Computer Science, Washington D.C., March.

Hollinger, Richard C. and Lonn Lanza-Kaduce. 1988. "The process of criminalization: The case of computer crime laws," *Criminology*, Vol. 26, No. 1.

Holmes, James P., R. L. Maxwell, and L. J. Wright. 1990. *A Performance Evaluation of Biometric Identification Devices*, Sandia National Laboratories, Albuquerque, N. Mex., July.

Honeywell, Secure Computing Technology Center. 1985-1988. *LOCK: Selected Papers*, Honeywell, St. Anthony, Minn.

Horning, James J., P. G. Neumann, D. D. Redell, J. Goldman, and D. R. Gordon. 1989. *A Review of NCIC 2000: The Proposed Design for the National Crime Information Center*, American Civil Liberties Union, Project on Privacy and Technology, Washington, D.C., February.

Horovitz, Bonna Lynn. 1985. "Computer software as a good under the uniform commercial code: Taking a byte out of the intangibility myth," *Boston University Law Review*, Vol. 65, pp. 129-164.

Houston, M. Frank. 1987. "What do the simple folks do? Software safety in the cottage industry," Food and Drug Administration, Center for Devices and Radiological Health, Rockville, Md., pp. S/20-S/24.

Houston, M. Frank. 1989. *Designing Safer, More Reliable Software Systems*, Food and Drug Administration, Center for Devices and Radiological Health, Rockville, Md.

Howden, William E. 1987. *Functional Program Testing and Analysis*, McGraw Hill, New York.

Independent European Programme Group (IEPG), Technical Area 13 (TA-13). 1989. "Introducing PCTE+," (April); and "Rationale for the changes between the PCTE+ specifications issue 3 dated 28 October 1988 and the PCTE specifications version 1.5 dated 15 November 1988," (January 6), IEPG, Eurogroup of NATO, Brussels.

Information Systems Security Association. 1988-1990. *ISSA Access*, Newport Beach, Calif.

*InfoWorld*. 1988. "What were simple viruses may fast become a plague," *Tech Talk*, May 2.

Institute for Defense Analyses (IDA). 1987. IDA memorandum reports: *Introduction to Information Protection* (M-379), *Operating Systems Security* (M-380), *Network Security* (M-381), *Database System Security* (M-382), *Formal Specification and Verification* (M-383), and *Risk Analysis* (M-384), IDA, Alexandria, Va., October.

Institute of Electrical and Electronics Engineers (IEEE). 1984. *IEEE Guide to Software Requirements Specifications*, ANSI/IEEE Std. 830-1984, IEEE, New York.

Institute of Electrical and Electronics Engineers (IEEE). 1988. *Proceedings: COMPASS '88 (Computer Assurance)*, June 27-July 1, IEEE, New York.

Institute of Electrical and Electronics Engineers (IEEE). 1988-1990. *Proceedings of the Computer Security Foundations Workshop*, Franconia, N.H., IEEE, New York.

Institute of Electrical and Electronics Engineers (IEEE). 1989a. *Proceedings: COMPASS '89 (Computer Assurance)*, June, IEEE, New York.

Institute of Electrical and Electronics Engineers (IEEE). 1989b. *Cipher*, Newsletter of the Technical Committee on Security & Privacy, IEEE Computer Society, Washington, D.C.

Institute of Electrical and Electronics Engineers (IEEE). 1990a. *Cipher*, Newsletter of the Technical Committee on Security & Privacy, Special Issue, "Minutes of the First Workshop on Covert Channels Analysis," IEEE Computer Society, Washington, D.C.

Institute of Electrical and Electronics Engineers (IEEE). 1990b. *IEEE Software* (issue on formal methods in software engineering), September.

Institute of Electrical and Electronics Engineers (IEEE). 1990c. *IEEE Transactions on Software Engineering* (issue on formal methods in software engineering), September.

International Standards Organization (ISO). 1989. "Security Architecture," Part 2 of 4, *Information Processing Systems Open System Interconnection Basic Reference Model*, ISO-7498-2, available from the American National Standards Institute, New York.

Jackson, Kelly. 1989a. "Plans grounded by FAA computer glitches," *Federal Computer Week*, November 20, p. 20.

Jackson, Kelly. 1989b. "Congress pushes computer crime law," *Federal Computer Week*, November 20, p. 23.

Jacobs, Jane. 1972. *The Death and Life of Great American Cities*, Penguin, Harmondsworth, United Kingdom.

Jaffe, Matthew S. and Nancy G. Leveson. 1989. *Completeness, Robustness, and Safety in Real-Time Software Requirements Specification*, Technical Report 89-01, Information and Computer Science, University of California, Irvine, February.

Japanese Ministry of International Trade and Industry (MITI). 1989. *The Present State and Problems of Computer Virus*, Agency of Industrial Science and Technology, Information-Technology Promotion Agency, Tokyo.

Johnson, David R. and David Post. 1989. *Computer Viruses*, a white paper on the legal and policy issues facing colleges and universities, American Council on Education and Wilmer, Cutler & Pickering, Washington, D.C.

Johnson, William. 1989. "Information espionage: An old problem with a new face," (Executive Report: Security in Open Times), *Computerworld*, October 23.

Joseph, Mark K. and Algirdas Avizienis. 1988. "A fault tolerance approach to computer viruses," *Computer*, IEEE, May.

Juitt, David. 1989. "Security assurance through system management," *Proceedings of the 12th National Computer Security Conference*, National Institute of Standards and Technology/National Computer Security Center, Baltimore, Md., October 10-13.

Kahn, David. 1967. *The Codebreakers: The Story of Secret Writing*, Macmillan, New York.

Karger, P. 1988. "Implementing commercial data integrity with secure capabilities," *Proceedings of the 1988 IEEE Symposium on Security and Privacy*, IEEE Computer Society, Oakland, Calif., April 18-21, pp. 130-139.

Karon, Paul. 1988. "The hype behind computer viruses: Their bark may be worse than their 'byte,'" *PC Week*, May 31, p. 49.

Kass, Elliot M. 1990. "Data insecurity," *Information Week*, March 19, p. 22.

Keller, John J. 1990. "Software glitch at AT&T cuts off phone service for millions," *Wall Street Journal*, January 16, p. B1.

Kemmerer, R. A. 1985. "Testing formal specifications to detect design errors," *IEEE Transactions on Software Engineering*, SE-11(1), pp. 32-43.

Kemmerer, R. A. 1986. *Verification Assessment Study Final Report, Volume I, Overview, Conclusions, and Future Directions*, Library No. S-228,204, National Computer Security Center, Fort Meade, Md., March 27.

Kemmerer, R. A. 1989a. "Analyzing encryption protocols using formal verification techniques," *IEEE Journal on Selected Areas in Communications*, Vol. 7, No. 4., pp. 448-457.

Kemmerer, R. A. 1989b. "Integration of formal methods into the development process," *IEEE Software*, September, pp. 37-50.

Kent, Stephen T. 1976. "Encryption-based protection protocols for interactive user-computer communication," Technical Report 162 (MIT-LCS TR-162), Laboratory for Computer Science, Massachusetts Institute of Technology, Cambridge, Mass., May.

Kent, Stephen T. 1981. *Protecting Externally Supplied Software in Small Computers*, Technical Report 255, Laboratory for Computer Science, Massachusetts Institute of Technology, Cambridge, Mass.

Kent, Stephen T., P. Sevcik, and J. Herman. 1982. "Personal authentication system for access control to the defense data network," *EASCON '82—15th Annual Electronics and Aerospace Systems Conference*, 82CH-182833, IEEE Washington Section and IEEE Aerospace and Electronics Systems Society, Washington, D.C., September 20-22.

King, Julia. 1989. "Executive tech briefing: Network security," *Federal Computer Week*, July 10, pp. 28-35.

Kolkhorst, B. G. and A. J. Macina. 1988. "Developing error-free software," *IEEE AES Magazine*, November.

Labaton, Stephen. 1989. "Rules weighed on transfer of big sums electronically," *New York Times*, October 31, pp. D1, D8.

Lamport, Leslie. 1989. "A simple approach to specifying concurrent systems," *Communications of the ACM*, Vol. 32, No. 1, January, pp. 32-45.

Lampson, Butler. 1973. "A note on the confinement problem," *Communications of the ACM*, Vol. 16, No. 10, October, pp. 613-615.

Lampson, Butler. 1985. "Protection," *ACM Operating Systems Review*, Vol. 19, No. 5, December, pp. 13-24.

Landry, John. 1990. Statement of ADAPSO, a computer software and services industry association, before the Senate Judiciary Subcommittee on Technology and the Law, July 31.

Lardner, Jr., George. 1990a. "CIA director: E. European spies at work," *Washington Post*, February 21, p. A15.

Lardner, Jr., George. 1990b. "National Security Agency: Turning on and tuning in," (two-part article), *Washington Post*, March 18-19, p. A1.

Law Commission. 1989. *Criminal Law, Computer Misuse*, HMSO, London, United Kingdom, October.

Leveson, Nancy G. 1986. "Software safety: Why, what, and how," *Computer Surveys*, Vol. 18, No. 2, June, pp. 125-164.

Lewis, Peter H. 1989. "Building a moat with software," *The New York Times*, September 3, p. F7.

Lewis, Peter H. 1990. "Privacy: The tip of the iceberg," *New York Times*, October 2, p. C8.

Lewyn, Mark. 1989. "Hackers: Is a cure worse than the disease?" *Business Week*, December 4, p. 37.

Lindsay, Peter. 1988. "Survey of theorem provers," *Software Engineering Journal*, IEEE, January.

Linger, R. C. and H. D. Mills. 1988. "A case study in cleanroom software engineering: The IBM COBOL structuring facility," *Proceedings of COMPSAC '88*, IEEE Computer Society, Washington, D.C.

Linn, John. 1989. "Privacy enhancement for Internet electronic mail," (memorandum—e-mail), Request for Comments 1113, Network Working Group, IAB Privacy Task Force, July 17.

Linowes, David F. 1989. *Privacy in America—Is Your Private Life in the Public Eye?* University of Illinois Press, Urbana and Chicago.

Lipner, S. B. 1982. "Non-discretionary controls for commercial applications," *Proceedings of the 1982 IEEE Symposium on Security and Privacy*, IEEE Computer Society, Oakland, Calif., April 26-28, pp. 2-10.

Lipton, R. J. 1989. *A New Approach to Testing*, Princeton University, Princeton, N.J.

Loew, Sue J. 1989. "Encrypted EDI: Scrambling to create a security product—sans standard," *Data Communications*, October, p. 50.

Luckham, David and Sriram Sankar. 1989. *Future Directions in Software Analysis and Testing*, Stanford University, Stanford, Calif.

Lunt, T. F. 1988. "Automated audit trail analysis and intrusion detection: A survey," *Proceedings of the 11th National Computer Security Conference*, National Institute of Standards and Technology/National Computer Security Center, Baltimore, Md.

Lunt, T. F., R. R. Schell, W. R. Shockley, M. Heckman, and D. Warren. 1988. "A near-term design for the SeaView multilevel database system," *Proceedings of the 1988 IEEE Symposium on Security and Privacy*, IEEE Computer Society, Oakland, Calif., April, pp. 234-244.

Lunt, Teresa F. 1989. "Aggregation and inference: Facts and fallacies," *Proceedings of the 1989 IEEE Symposium on Security and Privacy*, IEEE Computer Society, Oakland, Calif., May 1-3, pp. 102-109.

Lyons, John. 1990. Testimony before the Subcommittee on Transportation, Aviation, and Materials, U.S. House of Representatives, National Institute of Standards and Technology, Gaithersburg, Md.

Markoff, John. 1988a. "West German secretly gains access to U.S. military computers," *New York Times*, April 17.

Markoff, John. 1988b. "Breach reported in U.S. computers," *New York Times*, April 18, p. A1.

Markoff, John. 1989a. "Virus outbreaks thwart computer experts," *New York Times*, May 30.

Markoff, John. 1989b. "Paper on codes sent to 8,000 computers over U.S. objection," *New York Times*, August 9, A1.

Markoff, John. 1989c. "Computer virus cure may be worse than disease," *New York Times*, October 7, pp. A1, A35.

Markoff, John. 1990a. "Breakdown's lesson: Failure occurs on superhuman scale," *New York Times*, January 16, p. A24.

Markoff, John. 1990b. "Caller says he broke into U.S. computers to taunt the experts," *New York Times*, March 21, pp. A1, A21.

Markoff, John. 1990c. "Arrests in computer break-ins show a global peril," *New York Times*, April 4, pp. A1, A16.

Markoff, John. 1990d. "Washington is relaxing its stand on guarding computer security," *New York Times*, August 18, pp. 1, 20.

McIlroy, M. 1989. "Virology 101," *Computing Systems* (USENIX Association, Berkeley, Calif.), Vol. 2, No. 2, pp. 173-181.

McLoughlin, Glenn J. 1987. *Computer Crime and Security*, Science Policy Research Division, Congressional Research Service, Washington, D.C., January 3.

Meyer, C. and S. Matyas. 1983. *Cryptography: A New Dimension in Computer Data Security*, Wiley, New York.

Microelectronics and Computer Technology Corporation (MCC). 1989. *SpecTra: A Formal Methods Environment*, MCC Technical Report no. ACT-ILO-STP-324-89, MCC, Austin, Tex.

Millen, Jonathan K. 1987. "Covert channel capacity," *Proceedings of the 1987 IEEE Symposium on Security and Privacy*, IEEE Computer Society, Oakland, Calif., April 27-29, pp. 60-66.

Millen, J. K., S. C. Clark, and S. B. Freedman. 1987. "The interrogator: Protocol security analysis," *IEEE Transactions on Software Engineering*, Vol. SE-13, No. 2, February.

Miller, Donald V. and Robert W. Baldwin. 1989. "Access control by boolean expression evaluation," *Proceedings of the Computer Security Application Conference*, Tucson, Ariz., December 8, IEEE Computer Society, Washington, D.C.

Miller, Edward and W. E. Howden. 1981. *Software Testing and Validation Techniques*, 2nd rev. ed., IEEE Computer Society, Washington, D.C.

Miller, S. P., C. Neuman, J. I. Schiller, and J. H. Saltzer. 1987. "Kerberos authentication and authorization system," *Project Athena Technical Plan*, Section E.2.1, Massachusetts Institute of Technology, Cambridge, Mass., July.

Mitchell, J. G., W. Maybury, and R. Sweet. 1979. *Mesa Language Manual (version 5.0)*, CSL-79-3, Xerox Palo Alto Research Center, Palo Alto, Calif., April.

Mitchell, William. 1990. "Enterprise networks: The multivendor networks of the 1990s," *Networking Management*, Vol. 8, No. 2, February, pp. 69-72.

Moates, Jr., William H. and Karen A. Forcht. 1986. "Computer security education: Are business schools lagging behind?" *Data Management*, March.

Moeller, Robert R. 1989. *Computer Audit, Control and Security*, John Wiley & Sons, New York.

Morris, R. and K. Thompson. 1979. "UNIX password security: A case history," *Communications of the ACM*, Vol. 22, No. 11, November, pp. 594-597.

Mossbert, Walter S. and John Walcott. 1988. "U.S. redefines policy on security to place less stress on Soviets," *Wall Street Journal*, August 11.

Mosso, David. 1987. "Public policy and the FASB: As seen by one of its board members," *Bottomline*, December.

Munro, Neil. 1990. "NSA plan may stymie improved computer security," *Defense News*, September 10, pp. 3, 36.

Musolf, Lloyd. 1983. *Uncle Sam's Private, Profitseeking Corporations: Comsat, Fannie Mae, Amtrak, and Conrail*, Lexington Books, D.C. Heath and Company, Lexington, Mass.

National Academy of Sciences. 1987. *Balancing the National Interest: U.S. National Security Export Controls and Global Economic Competition*, (also known as the Allen Report), Committee on Science, Engineering, and Public Policy, National Academy Press, Washington, D.C.

National Aeronautics and Space Administration (NASA). 1984. *NASA ADP Risk Analysis Guideline*, (prepared by EDP Audit Controls, Inc.), Automated Information Systems Division: NASA Headquarters, July.

National Aeronautics and Space Administration (NASA). 1989a. *Automated Information Systems Security Plan*, Johnson Space Center, April.

National Aeronautics and Space Administration (NASA). 1989b. *Automated Information Systems Security Plan Executive Summary*, Goddard Space Flight Center, July.

National Aeronautics and Space Administration (NASA). 1989c. *Assuring the Security and Integrity of the GSFC Automated Information Resources*, Issuance Information Sheet GMI 2410.6B, Goddard Space Flight Center, May.

National Aeronautics and Space Administration (NASA). 1989d. *Assuring the Security and Integrity of NASA Automated Information Resources*, NMI: 2410.7A, NASA Management Instruction, Information Resources Management Office, Washington, D.C.

National Bureau of Standards (NBS). 1977. *Data Encryption Standard*, Federal Information Processing Standards Publication 46, NBS, Gaithersburg, Md., January. Reissued as Federal Information Processing Standards Publication 46-1, January 1988.

National Bureau of Standards (NBS). 1978. *Considerations in the Selection of Security Measures for Automatic Data Processing Systems*, NBS, Gaithersburg, Md., June.

National Bureau of Standards (NBS). 1980a. *Guidelines on User Authentication Techniques for Computer Network Access Control*, Federal Information Processing Standards

Publication 83, National Technical Information Service, Springfield, Va., September 29.

National Bureau of Standards (NBS). 1980b. *DES Modes of Operation*, Federal Information Processing Standards Publication 81, National Technical Information Service, Springfield, Va., December.

National Bureau of Standards (NBS). 1981a. *Guidelines for ADP Contingency Planning*, Federal Information Processing Standards Publication 87, National Technical Information Service, Springfield, Va., March 27.

National Bureau of Standards (NBS). 1981b. *Guideline on Integrity Assurance and Control in Database Administration*, Federal Information Processing Standards Publication 88, National Technical Information Service, Springfield, Va., August 14.

National Bureau of Standards (NBS). 1982. *Executive Guide to ADP Contingency Planning*, Stuart W. Katzke and James W. Shaw, NBS Special Publication 500-85, NBS, Washington, D.C., January.

National Bureau of Standards (NBS). 1983. *Guideline for Computer Security and Certification and Accreditation*, Federal Information Processing Standards Publication 102, National Technical Information Service, Springfield, Va., September 27.

National Bureau of Standards (NBS). 1984. *Security of Personal Computer Systems: A Growing Concern*, NBS, Gaithersburg, Md., April.

National Bureau of Standards (NBS). 1985a. *Security of Personal Computer Systems: A Management Guide*, NBS Special Publication 500-120, NBS, Gaithersburg, Md., January.

National Bureau of Standards (NBS). 1985b. *Security for Dial-Up Lines*, NBS Special Publication 500-137, NBS, Gaithersburg, Md., May.

National Bureau of Standards (NBS). 1986. *Work Priority Scheme for EDP Audit and Computer Security Review*, NBS, Gaithersburg, Md., March.

National Bureau of Standards (NBS). 1988. *Guide to Auditing for Controls and Security: A System Development Life Cycle Approach*, NBS Special Publication 500-153, NBS, Gaithersburg, Md., April.

National Bureau of Standards/National Computer Security Center (NBS/NCSC). 1987. *Proceedings of the 10th National Computer Security Conference*, NBS/NCSC, Baltimore, Md., September.

National Bureau of Standards/National Computer Security Center (NBS/NCSC). 1988. *Proceedings of the 11th National Computer Security Conference*, NBS/NCSC, Baltimore, Md., October.

National Center for Computer Crime Data (NCCCD) and RGC Associates. 1989. *Commitment to Security*, NCCCD, Los Angeles, Calif.

National Institute of Standards and Technology (NIST). 1988. *Smart Card Technology: New Methods for Computer Access Control*, NIST Special Publication 500-157, NIST, Gaithersburg, Md.

National Institute of Standards and Technology (NIST). 1989a. *Report of the Invitational Workshop on Integrity Policy in Computer Information Systems (WIPCIS)*, NIST Special Publication 500-160, NIST, Gaithersburg, Md., January.

National Institute of Standards and Technology (NIST). 1989b. *Computer Viruses and Related Threats: A Management Guide*, NIST Special Publication 500-166, NIST, Gaithersburg, Md., August.

National Institute of Standards and Technology (NIST). 1989c. *Report of the Invitational Workshop on Data Integrity*, NIST Special Publication 500-168, NIST, Gaithersburg, Md., September.

National Institute of Standards and Technology (NIST). 1990a. *Secure Data Network Systems (SDNS) Network, Transport, and Message Security Protocols* (NISTIR 90-4250), *Secure Data Network Systems (SDNS) Access Control Documents* (NISTIR 90-4259), *Se-*

*cure Data Network Systems (SDNS) Key Management Documents* (NISTIR 90-4262), NIST, Gaithersburg, Md.

National Institute of Standards and Technology (NIST). 1990b. "Data Encryption Standard Fact Sheet," NIST, Gaithersburg, Md., January.

National Institute of Standards and Technology (NIST). 1990c. *Computer Security Publications,* NIST Publication List 91, NIST, Gaithersburg, Md., March.

National Institute of Standards and Technology (NIST). 1990d. *Security Requirements for Cryptographic Modules,* draft, Federal Information Processing Standards Publication 140-1, National Technical Information Service, Springfield, Va., July 13.

National Institute of Standards and Technology (NIST). 1990e. *Guidelines and Recommendations on Integrity,* draft, NIST, Gaithersburg, Md., July 23.

National Institute of Standards and Technology/National Computer Security Center (NIST/NCSC). 1989. *Proceedings of the 12th National Computer Security Conference,* NIST/NCSC, Baltimore, Md., October.

National Institute of Standards and Technology/National Computer Security Center (NIST/NCSC). 1990. *Analysis and Comments on the Draft Information Technology Security Evaluation Criteria (ITSEC),* NIST, Gaithersburg, Md., August 2.

National Institute of Standards and Technology/National Security Agency (NIST/NSA). 1989. *Memorandum of Understanding Between Directors Concerning the Implementation of Public Law 100-235,* Washington, D.C., March 24.

National Research Council (NRC). 1983. *Multilevel Data Management Security,* Air Force Studies Board, National Academy Press, Washington, D.C.

National Research Council (NRC). 1984. *Methods for Improving Software Quality and Life Cycle Cost,* Air Force Studies Board, National Academy Press, Washington, D.C.

National Research Council (NRC). 1988a. *Global Trends in Computer Technology and Their Impact on Export Control,* Computer Science and Technology Board, National Academy Press, Washington, D.C.

National Research Council (NRC). 1988b. *Toward a National Research Network,* Computer Science and Technology Board, National Academy Press, Washington, D.C.

National Research Council (NRC). 1988c. *Selected Issues in Space Science Data Management and Computation,* Space Sciences Board, National Academy Press, Washington, D.C.

National Research Council (NRC). 1989a. *Scaling Up: A Research Agenda for Software Engineering,* Computer Science and Technology Board, National Academy Press, Washington, D.C.

National Research Council (NRC). 1989b. *Growing Vulnerability of the Public Switched Networks: Implications for National Security Emergency Preparedness,* Board on Telecommunications and Computer Applications, National Academy Press, Washington, D.C.

National Research Council (NRC). 1989c. *NASA Space Communications R&D: Issues, Derived Benefits, and Future Directions,* Space Applications Board, National Academy Press, Washington, D.C., February.

National Research Council (NRC). 1989d. *Use of Building Codes in Federal Agency Construction,* Building Research Board, National Academy Press, Washington, D.C.

National Research Council (NRC). 1990. *Keeping the U.S. Computer Industry Competitive: Defining the Agenda,* Computer Science and Technology Board, National Academy Press, Washington, D.C.

National Security Agency (NSA). 1985. *Personal Computer Security Considerations,* NCSC-WA-002—85, National Computer Security Center, Fort Meade, Md., December.

National Security Agency (NSA). 1990a. "Press Statement: NCSC's Restructuring," NSA, Fort Meade, Md., August.

National Security Agency (NSA). 1990b. "Evaluated products list for trusted computer systems," *Information Security Products and Services Catalogue*, National Computer Security Center, Fort Meade, Md.

National Security Agency/Central Security Service (NSA/CSS). 1986. *Software Acquisition Manual*, NSAM 81-2, Fort Meade, Md., May 15.

National Security Agency/Central Security Service (NSA/CSS). 1987. *Software Product Standards Manual*, NSAM 81-3/DOD-STD-1703(NS), Fort Meade, Md., April 15.

National Technical Information Service (NTIS). January 1988/October 1989. U.S. Department of Commerce, Published Search. Citations from the Computer Database: *Computer Viruses and Computer Software Vaccines for Software Protection*, NTIS, Washington, D.C.

Needham, R. and M. Schroeder. 1978. "Using encryption for authentication in large networks of computers," *Communications of the ACM*, Vol. 21, No. 12, December, pp. 993-998.

*Network World*. 1990. "Network security still slack," (art captioned "Computer Intelligence"), February 5, p. 33.

Neumann, Peter G. 1986. "On hierarchical design of computer systems for critical applications," *IEEE Transactions on Software Engineering*, Vol. 12, No. 9, September, pp. 905-920.

Neumann, Peter G. 1988. "A glitch in our computer thinking: We create powerful systems with pervasive vulnerabilities," *Los Angeles Times*, August 2, p. 7.

Neumann, Peter G. 1989. "RISKS: Cumulative index of software engineering notes— Illustrative risks to the public in the use of computer systems and related technology," *ACM Software Engineering Notes*, Vol. 14, No. 1, January, pp. 22-26. (An updated index is to be published in the January 1991 issue, Vol. 16, No. 1.)

Neumann, Peter G. 1990a. "Rainbows and arrows: How the security criteria address computer misuse," *Proceedings of the 13th National Computer Security Conference*, National Institute of Standards and Technology/National Computer Security Center, Washington, D.C., October.

Neumann, Peter G. 1990b. "A perspective from the RISKS forum," *Computers Under Attack: Intruders, Worms, and Viruses*, Peter J. Denning (Ed.), ACM Press, New York.

Neumann, Peter G. and D. B. Parker. 1989. "A summary of computer misuse techniques," *Proceedings of the 12th National Computer Security Conference*, National Institute of Standards and Technology/National Computer Security Center, Baltimore, Md., October 10-13, pp. 396-407.

New York State, Committee on Investigations, Taxation, and Government Operations. 1989. *Beware Computer 'Virus Attack'*, a staff report on the lack of security in state owned and operated computers, Albany, N.Y., July 28.

*New York Times*. 1987. "German computer hobbyists rifle NASA's files," September 16.

*New York Times*. 1988. "Computer systems under siege, here and abroad," January 31.

*New York Times*. 1988. "Top secret, and vulnerable," April 15.

*New York Times*. 1988. "Computer users fall victim to a new breed of vandals," May 19.

*New York Times*. 1988. "Newspaper computer infected with a 'virus,'" May 25.

*New York Times*. 1988. "Sabotage aimed at computer company destroys government computer data," July 4.

*New York Times*. 1988. "Programmer convicted after planting a 'virus,'" September 21, p. D15.

*New York Times*. 1988. "Car computer inquiry begun," November 17.

*New York Times*. 1988. "Cyberpunks seek thrills in computerized mischief," November 26.

*New York Times*. 1989. "2 accused of computer crimes in TV rivalry," May 11, p. A21.

*New York Times*. 1990. "G.A.O. study of computers," February 21, p. D4.

*Newsweek*. 1988. "Is your computer infected?" February 1.

Nordwall, Bruce D. 1989. "ITT avionics emphasizes development of software, improves electronic systems," *Aviation Week & Space Technology*, July 17, pp. 83, 85.

Norman, Adrian R. D. 1983. *Computer Insecurity*, Chapman and Hall, New York.

Nycum, Susan H. 1989. "Legal Exposures of the Victim of Computer Abuse under U.S. Law," International Bar Association (IBA) SBL Conference, Strasbourg, October 2-6, IBA, London, England.

Nycum, Susan Hubbell. 1976. "The criminal law aspects of computer abuse, Part 1: State penal laws," *Journals of Computers and Law*, Vol. 5, pp. 271-295.

Office of Management and Budget (OMB). 1988. *Guidance for Preparation of Security Plans for Federal Computer Systems Containing Sensitive Information*, OMB Bulletin No. 88-16, Washington, D.C., July.

Office of Management and Budget (OMB). 1990. *Guidance for Preparation of Security Plans for Federal Computer Systems that Contain Sensitive Information*, OMB Bulletin No. 90-08, Washington, D.C., July.

Office of Science and Technology Policy (OSTP). 1989. *The Federal High-Performance Computing Program*, Washington, D.C., September 8.

Office of Technology Assessment (OTA). 1985. *Federal Government Information Technology: Electronic Surveillance and Civil Liberties*, OTA-CIT-293, October, U.S. GPO, Washington, D.C.

Office of Technology Assessment (OTA). 1986a. *Federal Government Information Technology: Management, Security, and Congressional Oversight*, OTA-CIT-297, February, U.S. GPO, Washington, D.C.

Office of Technology Assessment (OTA). 1986b. *Federal Government Information Technology: Electronic Record Systems and Individual Privacy*, OTA-CIT-296, June, U.S. GPO, Washington, D.C.

Office of Technology Assessment (OTA). 1987a. *The Electronic Supervisor: New Technology, New Tensions*, OTA-CIT-333, September, U.S. GPO, Washington, D.C.

Office of Technology Assessment (OTA). 1987b. *Defending Secrets, Sharing Data: New Locks and Keys for Electronic Information*, OTA-CIT-310, October, U.S. GPO, Washington, D.C.

Office of Technology Assessment (OTA). 1990. *Critical Connections: Communications for the Future*, OTA-CIT-407, January, U.S. GPO, Washington, D.C.

Office of the Federal Register, National Archives and Records Administration. 1990. *Code of Federal Regulations*, Foreign Relations, Title 22, Parts 1 to 299, Subchapter M—International Traffic in Arms Regulations, revised April 1, pp. 333-390.

Parker, Donn B. 1976. *Crime by Computer*, Charles Scribner's Sons, New York.

Parker, Donn B. 1983. *Fighting Computer Crime*, Charles Scribner's Sons, New York.

Parnas, David L., A. J. van Schouwen, and S. P. Kwan. 1990. "Evaluation of safety critical software," *Communications of the ACM*, Vol. 33, No. 6, June, pp. 636-648.

Paul, Bill. 1989. "Electronic theft is routine and costs firms billions, security experts say," *Wall Street Journal*, October 20, p. 1.

Paul, Bill. 1990. "Blackouts on East Coast are called unavoidable," *Wall Street Journal*, February 28, p. B4.

Paul, James. 1989. *Bugs in the Program—Problems in Federal Government Computer Software Development and Regulation*, Subcommittee on Investigations and Oversight, U.S. House of Representatives, September.

Paulk, Mark C. 1989. "Review of the computer virus crisis," *IEEE Computer*, July, p. 122.

*PC Magazine*. 1988a. "Virus wars: A serious warning," February 29.

*PC Magazine*. 1988b. "Why it's time to talk about viruses," June 28, pp. 33-36.

Pearson, Dorothy. 1988. "MIS mangers launch counterattack to stem rising virus epidemic," *PC Week*, August 29, pp. 23-24.

Pellerin, Cheryl. 1990. "Lights-out computing: Agencies are discovering the benefits of unattended computer centers," *Federal Computer Week*, March 19.

Peterson, Ivars. 1988. "A digital matter of life and death," *Science News*, March 12, pp. 170-171.

Pittelli, Frank M. and Hector Garcia-Molina. 1989. "Reliable scheduling in a TMR database system," *ACM Transactions on Computer Systems*, Vol. 7, No. 1, February.

Podell, Harold J. and Marshall D. Abrams. 1989. "A computer security glossary for the advanced practitioner," *Computer Security Journal*, Vol. IV, No. 1, pp. 69-88.

Pollack, Andrew. 1990. "Revlon sues supplier over software disabling," *New York Times*, October 25, pp. D1, D4.

Ponting, Bob. 1988. "Some common sense about network viruses, and what to do about them," (Newsfront section), *Data Communications*, April, p. 60.

Poore, Jesse H. and Harlan D. Mills. 1989. *An Overview of the Cleanroom Software Development Process*, unpublished paper presented at the Formal Methods Workshop, Halifax, Nova Scotia, July. Available from the Department of Computer Science, University of Tennessee, Knoxville.

Poos, Bob. 1990. "AF amends RFP to clarify security needs," *Federal Computer Week*, February 19, p. 4.

Potts, Mark. 1989. "When computers go down, so can firms' bottom lines," *Washington Post*, November 2.

Prefontaine, Daniel C., Canadian Department of Justice. 1990. "Future trends," presented at the Forum on the International Legal Vulnerability of Financial Information, Royal Bank of Canada, Toronto, February 26-28.

President's Council on Integrity and Efficiency. 1988. *Review of General Controls in Federal Computer Systems*, U.S. GPO, Washington, D.C., October.

President's Council on Management Improvement & President's Council on Integrity and Efficiency. 1988. *Model Framework for Management Control Over Automated Information Systems*, U.S. GPO, Washington, D.C., January.

*Privacy Times* (Evan Hendricks, Ed.). 1989. Vol. 9, No. 16, September 19, Washington, D.C.

Rabin, Michael O. and J. D. Tygar. 1987. *An Integrated Toolkit for Operating System Security*, Harvard University, Cambridge, Mass., May.

Reuter. 1990. "Man faces charges of computer fraud," *Washington Post*, February 4, p. A18.

Richards, Evelyn. 1989. "Study: Software bugs costing U.S. billions," *Washington Post*, October 17, pp. D1, D5.

Richardson, Jennifer. 1990a. "Federal reserve defends Fedwire security," *Federal Computer Week*, February 26, p. 4.

Richardson, Jennifer. 1990b. "Federal reserve adds security to Fedwire," *Federal Computer Week*, April 9.

Rinkerman, Gary. 1983. "Potential liabilities of independent software testing and certification organizations," *Computer Law Reporter*, Vol. 1, No. 5, March, pp. 725-727.

Rivest, R., A. Shamir, and L. Adelman. 1978. "A method for obtaining digital signatures and public-key cryptosystems," *Communications of the ACM*, Vol. 21, No. 2, February, pp. 120-126.

Rochlis, Jon A. and Mark W. Eichin. 1989. "With microscope and tweezers: The worm from MIT's perspective," *Communications of the ACM*, Vol. 32, No. 6, June, pp. 689-698.

Rothfeder, Jeffrey, et al. 1990. "Is your boss spying on you?" *Business Week*, January 15, p. 74.

Rumbelow, Clive. 1981. "Liability for programming errors," *International Business Lawyer*, Vol. 9, (vii/viii), United Kingdom.

Rutz, Frank. 1988. "DOD fights off computer virus," *Government Computer News*, Vol. 7, No. 3, February 5, p. 1.

Safire, William. 1990. "Spies of the future," *New York Times*, March 16, p. A35.

Salpukas, Agis. 1989. "Computer chaos for air travelers," *New York Times*, May 13, p. A1.

Saltman, Roy. 1988. "Accuracy, integrity and security in computerized vote-tallying," *Communications of the ACM*, Vol. 31, No. 10, October, pp. 1184-1191.

Saltzer, J. and M. Schroeder. 1975. "The protection of information in computer systems," *Proceedings: IEEE*, Vol. 63, No. 9, September, pp. 1278-1308.

Savage, J. A. 1990. "Apollo blasted by users over system security glitches," *Computerworld*, October 8, p. 49.

Saydjari, O. Sami, Joseph M. Beckman, and Jeffrey R. Leaman. 1987. "Locking computers securely," *Proceedings of the 10th National Computer Security Conference*, National Bureau of Standards/National Computer Security Center, Baltimore, Md., September 21-24, pp. 129-141.

Saydjari, O. Sami, J. M. Beckman, and J. R. Leaman. 1989. "LOCK trek: Navigating uncharted space," *Proceedings of the 1989 IEEE Computer Society Symposium on Security and Privacy*, IEEE Computer Society, Oakland, Calif., May, pp. 167-175.

Scherlis, William L., Stephen L. Squires, and Richard D. Pethia. 1990. "Computer Emergency Response," *Computers Under Attack: Intruders, Worms, and Viruses*, Peter Denning (Ed.), ACM Press, New York.

Schlichting, R. and R. Schneider. 1983. "Fail-stop processors: An approach to designing fault-tolerant computing systems," *ACM Transactions on Computer Systems*, Vol. 1, No. 3, August, pp. 222-238.

Schmitt, Warren. 1990. *Information Classification and Control*, Sears Technology Services, Schaumburg, Ill., January.

Schultz, Eugene. 1990. "Forming and managing CIAC: Lessons learned," unpublished presentation at CERT Workshop, June 20, Pleasanton, Calif., Lawrence Livermore National Laboratory, Livermore, Calif.

Schuman, Evan. 1989. "Never mind OSF/1, here's OSF/2," *UNIX Today*, November 27, pp. 1, 26.

Selby, R. W., V. R. Basili, and F. T. Baker. 1987. "Cleanroom software development: An empirical evaluation," *IEEE Transactions on Software Engineering*, Vol. SE-13, No. 9.

Selz, Michael. 1989. "Computer vaccines or snake oil?" *Wall Street Journal*, October 13, p. B6.

Sennett, C. T. 1989. *Formal Methods in the Production of Secure Software*, Royal Signals and Radar Establishment, Malvern, United Kingdom, pp. 1-2.

Seymour, Jim, and Jonathan Matzkin. 1988. "Confronting the growing threat of computer software viruses," *PC Magazine*, June 28, pp. 33-36.

Shatz, Willie. 1990. "The terminal men: Crackdown on the 'Legion of Doom' ends an era for computer hackers," *Washington Post*, June 24, pp. H1, H6.

Shoch, John F. and Jon A. Hupp. 1982. "The 'worm' programs—Early experience with a distributed computation," *Computing Practices*, March, pp. 172-180.

Shore, John. 1988. "Why I never met a programmer I could trust," *Communications of the ACM*, Vol. 31, No. 4, April, p. 372.

Simitis, S. (Ed.). 1987. *The Hessian Data Protection Act*, Editor: the Hessian Data Protection Commissioner, Uhlandstrasse 4, 6200 Wiesbaden, Federal Republic of Germany. Publisher: Wiesbadener Graphische Betriebe GmbH, Wiesbaden.

Simmons, G. 1988. "A survey of information authentication," *Proceedings: IEEE*, Vol. 76, No. 5, May, pp. 603-620.

Simpson, Glenn. 1989. "Can you count on the vote count?" *Insight*, January 9, p. 23.

Sims, Calvin. 1989. "Not everyone applauds new phone services," *New York Times*, December 13, p. 6.

Sims, Calvin. 1990. "Computer failure disrupts AT&T long distance," *New York Times*, January 16, pp. A1, A24.

Sloan, Irving J. 1984. *Computers and the Law*, Oceana Publications, New York.

Smith, Kerry M. L. 1988. "Suing the provider of computer software: How courts are applying U.C.C. Article Two, strict tort liability, and professional malpractice," *Willamette Law Review*, Vol. 24, No. 3, Summer, pp. 743-766.

Smith, Tom. 1989. "IBM's new release of RACF, other security tools bow," *Network World*, October 30, pp. 4, 60.

Snyders, Jan. 1983. "Security software doubles your protection," *Computer Decisions*, Vol. 15, No. 9, September, pp. 46, 50-56.

Solomon, J. 1982. "Specification-to-code correlation," *Proceedings of the 1982 IEEE Symposium on Security and Privacy*, IEEE Computer Society, Oakland, Calif., April.

Soma, John T. 1983. *Computer Technology and the Law*, Shepard's/McGraw-Hill, Colorado Springs, Colo.

Soper, Keith. 1989. "Integrity vs. security: Avoiding the trade-off," *Computerworld*, June 12, pp. 79-83.

Spafford, Eugene H. 1989a. *The Internet Worm Program: An Analysis*, Purdue Technical Report CSD-TR-823, Department of Computer Science, Purdue University, West Lafayette, Ind.

Spafford, Eugene H. 1989b. "Crisis and aftermath," *Communications of the ACM*, Vol. 32, No. 6, June, pp. 678-687.

Specter, Michael. 1990. "Revenge on the nerds," *Washington Post*, February 11, p. C5.

Sprouse, Robert T. 1987. "Commentary: On the SEC-FASB partnership," *Accounting Horizons*, December, pp. 92-95.

SRI International. 1989. *International Information Integrity Institute (I-4) Annual Report 1989*, Menlo Park, Calif.

Steiner, Jennifer, C. Neuman, and J. I. Schiller. 1988. "Kerberos: An authentication service for open network systems," *USENIX Dallas Winter 1988 Conference Proceedings*, USENIX Association, Berkeley, Calif., pp. 191-202.

Stipp, David. 1990. "Virus verdict likely to have limited impact," *Wall Street Journal*, January 24, pp. B1, B7.

Stoll, Clifford. 1988. "Stalking the Wily Hacker," *Communications of the ACM*, Vol. 31, No. 5, May, pp. 484-497.

Stoll, Clifford. 1989. *The Cuckoos's Egg*, Doubleday, New York.

Strauss, Paul R. 1989. "Lesson of the lurking software glitch," *Data Communications*, June 21, p. 9.

Streitfeld, David. 1989. "Personal data, on the record," *Washington Post*, September 26, p. D5.

Sweet, Walter. 1990. "Global nets elevate security concerns," *Network World*, July 30, pp. 23-24.

Tanebaum, A. 1981. *Computer Networks*, Prentice-Hall, Englewood Cliffs, N.J.

Thackeray, Gail. 1985. "Computer-related crimes: An outline," *Jurimetrics Journal*, Spring, pp. 300-318.

Thompson, K. 1984. "Reflections on trusting trust," (1983 Turing Award Lecture), *Communications of the ACM*, Vol. 27, No. 8, August, pp. 761-763.

*Time*. 1988. "Computer viruses," (cover story), September 26.

Toigo, Jon William. 1990. "SECURITY: Biometrics creep into business," *Computerworld*, June 11, pp. 75-78.

Tompkins, F. G. 1984. *NASA Guidelines for Assuring the Adequacy and Appropriateness of Security Safeguards in Sensitive Applications*, MTR-84W179, The MITRE Corp., Metrek Division, McLean, Va., September.

Turn, Rein. 1980. "An overview of transborder data flow issues," *Proceedings of the 1980*

*IEEE Computer Society Symposium on Security and Privacy,* IEEE Computer Society, Oakland, Calif., April 14-16, pp. 3-8.

Turn, Rein. 1990. "Information privacy issues for the 1990s," *Proceedings of the 1990 IEEE Computer Society Symposium on Security and Privacy,* IEEE Computer Society, Oakland, Calif., May 7-8.

Turner, Judith Axler. 1988. "Security officials ask researchers not to make 'virus' copies available," *The Chronicle of Higher Education,* No. 13, November 23, pp. 1, A12.

Tzu, Sun. 1988. *The Art of War,* (translated by Thomas Cleary), Shambhala, Boston.

U.K. Communications-Electronics Security Group/Department of Trade and Industry (CESG/DTI). 1990. *UK IT Security Evaluation and Certification Scheme,* Publication No. 1: Description of the Scheme, Final Draft Version 2.3, UKSP 01, Cheltenham, England, July 13.

U.K. Department of Trade and Industry (DTI). 1989. *Overview Manual* (V01), *Glossary* (V02), *Index* (V03), *Users' Code of Practice* (V11), *Security Functionality Manual* (V21), *Evaluation Levels Manual* (V22), *Evaluation and Certification Manual* (V23), *Vendors' Code of Practice* (V31), Version 3.0, Commercial Computer Security Centre, London, England, February.

U.K. Ministry of Defence. 1989a. *Requirements for the Procurement of Safety Critical Software in Defense Equipment,* Interim Defense Standard 00-55, Glasgow, United Kingdom, May.

U.K. Ministry of Defence. 1989b. *Requirements for the Analysis of Safety Critical Hazards,* Interim Defense Standard 00-56, Glasgow, United Kingdom, May.

Ulbrich, B. and J. Collins. 1990. "Announcing Sun Microsystem's Customer Warning System for security incident handling," *X-Sun-Spots-Digest,* Vol. 9, No. 308, message 13.

Underwriters Laboratories, Inc. 1989. *Underwriters Laboratories, Inc. 1988 Annual Report,* Underwriters Laboratories, Inc., Northbrook, Ill.

Underwriters Laboratories, Inc. 1990a. The Proposed First Edition of the Standards for Safety-related Software, UL-1998, Underwriters Laboratories, Inc., Northbrook, Ill., August 17.

Underwriters Laboratories, Inc. 1990b. *UL Yesterday today tomorrow,* Underwriters Laboratories, Inc., Northbrook, Ill.

University of California, Los Angeles (UCLA). 1989. *Sixth Annual UCLA Survey of Business School Computer Usage,* John E. Anderson Graduate School of Management, UCLA, Los Angeles, Calif., September.

U.S. Bureau of Alcohol, Tobacco and Firearms. 1988. "Explosive Incidents Report 1987," Washington, D.C.

U.S. Congress, House, Committee on the Judiciary, Subcommittee on Crime. 1983. *Counterfeit Access Device and Computer Crime: Hearings on H.R. 3181, H.R. 3570, and H.R. 5112,* 98th Cong., 1st and 2nd sess., September 29 and November 10, 1983, and March 28, 1984, U.S. GPO, Washington, D.C.

U.S. Congress, House, Committee on the Judiciary, Subcommittee on Crime. 1985. *Computer Crime and Computer Security: Hearing on H.R. 1001 and H.R. 930,* 99th Cong., 1st sess., May 25, U.S. GPO, Washington, D.C.

U.S. Congress, House. 1986. *Computer Fraud and Abuse Act of 1986,* Public Law 99-474, H.R. 4718, October 16, H. Rept. 100-153(I), U.S. GPO, Washington, D.C.

U.S. Congress, House, Committee on the Judiciary. 1986. *Computer Fraud and Abuse Act of 1986: Report to Accompany H.R. 4712,* 99th Cong., 2nd sess., U.S. GPO, Washington, D.C.

U.S. Congress, House, Committee on the Judiciary. 1986. *Computer Fraud and Abuse Act of 1986: Report to Accompany H.R. 5616,* 99th Cong., 2nd sess., U.S. GPO, Washington, D.C.

U.S. Congress, House, Committee on Government Operations, Legislation and National Security Subcommittee. 1987. *Computer Security Act of 1987: Hearings on H.R. 145 Before a Subcommittee of the Committee on Government Operations*, 100th Cong., 1st sess., February 25 and 26 and March 17, U.S. GPO, Washington, D.C.

U.S. Congress, House, Committee on Science, Space, and Technology. 1987. *Computer Security Act of 1987: Report to Accompany H.R. 145*, 100th Cong., 1st sess., U.S. GPO, Washington, D.C.

U.S. Congress, House, Technology Policy Task Force of the Committee on Science, Space, and Technology. 1987. *Communications and Computers in the 21st Century: Hearing*, 100th Cong., 1st sess., June 25, U.S. GPO, Washington, D.C.

U.S. Congress, House. 1989. *Computer Protection Act of 1989*, H.R. 287, 101st Cong., 1st sess., January 3, U.S. GPO, Washington, D.C.

U.S. Congress, House, Committee on Energy and Commerce, Subcommittee on Telecommunications and Finance. 1989. *Hearing to Examine the Vulnerability of National Telecommunications Networks to Computer Viruses*, 101st Cong., 1st sess., July 20, U.S. GPO, Washington, D.C.

U.S. Congress, House. 1989. *Computer Network Protection Act of 1989*, H.R. 3524, 101st Cong., 1st sess., October 25, U.S. GPO, Washington, D.C.

U.S. Congress, House. 1989. *Data Protection Act of 1989*, H.R. 3669, 101st Cong., 1st sess., November 15, U.S. GPO, Washington, D.C.

U.S. Congress, House. 1989. *Computer Virus Eradication Act of 1989*, H.R. 55, 101st Cong., 1st sess., U.S. GPO, Washington, D.C.

U.S. Congress, House, Committee on Energy and Commerce, Subcommittee on Telecommunications and Finance. 1990. *Oversight Hearing to Receive the Findings of the U.S. General Accounting Office on the Vulnerability of United States Securities Trading, Electronic Funds Transfer, and Financial Message Systems to Computer Viruses*, 101st Cong., 2nd sess., February 21, U.S. GPO, Washington, D.C.

U.S. Congress, Senate, Committee on the Judiciary. 1986. *Electronic Communications Privacy Act of 1986: Report to Accompany S. 2575*, 99th Cong., 2nd sess., U.S. GPO, Washington, D.C.

U.S. Congress, Senate, Judiciary Subcommittee on Patents, Copyrights, and Trademarks. 1989. *Computer Software Rental Amendments Act (S. 198): Hearings*, 101st Cong., 1st sess., April 19, U.S. GPO, Washington, D.C.

U.S. Congress, Senate, Judiciary Subcommittee on Technology and the Law. 1989. Hearing on Computer Viruses, 101st Cong., 1st sess., May 15, U.S. GPO, Washington, D.C.

U.S. Congress, Senate. 1990. *Computer Abuse Amendment Act of 1990*, S. 2476, 101st Cong., 2nd sess., April 19, U.S. GPO, Washington, D.C.

U.S. Department of Defense (DOD). 1985a. *Password Management Guideline*, CSC-STD-002-85, also known as the Green Book, National Computer Security Center, Fort Meade, Md., April 12.

U.S. Department of Defense (DOD). 1985b. *Technical Rationale Behind CSC-STD-003-85: Computer Security Requirements, Guidance for Applying the Department of Defense Trusted Computer System Evaluation Criteria in Specific Environments*, also known as the Yellow Book, National Computer Security Center, Fort Meade, Md., June 25.

U.S. Department of Defense (DOD). 1985c. *Keeping the Nation's Secrets*, Commission to Review DOD Security Policies and Practices, Washington, D.C., November.

U.S. Department of Defense (DOD). 1985d. *Trusted Computer System Evaluation Criteria*, DOD 5200.28-STD, also known as the Orange Book, National Computer Security Center, Fort Meade, Md., December (superseded CSC-STD-001-83 dated August 15, 1983).

U.S. Department of Defense (DOD). 1987. *Trusted Network Interpretation of the Trusted*

*Computer System Evaluation Criteria*, NCSC-TG-005, Version 1, also known as the Red Book, or TNI, National Computer Security Center, Fort Meade, Md., July 31.

U.S. Department of Defense (DOD). 1988a. "Improvements in computer security procedures," Office of Assistant Secretary of Defense, Public Affairs, Washington, D.C., January 6.

U.S. Department of Defense (DOD). 1988b. *Glossary of Computer Security Terms*, NCSC-TG-004, Version 1, National Computer Security Center, Fort Meade, Md., October 21.

U.S. Department of Defense (DOD). 1988c. "DARPA establishes computer emergency response team," Office of Assistant Secretary of Defense, Public Affairs, Washington, D.C., December 6.

U.S. Department of Defense (DOD), Defense Acquisition Board. 1990. *Department of Defense Software Master Plan*, draft, February 9.

U.S. Department of Energy. 1985. *Sensitive Unclassified Computer Security Program Compliance Review Guidelines*, DOE/MA-0188/1, Assistant Secretary, Management and Administration, Directorate of Administration, Office of ADP Management, Washington, D.C., June (revised September 1985).

U.S. Department of Energy, Energy Information Administration. 1986. *Sensitive Computer Applications Certification/Recertification Policy and Procedures*, EI 5633.1, initiated by ADP Services Staff, Washington, D.C., October.

U.S. Department of Energy. 1988. *Unclassified Computer Security Program*, DOE 1360.2A, initiated by Office of ADP Management, Washington, D.C., May.

U.S. Department of Justice (DOJ), National Institute of Justice. 1989. *Computer Crime: Criminal Justice Resource Manual*, Washington, D.C., August.

U.S. Department of the Treasury. 1989. "Reports of crimes and suspected crimes," *Federal Register*, Vol. 54, No. 117, June 20.

U.S. Food and Drug Administration (FDA). 1987. *Policy for the Regulation of Computer Products*, draft, FDA, Rockville, Md., September 9.

U.S. Food and Drug Administration (FDA). 1988. *Reviewer Guidance for Computer-Controlled Medical Devices*, draft, FDA, Rockville, Md., July 25.

Veterans Administration, Office of Information, Systems, and Telecommunications. 1987. *Computer Security: A Handbook for VA Managers and End-Users*, July. Available from U.S. Department of Veterans Affairs, Washington, D.C.

Voelcker, John. 1988. "Spread of computer viruses worries users," *The Institute* (a publication of the Institute of Electrical and Electronics Engineers), Vol. 12, No. 6, June, p. 1.

Wald, Matthew L. 1990. "Experts diagnose telephone 'crash'," *New York Times*, January 16, p. A25.

Waldrop, Mitchell M. 1989. "Flying the electric skies," *Science*, Vol. 244, pp. 1532-1534.

Walker, B. J., R. A. Kemmerer, and G. J. Popek. 1980. "Specification and verification of the UCLA Unix security kernel," *Communications of the ACM*, Vol. 23, No. 2, 1980, pp. 118-131.

Walker, Stephen T. 1985. "Network security overview," *Proceedings of the 1985 IEEE Symposium on Security and Privacy*, IEEE Computer Society, Oakland, Calif., April 22-24, pp. 62-76.

*Wall Street Journal*. 1988. "First computer message on stopping virus took 48 hours to reach target," November 8, p. B5.

Wall, Wendy L. 1989. "Few firms plan well for mishaps that disable computer facilities," *Wall Street Journal*, May 31.

*Washington Post*. 1988. "Searching for a better computer shield," November 13, pp. H1, H6.

*Washington Post*. 1989. "Computer virus strikes Michigan hospital," March 23.

*Washington Post*. 1990. "Man faces charges of computer fraud," February 4, p. A18.

*Washington University Law Quarterly*. 1977. "Potential liability: Conclusion," Vol. 405, No. 3, p. 433.

Webb, Ben. 1989. "Plan to outlaw hacking," *Nature*, Vol. 341, October 19, p. 559.

Weil, Martin. 1989. "Double malfunction grounds thousands," *Washington Post*, November 4, pp. B1, B4.

Williams, Gurney III. 1988. "UL: What's behind the label," *Home Mechanix*, pp. 78-80, 87-88.

Winans, Christopher. 1990. "Personal data travels, too, through agencies," *Wall Street Journal*, March 27, p. B1.

Wines, Michael. 1990. "Security agency debates new role: Economic spying," *New York Times*, June 18, p. A1.

Wing, Jeannette. 1990. "A specifier's introduction to formal methods," *IEEE Computer*, September.

Wright, Karen. 1990. "The road to the global village," *Scientific American*, March, pp. 83-94.

Young, Catherine L. 1987. "Taxonomy of computer virus defense mechanisms," *Proceedings of the 10th National Computer Security Conference*, National Bureau of Standards/National Computer Security Center, Baltimore, Md., September 21-24, pp. 220-225.

Young, W. D. and J. McHugh. 1987. "Coding for a believable specification to implementation mapping," *Proceedings of the 1987 IEEE Symposium on Security and Privacy*, IEEE Computer Society, Oakland, Calif., April 27-29, pp. 140-148.

Youngblut, Christine, et al. 1989. "SDS Software Testing and Evaluation," IDA Paper P-2132, Institute for Defense Analyses, Alexandria, Va., February.

Zachary, G. Pascal. 1990. "U.S. agency stands in way of computer-security tool," *Wall Street Journal*, July 9, pp. B1, B3.

Zeil, Steven J. 1989. *Constraint Satisfaction and Test Data Generation*," Old Dominion University, Norfolk, Va.

# Appendixes

# Appendix A

# The Orange Book

The Department of Defense's *Trusted Computer System Evaluation Criteria*, or Orange Book, contains criteria for building systems that provide specific sets of security features and assurances (U.S. DOD, 1985d; see Box A.1). However, the Orange Book does not provide a complete basis for security:

- Its origin in the defense arena is associated with an emphasis on disclosure control that seems excessive to many commercial users of computers. There is also a perception in the marketplace that it articulates defense requirements only.
- It specifies a coherent, targeted set of security functions that may not be general enough to cover a broad range of requirements in the commercial world. For example, it does not provide sufficient attention to information integrity and auditing. It says little about networked systems (despite the attempts made by the current and anticipated versions of the *Trusted Network Interpretation*, or Red Book (U.S. DOD, 1987). Also, it provides only weak support for management control practices, notably individual accountability and separation of duty.
- The Orange Book process combines published system criteria with system evaluation and rating (relative to the criteria) by the staff of the National Computer Security Center. This process provides no incentive or reward for security capabilities that go beyond, or do not literally answer, the Orange Book's specific requirements.
- Familiarity with the Orange Book is uneven within the broader community of computer manufacturers, managers, auditors, and insurers, and system users. Its definitions and concepts have not been expressed in the vocabulary typically used in general information

BOX A.1  SUMMARY OF EVALUATION CRITERIA CLASSES

The classes of systems recognized under the trusted computer systems evaluation criteria are as follows.  They are presented in the order of increasing desirability from a computer security point of view.

Class (D):  Minimal Protection

This class is reserved for those systems that have been evaluated but that fail to meet the requirements for a higher evaluation class.

Class (C1):  Discretionary Security Protection

The Trusted Computing Base (TCB) of a class (C1) system nominally satisfies the discretionary security requirements by providing separation of users and data.  It incorporates some form of credible controls capable of enforcing access limitations on an individual basis, i.e., ostensibly suitable for allowing users to be able to protect project or private information and to keep other users from accidentally reading or destroying their data.  The class (C1) environment is expected to be one of cooperating users processing data at the same level(s) of sensitivity.

Class (C2):  Controlled Access Protection

Systems in this class enforce a more finely grained discretionary access control than (C1) systems, making users individually accountable for their actions through login procedures, auditing of security-relevant events, and resource isolation.

Class (B1): Labeled Security Protection

Class (B1) systems require all the features required for class (C2).  In addition, an informal statement of the security policy model, data labeling, and mandatory access control over named subjects and objects must be present.  The capability must exist for accurately labeling exported information.  Any flaws identified by testing must be removed.

Class (B2):  Structured Protection

In class (B2) systems, the TCB is based on a clearly defined and documented formal security policy model that requires the discretionary and mandatory access control enforcement found in class (B1) systems to be extended to all subjects and objects in the ADP system.  In addition, covert channels are addressed.  The TCB must be carefully structured into protection-critical and non-protection-critical elements.  The TCB interface is well-defined and the TCB design and implementation enable it to be subjected to more thorough testing and more complete review.  Authentication mechanisms are strengthened, trusted facility management is provided in the form of support for system administrator and operator functions, and stringent configuration management controls are imposed.  The system is relatively resistant to penetration.

Class (B3): Security Domains

The class (B3) TCB must satisfy the reference monitor requirements that it mediate all accesses of subjects to objects, be tamperproof, and be small enough to be subjected to analysis and tests. To this end, the TCB is structured to exclude code not essential to security policy enforcement, with significant system engineering during TCB design and implementation directed toward minimizing its complexity. A security administrator is supported, audit mechanisms are expanded to signal security-relevant events, and system recovery procedures are required. The system is highly resistant to penetration.

Class (A1): Verified Design

Systems in class (A1) are functionally equivalent to those in class (B3) in that no additional architectural features or policy requirements are added. The distinguishing feature of systems in this class is the analysis derived from formal design specification and verification techniques and the resulting high degree of assurance that the TCB is correctly implemented. This assurance is developmental in nature, starting with a formal model of the security policy and a formal top-level specification (FTLS) of the design. In keeping with extensive design and development analysis of the TCB required of systems in class (A1), more stringent configuration management is required and procedures are established for securely distributing the system to sites. A system security administrator is supported.

SOURCE: Department of Defense *Trusted Computer System Evaluation Criteria*, DOD 5200.28-STD, December 1985, Appendix C, pp. 93-94.

processing. It has been codified as a military standard, making it a requirement for defense systems, and its dissemination has been directed largely to major vendors of centralized systems, notably vendors who are or who supply government contractors.

Because of its shortcomings, which have been debated in the computer security community for several years, the Orange Book must be regarded as only an interim stage in the codification of prudent protection practices.

# Appendix B
## Selected Topics in
## Computer Security Technology

This appendix discusses in considerable detail selected topics in computer security technology chosen either because they are well understood and fundamental, or because they are solutions to current urgent problems. Several sections expand on topics presented in Chapter 3.

## ORANGE BOOK SECURITY

A security policy is a set of rules by which people are given access to information and/or resources. Usually these rules are broadly stated, allowing them to be interpreted somewhat differently at various levels within an organization. With regard to secure computer systems, a security policy is used to derive a security model, which in turn is used to develop the requirements, specifications, and implementation of a system.

### Library Example

A "trusted system" that illustrates a number of principles related to security policy is a library. In a very simple library that has no librarian, anyone (a subject) can take out any book (an object) desired: no policy is being enforced and there is no mechanism of enforcement. In a slightly more sophisticated case, a librarian checks who should have access to the library but does not particularly care who takes out which book: the policy enforced is, "Anyone allowed in the room is allowed access to anything in the room." Such a policy requires only identification of the subject. In a third case, a simple extension of the previous one, no one is allowed to take out more than five books at a time. In a sophisticated version of this system, a librarian first determines how many books a subject already has out before allowing that subject to take more out. Such a policy requires a check of the subject's identity and current status.

In a library with an even more complex policy, only certain people are allowed to access certain books. The librarian performs a check by name of who is allowed to access which books. This policy frequently involves the development of long lists of names and may evolve toward, in some cases, a negative list, that is, a list of people who should not be able to have access to specific information. In large organizations, determining which users have access to specific information frequently is based on the project they are working on or the level of sensitivity of data for which they are authorized. In each of these cases, there is an access control policy and an enforcement mechanism. The policy defines the access that an individual will have to information contained in the library. The librarian serves as the policy-enforcing mechanism.

## Orange Book Security Models

The best-known and most widely used formal models of computer security functionality, the Bell and LaPadula model and its variants (Bell and LaPadula, 1976), emphasize confidentiality (protection from unauthorized disclosure of information) as their primary security service. In particular, these models attempt to capture the "mandatory" (what ISO Standard 7498-2 (ISO, 1989) refers to as "administratively directed, label-based") aspects of security policy. This is especially important in providing protection against "Trojan horse" software, a significant concern among those who process classified data. Mandatory controls are typically enforced by operating-system mechanisms at the relatively coarse granularity of processes and files. This state of affairs has resulted from a number of factors, several of which are noted below:

1. The basic security models were accurately perceived to represent Department of Defense (DOD) security concerns for protecting classified information from disclosure, especially in the face of Trojan horse attacks. Since it was under the auspices of DOD funding that the work in formal security policy models was carried out, it is not surprising that the emphasis was on models that reflected DOD requirements for confidentiality.

2. The embodiment of the model in the operating system has been

deemed essential in order to achieve a high level of assurance and to make available a secure platform on which untrusted (or less trusted) applications could be executed without fear of compromising overall system security. It was recognized early that the development of trusted software, that is, software that is trusted to not violate the security policy imposed on the computer system, is a very difficult and expensive task. This is especially true if a security policy calls for a high level of assurance in a potentially "hostile" environment, for example, execution of software from untrusted sources.

The strategy evolved of developing trusted operating systems that could segregate information and processes (representing users) to allow controlled sharing of computer system resources. If trusted application software were written, it would require a trusted operating system as a platform on top of which it would execute. (If the operating system were not trusted, it, or other untrusted software, could circumvent the trusted operation of the application in question.) Thus development of trusted operating systems is a natural precursor to the development of trusted applications.

At the time this strategy was developed, in the late 1960s and in the 1970s, computer systems were almost exclusively time-shared computers (mainframes or minis), and the resources to be shared (memory, disk storage, and processors) were expensive. With the advent of trusted operating systems, these expensive computing resources could be shared among users who would develop and execute applications without requiring trust in each application to enforce the system security policy. This has become an accepted model for systems in which the primary security concern is disclosure of information and in which the information is labeled in a fashion that reflects its sensitivity.

3. The granularity at which the security policy is enforced is determined largely by characteristics of typical operating system interfaces and concerns for efficient implementation of the mechanisms that enforce security. Thus, for example, since files and processes are the objects managed by most operating systems, these were the objects protected by the security policy embodied in the operating system. In support of Bell-LaPadula, data sensitivity labels are associated with files, and authorizations for data access are associated with processes operating on behalf of users. The operating system enforces the security policy by controlling access to data based on file labels and process (user) authorizations. This type of security policy implementation is the hallmark of high-assurance systems as defined by the Orange Book.

Concerning integrity in the Orange Book, note that if an integrity *policy* (like Clark-Wilson) and an integrity *mechanism* (like type enforcement or rings) are then differentiated, an invariant property of mechanisms is that they enforce a "protected subsystem" kind of property. That is, they undertake to ensure that certain data is touchable only by certain code irrespective of the privileges that code inherits because of the person on whose behalf it is executing. Thus a proper integrity mechanism would ensure that one's personal privilege to update a payroll file could not be used to manipulate payroll data with a text editor, but rather that the privilege could be used only to access payroll data through the payroll subsystem, which presumably performs application-dependent consistency checks on what one does.

While the Orange Book does not explicitly call out a set of integrity-based access rules, it does require that B2-level[1] systems and those above execute out of a protected domain, that is, that the trusted computing base (TCB) itself be a protected subsystem. The mechanism used to do this (e.g., rings) is usually, but not always, exported to applications. Thus an integrity mechanism is generally available as a byproduct of a system operating at the B2 level.

The Orange Book does not mandate mechanisms to support data integrity, but it easily could do so at the B2 level and above, because it mandates that such a mechanism exist to protect the TCB. It is now possible to devise mechanisms that protect the TCB but that cannot be made readily available to applications; however, such cases are in the minority and can be considered pathological.

## HARDWARE ENFORCEMENT OF
## SECURITY AND INTEGRITY

The complexity and difficulty of developing secure applications can be reduced by modifying the hardware on which those applications run. Such modifications may add functionality to the operating system or application software, they may guarantee specific behavior that is not normally provided by conventional hardware, or they may enhance the performance of basic security functions, such as encryption. This section describes two projects that serve as worked examples of what can be accomplished when hardware is designed with security and/or integrity in mind, and what is gained or lost through such an approach.

### VIPER Microprocessor

The VIPER microprocessor was designed specifically for high-integrity control applications at the Royal Signals and Radar Establishment (RSRE), which is part of the U.K.'s Ministry of Defence (MOD). VIPER attempts to achieve high integrity with a simple architecture and instruction set designed to meet the requirements of formal verification and to provide support for high-integrity software.

VIPER 1 was designed as a primitive building block that could be used to construct complete systems capable of running high-integrity applications. Its most important requirement is the ability to stop immediately if any hardware error is detected, including illegal instruction codes and numeric underflow and overflow. By stopping when an error is detected, VIPER assures that no incorrect external actions are taken following a failure. Such "fail-stop" operation (Schlichting and Schneider, 1983) simplifies the design of higher-level algorithms used to maintain the reliability and integrity of the entire system.

VIPER 1 is a memory-based processor that makes use of a uniform instruction set (i.e., all instructions are the same width). The processor has only three programmable 32-bit registers. The instruction set limits the amount of addressable memory to 1 megaword, with all access on word boundaries. There is no support for interrupts, stack processing, or micro-pipelining.

The VIPER 1 architecture provides only basic program support. In fact, multiplication and division are not supported directly by the hardware. This approach was taken primarily to simplify the design of VIPER, thereby allowing it to be verified. If more programming convenience is desired, it must be handled by a high-level compiler, assuming that the resulting loss in performance is tolerable.

The VIPER 1A processor allows two chips to be used in tandem in an active-monitor relationship. That is, one of the chips can be used to monitor the operation of the other. This is achieved by comparing the memory and input/output (I/O) addresses generated by both chips as they are sent off-chip. If either chip detects a difference in this data, then both chips are stopped. In this model, a set of two chips is used to form a single fail-stop processor making use of a single memory module and an I/O line.

It is generally accepted that VIPER's performance falls short of conventional processors' performance, and always will. Because it is being developed for high-integrity applications, the VIPER processor must always depend on well-established, mature implementation techniques and technologies. Many of the decisions about VIPER's design were made with static analysis in mind. Consequently, the instruction set was kept simple, without interrupt processing, to allow static analysis to be done effectively.

## LOCK Project

The LOgical Coprocessing Kernel (LOCK) Project intends to develop a secure microcomputer prototype by 1990 that provides A1-level security for general-purpose processing. The LOCK design makes use of a hardware-based reference monitor, known as SIDEARM, that can be used to build new, secure variants of existing architectures or can be included in the design of new architectures as an option. The goal is to provide the highest level of security as currently defined by National Computer Security Center (NCSC) standards, while providing 80 percent of the performance achievable by an unmodified, insecure computer. SIDEARM is designed to achieve this goal by controlling the memory references made by applications running on the processor to which it is attached. Assuming that SIDEARM is always working properly and has been integrated into the host system in a manner that guarantees its controls cannot be circumvented, it provides high assurance that applications can access data items only in accordance with a well-understood security policy. The LOCK Project centers on guaranteeing that these assumptions are valid.

The SIDEARM module is the basis of the LOCK architecture and is itself an embedded computer system, making use of its own processor, memory, communications, and storage subsystems, including a laser disk for auditing. It is logically placed between the host processor and memory, and integrated into those existing host facilities, such as memory management units, that control access into memory. Since it is a separate hardware component, applications can not modify any of the security information used to control SIDEARM directly.

Security policy is enforced by assigning security labels to all subjects (i.e., applications or users) and objects (i.e., data files and programs) and making security policy decisions without relying on the host system. The security policy enforced by SIDEARM includes type-enforcement controls, providing configurable, mandatory integrity. That is, "types" can be assigned to data objects and used to restrict access to subjects that are performing functions appropriate to that type. Thus type-enforcement can be used, for example, to ensure that a payroll data file is accessed only by payroll programs, or that specific transforms, such as labeling or encryption, are performed on data prior to output. Mandatory access control (MAC), discretionary access control (DAC), and type enforcement are "additive" in that a subject must pass all three criteria before being allowed to access an object.

The LOCK Project makes use of multiple TEPACHE-based TYPE-I

encryption devices to safeguard SIDEARM media (security databases and audit) and data stored on host system media, and to close covert channels. As such, LOCK combines aspects of both COMSEC (communications security) and COMPUSEC (computer security) in an interdependent manner. The security provided by both approaches is critical to LOCK's proper operation.

The LOCK architecture requires few but complex trusted software components, including a SIDEARM device driver and software that ensures that decisions made by the SIDEARM are enforced by existing host facilities such as a memory management unit. An important class of trusted software comprises "kernel extensions," security-critical software that runs on the host to handle machine-dependent support, such as printer and terminal security labeling, and application-specific security policies, such as that required by a database management system. Kernel extensions are protected and controlled by the reference monitor and provide the flexibility needed to allow the LOCK technology to support a wide range of applications, without becoming too large or becoming architecture-dependent.

One of LOCK's advantages is that a major portion of the operating system, outside of the kernel extensions and the reference monitor, can be considered "hostile." That is, even if the operating system is corrupted, LOCK will not allow an unauthorized application to access data objects. However, parts of the operating system must still be modified or removed to make use of the functionality provided by SIDEARM. The LOCK Project intends to support the UNIX System V interface on the LOCK architecture and to attain certification of the entire system at the A1 level.

## CRYPTOGRAPHY

Cryptography is the art of keeping data secret, primarily through the use of mathematical or logical functions that transform intelligible data into seemingly unintelligible data and back again. Cryptography is probably the most important aspect of communications security and is becoming increasingly important as a basic building block for computer security.

### Fundamental Concepts of Encryption

Cryptography and cryptanalysis have existed for at least 2,000 years, perhaps beginning with a substitution algorithm used by Julius Caesar (Tanebaum, 1981). In his method, every letter in the original message, known now as the plaintext, was replaced by the letter that occurred three places later in the alphabet. That is, A was replaced by D, B was replaced by E, and so on. For example, the plaintext "VENI VIDI VICI" would yield "YHQL YLGL YLFL." The resulting message, now known as the ciphertext, was then couriered to an awaiting centurion, who decrypted it by replacing each letter with the letter that occurred three places "before" it in the alphabet. The encryption and decryption algorithms were essentially controlled by the number three, which thus was the encryption and decryption key. If Caesar suspected that an unauthorized person had discovered how to decrypt the ciphertext, he could simply change the key value to another number and inform the field generals of that new value by using some other method of communication. Although Caesar's cipher is a relatively simple example of cryptography, it clearly depends on a number of essential components: the encryption and decryption algorithms, a key that is known by all authorized parties, and the ability to change the key. Figure B.1 shows the encryption process and how the various components interact.

|  | Encryption Key | | Decryption Key | |
|---|---|---|---|---|
|  | ↓ | | ↓ | |
| Plaintext → | Encryption →<br>Algorithm | Ciphertext → | Decryption →<br>Algorithm | Plaintext |

FIGURE B.1 The encryption process.

If any of these components is compromised, the security of the information being protected decreases. If a weak encryption algorithm is chosen, an opponent may be able to guess the plaintext once a copy of the ciphertext is obtained. In many cases, the cryptanalyst need only know the type of encryption algorithm being used in order to break it. For example, knowing that Caesar used only a cyclic substitution of the alphabet, one could simply try every key value from 1 to 25, looking for the value that resulted in a message containing Latin words. Similarly, many encryption algorithms that appear to be very complicated are rendered ineffective by an improper choice of a key value. In a more practical sense, if the receiver forgets the key value or uses the wrong one, then the resulting message will probably be unintelligible, requiring additional effort to retransmit the message and/or the key. Finally, it is possible that the enemy will break the code even if the strongest possible combination of algorithms and key values is used. Therefore, keys and possibly even the algorithms need to be changed over a period of time to limit the loss of security when the enemy has broken the current system. The process of changing keys and distributing them to all parties concerned is known as *key management* and is the most difficult aspect of security management after an encryption method has been chosen.[2]

In theory, any logical function can be used as an encryption algorithm. The function may act on single bits of information, single letters in some alphabet, or single words in some language or groups of words. The Caesar cipher is an example of an encryption algorithm that operates on single letters within a message. Throughout history a number of "codes" have been used in which a two-column list of words is used to define the encryption and decryption algorithms. In this case, plaintext words are located in one of the columns and replaced by the corresponding word from the other column to yield the ciphertext. The reverse process is performed to regenerate the plaintext from the ciphertext. If more than two columns are distributed, a key can be used to designate both the plaintext and ciphertext columns to be used. For example, given 10 columns, the key [3,7] might designate that the third column represents plaintext words and the seventh column represents ciphertext words. Although code books (e.g., multicolumn word lists) are convenient for manual enciphering and deciphering, their very existence can lead to compromise. That is, once a code book falls into enemy hands, ciphertext is relatively simple to decipher. Furthermore, code books are difficult to produce and to distribute, requiring accurate accounts of who has which books and which parties can communicate using those books. Consequently, mechanical and electronic devices have been developed to automate the encryption and decryption process, using primarily mathematical functions on single bits of information or single letters in a given alphabet.

## Private vs. Public Crypto-Systems

The security of a given crypto-system depends on the amount of information known by the cryptanalyst about the algorithms and keys in use. In theory, if the encryption algorithm and keys are independent of the decryption algorithm and keys, then full knowledge of the encryption algorithm and key will not help the cryptanalyst break the code. However, in many practical crypto-systems, the same algorithm and key are used for both encryption and decryption. The security of these symmetric cipher systems depends on keeping at least the key secret from others, making such systems private-key crypto-systems. An example of a symmetric, private-key crypto-system is the Data Encryption Standard (DES) (see below, "Data Encryption Standard").

In this case, the encryption and decryption algorithm is widely known and has been widely studied; the privacy of the encryption and decryption key is relied on to ensure security. Other private-key systems have been implemented and deployed by the National Security Agency (NSA) for the protection of classified government information. In contrast to the DES, the encryption and decryption algorithms within those crypto-systems have been kept classified, to the extent that the computer chips on which they are implemented are coated in such a way as to prevent them from being examined.

Users are often intolerant of private encryption and decryption algorithms because they do not know how the algorithms work or if a "trapdoor" exists that would allow the algorithm designer to read the user's secret information. In an attempt to eliminate this lack of trust, a number of crypto-systems have been developed around encryption and decryption algorithms based on fundamentally difficult problems, or one-way functions, that have been studied extensively by the research community. Another approach used in public-key systems, such as that taken by the RSA (see the section below headed "RSA"), is to show that the most obvious way to break the system involves solving a hard problem (although this means that such systems may be broken by simpler means).

For practical reasons, it is desirable to use different encryption and decryption keys in a crypto-system. Such asymmetric systems allow the encryption key to be made available to anyone, while preserving confidence that only people who hold the decryption key can decipher the information. These systems, which depend solely on the privacy of the decryption key, are known as public-key crypto-systems. An example of an asymmetric, public-key cipher is the patented RSA system.

## Digital Signatures

Society accepts handwritten signatures as legal proof that a person has agreed to the terms of a contract as stated on a sheet of paper, or that a person has authorized a transfer of funds as indicated on a check. But the use of written signatures involves the physical transmission of a paper document; this is not practical if electronic communication is to become more widely used in business. Rather, a digital signature is needed to allow the recipient of a message or document to irrefutably verify the originator of that message or document.

A written signature can be produced by one person (although forgeries certainly occur), but it can be recognized by many people as belonging uniquely to its author. To be accepted as a replacement for a written signature, a digital signature, then, would have to be easily authenticated by anyone, but be producible only by its author.

A digital signature system consists of three elements, each carrying out a procedure:

1. The generator, which produces two numbers called the mark (which should be unforgeable) and the secret;

2. The signer, which accepts a secret and an arbitrary sequence of bytes called the input, and produces a number called the signature; and

3. The checker, which accepts a mark, an input, and a signature and says whether or not the signature matches the input for that mark.

The procedures have the following properties:

• If the generator produces a mark and a secret, and the signer produces a signature when given the secret and an input, then the checker will say that the signature matches the input for that mark.

• If one has a mark produced by the generator but does not have the secret, then even with a large number of inputs and matching signatures for that mark, one still cannot produce an additional input and matching signature for that mark. In particular, even if the signature matches one of the inputs, one cannot produce another input that it matches. A digital signature system is useful because if one has a mark produced by the generator, as well as an input and matching signature, then one can be sure that the signature was computed by a system that knew the corresponding secret, because a system that did not know the secret could not have computed the signature.

For instance, one can trust a mark to certify an uninfected program if

• one believes that it came from the generator, and

• one also believes that any system that knows the corresponding secret is one that can be trusted not to sign a program image if it is corrupted.

Known methods for digital signatures are often based on computing a secure checksum (see below) of the input to be signed and then encrypting the checksum with the secret. If the encryption uses public-key encryption, the mark is the public key that matches the secret, and the checker simply decrypts the signature.

For more details, see Chapter 9 in Davies and Price (1984).

## Cryptographic Checksums

A cryptographic checksum or one-way hash function accepts any amount of input data (in this case a file containing a program) and computes a small result (typically 8 or 16 bytes) called the checksum. Its important property is that it requires that much work be done to find a different input with the same checksum. Here "a lot of work" means "more computing than an adversary can afford." A cryptographic checksum is useful because it identifies the input: any change to the input, even a very clever one made by a malicious person, is sure to change the checksum. Suppose a trusted person tells another that the program with checksum 7899345668823051 does not have a virus (perhaps he does this by signing the checksum with a digital signature). One who computes the checksum of file WORDPROC.EXE and gets 7899345668823051 should believe that he can run WORDPROC.EXE without worrying about a virus.

For more details, see Davies and Price (1984), Chapter 9.

## Public-Key Crypto-systems and Digital Signatures

Public-key crypto-systems offer a means of implementing digital signatures. In a public-key system the sender enciphers a message using the receiver's public key, creating ciphertext1. To sign the message he enciphers ciphertext1 with his private key, creating ciphertext2. Ciphertext2 is then sent to the receiver. The receiver applies the sender's public key to decrypt ciphertext2, yielding ciphertext1. Finally, the receiver applies his private key to convert ciphertext1 to plaintext. The authentication of the sender is evidenced by the fact that the receiver successfully applied the sender's public key and was able to create plaintext. Since encryption and decryption are opposites, using the sender's public key to decipher the sender's private key proves that only the sender could have sent it.

To resolve disputes concerning the authenticity of a document, the receiver can save the ciphertext, the public key, and the plaintext as proof of the sender's signature. If the sender later denies that the message was sent, the receiver can present the signed message to a court of law where the judge then uses the sender's public key to check that the ciphertext corresponds to a meaningful plaintext message with the sender's name, the proper time sent, and so forth. Only the sender could have generated the message, and therefore the receiver's claim would be upheld in court.

## Key Management

In order to use a digital signature to certify a program (or anything else, such as an electronic message), it is necessary to know the mark that should be trusted. Key management is the process of reliably distributing the mark to everyone who needs to know it. When only one mark needs to be trusted, this is quite simple: a trusted person tells another what the mark is. He cannot do this using the computer system, which cannot guarantee that the information actually came from him. Some other communication channel is needed: a face-to-face meeting, a telephone conversation, a letter written on official stationery, or anything else that gives adequate assurance. When several agents are certifying programs, each using its own mark, things are more complex. The solution is for one trusted agent to certify the marks of the other agents, using the same digital signature scheme used to certify anything else. Consultative Committee on International Telephony and Telegraphy (CCITT) standard X.509 describes procedures and data formats for accomplishing this multilevel certification (CCITT, 1989b).

## Algorithms

### One-Time Pads

There is a collection of relatively simple encryption algorithms, known as one-time pad algorithms, whose security is mathematically provable. Such algorithms combine a single plaintext value (e.g., bit, letter, or word) with a random key value to generate a single ciphertext value. The strength of one-time pad algorithms lies in the fact that separate random key values are used for each of the plaintext values being enciphered, and the stream of key values used for one message is never used for another, as the name implies. Assuming there is no relationship between the stream of key values used during the process, the cryptanalyst has to try every possible key value for every ciphertext value, a task that can be made very difficult simply by the use of different representations for the plaintext and key values.

The primary disadvantage of a one-time pad system is that it requires an amount of key information equal to the size of the plaintext being enciphered. Since the key information must be known by both parties and is never reused, the amount of information exchanged between parties is twice that contained in the message itself. Furthermore, the key information must be transmitted using mechanisms different from those for the message, thereby doubling the resources required.

Finally, in practice, it is relatively difficult to generate large streams of "random" values effectively and efficiently. Any nonrandom patterns that appear in the key stream provide the cryptanalyst with valuable information that can be used to break the system.

One-time pads can be implemented efficiently on computers using any of the primitive logical functions supported by the processor. For example, the Exclusive-Or (XOR) operator is a convenient encryption and decryption function. When two bits are combined using the XOR operator, the result is 1 if one and only one of the input bits is 1; otherwise the result is 0, as defined by the table in Figure B.2

1 XOR 0 = 1
0 XOR 1 = 1
0 XOR 0 = 0
1 XOR 1 = 0

FIGURE B.2 The XOR function.

The XOR function is convenient because it is fast and permits decrypting the encrypted information simply by "XORing" the ciphertext with the same data (key) used to encrypt the plaintext, as shown in Figure B.3.

| ENCRYPTION: | Plaintext | 0101 0100 0100 0101 |
| | Key | 0100 0001 0100 0001 |
| | | —— —— —— —— —— —— |
| | Ciphertext | 0001 0101 0000 0100 |
| DECRYPTION: | Ciphertext | 0001 0101 0000 0100 |
| | Key | 0100 0001 0100 0001 |
| | | —— —— —— —— —— —— |
| | Plaintext | 0101 0100 0100 0101 |

FIGURE B.3 Encryption and decryption using the XOR function.

## Data Encryption Standard

In 1972, the National Bureau of Standards (NBS; now the National Institute of Standards and Technology (NIST)) identified a need for a standard crypto-system for unclassified applications and issued a call for proposals. Although it was poorly received at first, IBM proposed, in 1975, a private-key crypto-system that operated on 64-bit blocks of information and used a single 128-bit key for both encryption and decryption. After accepting the initial proposal, NBS sought both industry and NSA evaluations. Industry evaluation was desired because NBS wanted to provide a secure encryption that industry would want to use, and NSA's advice was requested because of its historically strong background in cryptography and cryptanalysis. NSA responded with a generally favorable evaluation but recommended that some of the fundamental components, known as S-boxes, be redesigned. Based primarily on that recommendation, the Data Encryption Standard (DES; NBS, 1977) became a federal information processing standard in 1977 and an American National Standards Institute (ANSI) standard (number X3.92-1981/R1987) in 1980, using a 56-bit key.

The Data Encryption Standard (DES) represents the first cryptographic algorithm openly developed by the U.S. government. Historically, such algorithms have been developed by the NSA as highly classified projects. However, despite the openness of its design, many researchers believed that NSA's influence on the S-box design and the length of the key introduced a trapdoor that allowed the NSA to read any message encrypted using the DES. In fact, one researcher described the design of a special-purpose parallel processing computer that was capable of breaking a DES system using 56-bit keys and that, according to the researcher, could be built by the NSA using conventional technology. Nonetheless, in over ten years of academic and industrial scrutiny, no flaw in the DES has been made public (although some examples of weak keys have been discovered). Unfortunately, as with all crypto-systems, there is no way of knowing if the NSA or any other organization has succeeded in breaking the DES.

The controversy surrounding the DES was reborn when the NSA announced that it would discontinue the FS-1027 DES device certification program after 1987, although it did recertify the algorithm (until 1993) for use primarily in unclassified government applications and for electronic funds transfer applications, most notably FedWire, which had invested substantially in the use of DES. NSA cited the widespread use of the DES as a disadvantage, stating that if it were used too much it would become the prime target of criminals and foreign adversaries. In its place, NSA has offered a range of private-key algorithms based on classified algorithms that make use of keys generated and managed by NSA.

The Data Encryption Standard (DES) algorithm has four approved modes of operation: the electronic codebook, cipher block chaining, cipher feedback, and output feedback. Each of these modes has certain characteristics that make it more appropriate than the others for specific purposes. For example, the cipher block chaining and cipher feedback modes are intended for message authentication purposes, while the electronic codebook mode is used primarily for encryption and decryption of bulk data (NBS, 1980b).

## RSA

The RSA is a public key crypto-system, invented and patented by Ronald Rivest, Adi Shamir, and Leonard Adelman, that is based on large prime numbers (Rivest et al., 1978). In their method, the decryption key is generated by selecting a pair of prime numbers, $P$ and $Q$, (i.e., numbers that are not divisible by any other) and another number, $E$, which must pass a special mathematical test based on the values of the pair of primes. The encryption key consists of the product of $P$ and $Q$, which is called $N$, and the number $E$, which can be made publicly available. The decryption key consists of $N$ and another number, called $D$, which results from a mathematical calculation using $N$ and $E$. The decryption key must be kept secret.

A given message is encrypted by converting the text to numbers (using conventional conversion mechanisms) and replacing each number with a number computed using $N$ and $E$. Specifically, each number is multiplied by itself $E$ times, with the result being divided by $N$, yielding a quotient, which is discarded, and a remainder. The remainder is used to replace the original number as part of the ciphertext. The decryption process is similar, multiplying the ciphertext number by itself $D$ times (versus $E$ times) and dividing it by $N$, with the remainder representing the desired plaintext number (which is converted back to a letter). RSA's security depends on the fact that, although finding large prime numbers is computationally easy, factoring large integers into their component primes is not, and it is computationally intensive.[3] However, in recent years, parallel processing techniques and improvements in factoring algorithms have significantly increased the size of numbers (measured as the number of decimal digits in its representation) that can be factored in a relatively short period of time (i.e., less than 24 hours). Seventy-digit numbers are well within reach of modern computers and processing techniques, with 80-digit numbers on the horizon. Most commercial RSA systems use 512-bit keys (i.e., 154 digits), which should be out of the reach of conventional computers and algorithms for quite some time. However, the best factoring approaches currently use networks of workstations (perhaps several hundred or thousand of them), working part-time for weeks on end (Browne, 1988). This suggests that factoring numbers up to 110 digits is on the horizon.

## PROTECTION OF PROPRIETARY
## SOFTWARE AND DATABASES

The problem of protecting proprietary software or proprietary databases is an old and difficult one. The blatant copying of a large commercial program, such as a payroll program, and its systematic use within the pirating organization are often detectable and will then lead to legal action. Similar considerations apply to large databases, and for these the pirating organization has the additional difficulty of obtaining the vendor-supplied periodic updates, without which the pirated database will become useless.

The problem of software piracy is further exacerbated in the context of personal computing. Vendors supply programs for word processing, spreadsheets, game-playing programs, compilers, and so on, and these are systematically copied by pirate vendors and by private users. While large-scale pirate vendors may eventually be detected and stopped, there is no hope of preventing, through detection and legal action, the mass of individual users from copying from each other.

Various technical solutions have been proposed for the problem of software piracy in the personal computing world. Some involve a machine-customized layout of the data on a disk. Others involve the use of volatile transcription of certain parts of a program text. Cryptography employing machine- or program-instance customized keys has been suggested, in conjunction with coprocessors that are physically impenetrable so that cryptographic keys and crucial decrypted program text cannot be captured. Some of these approaches, especially those employing special hardware, and hence requiring cooperation between hardware and software manufacturers, have not penetrated the marketplace. The safeguards deployed by software vendors are usually incomplete and after a while succumb to attacks by talented amateur hackers who produce copyable versions of the protected disks. There even exist programs to help a user overcome the protections of many available proprietary programs. (These thieving programs are then presumably themselves copied through use of their own devices!) It should be pointed out that there is even a debate as to whether the prevalent theft of proprietary personal computing software by individuals is sufficiently harmful to warrant the cost of developing and deploying really effective countermeasures (Kent, 1981).

The problem of copying proprietary software and databases, while important, lies outside the purview of system security. Software piracy is an issue between the rightful owner and the thief, and its resolution depends on tools and methods, and represents a goal, which are separate from those associated with system security.

There is, however, an important aspect of protection of proprietary software and/or databases that lies directly within the domain of system security as it is commonly understood. It involves the unauthorized use of proprietary software and databases by parties other than the organization licensed to use such software or databases, and in systems other than within the organization's system where the proprietary software is legitimately installed. Consider, for example, a large database with the associated complex-query software that is licensed by a vendor to an organization. This may be done with the contractual obligation that the licensee obtains the database for his own use and not for making query services available to outsiders. Two modes of transgression against the proprietary rights of the vendor are possible. The organization itself may breach its obligation not to provide the query services to others, or some employee who himself may have legitimate access to the database may provide or even sell query services to outsiders. In the latter case the licensee organization may be held responsible, under certain circumstances, for not having properly guarded the proprietary rights of the vendor. Thus there is a security issue associated with the prevention of unauthorized use of proprietary software or databases legitimately installed in a computing system. In the committee's classification of security services, it comes under the heading of resource (usage) control. Namely, the proprietary software is a resource and its owners wish to protect against its unauthorized use (say, for sale of services to outsiders) by a user who is otherwise authorized to access that software.

Resource control as a security service has inspired very few, if any, research and implementation efforts. It poses some difficult technical problems, as well as possible privacy problems. The obvious approach is to audit, on a selective and possibly random basis, access to the proprietary resource in question. Such an audit trail can then be evaluated by human scrutiny, or automatically, for indications of unauthorized use as defined in the present context. It may well be that effective resource control will require recording, at least on a spot-check basis, aspects of the content of a user's interaction with software and/or a database. For obvious reasons, this may provoke resistance.

Another security service that may come into play in this context of resource control is nonrepudiation. The legal aspects of the protection of proprietary rights may require that certain actions taken by a user in connection with the proprietary resource be such that once the actions are recorded, the user is barred from later repudiating his connection to these actions.

It is clear that such measures for resource control, if properly implemented and installed, will serve to deter the unauthorized use of proprietary resources by individual users. But what about the organization controlling the trusted system in which the proprietary resource is embedded? On the one hand, such an organization may well have the ability to dismantle the very mechanisms designed to control the use of proprietary resources, thereby evading effective scrutiny by the vendor or its representations. On the other hand, the design and nature of security mechanisms are such that the mechanisms are difficult to change selectively, and especially in a manner ensuring that their subsequent behavior will emulate the untampered-with mode, thus making the change undetectable. Thus the expert effort and people involved in effecting such changes will open the organization to danger of exposure.

There is now no documented major concern about the unauthorized use, in the sense of the present discussion, of proprietary programs or databases. It may well be that in the future, when the sale of proprietary databases assumes economic significance, the possibility of abuse of proprietary rights by licensed organizations and authorized users will be an important issue. At that point an appropriate technology for resource control will be essential.

## USE OF PASSWORDS FOR AUTHENTICATION

Passwords have been used throughout military history as a mechanism to distinguish friends from foes. When sentries were posted, they were told the daily password that would be given by any friendly soldier who attempted to enter the camp. Passwords represent a shared secret that allows strangers to recognize each other, and they have a number of advantageous properties. They can be chosen to be easily remembered (e.g., "Betty Boop") without being easily guessed by the enemy (e.g., "Mickey Mouse"). Furthermore, passwords allow any number of people to use the same authentication method, and they can be changed frequently (as opposed to physical keys, which must be duplicated). The extensive use of passwords for user authentication in human-to-human interactions has led to their extensive use in human-to-computer interactions.

According to the NCSC *Password Management Guideline*, "A password is a character string used to authenticate an identity. Knowledge of the password that is associated with a user ID is considered proof of authorization to use the capabilities associated with that user ID" (U.S. DOD, 1985a).

Passwords can be issued to users automatically by a random generation routine, providing excellent protection against commonly used passwords. However, if the random password generator is not good, breaking one may be equivalent to breaking all. At one installation, a person reconstructed the entire master list of passwords by guessing the mapping from random numbers to alphabetic passwords and inferring the random number generator (McIlroy, 1989). For that reason, the random generator must base its seed on a varying source, such as the system clock. Often the user will not find a randomly selected password acceptable because it is too difficult to memorize. This can significantly decrease the advantage of random passwords, because the user may write the password down somewhere in an effort to remember it. This may cause infinite exposure of the password, thus thwarting all attempts to maintain security. For this reason it can be helpful to give a user the option to accept or reject a password, or choose one from a list. This may increase the probability that the user will find an acceptable password.

User-defined passwords can be a positive method for assigning passwords if the users are aware of the classic weaknesses. If the password is too short, say, four digits, a potential intruder can exhaust all possible password combinations and gain access quickly. That is why every system must limit the number of tries any user can make toward entering his password successfully. If the user picks very simple passwords, potential intruders can break the system by using a list of common names or a dictionary. A dictionary of 100,000 words has been shown to raise the intruder's chance of success by 50 percent (McIlroy, 1989). Specific guidelines on how to pick passwords are important if users are allowed to pick their own passwords. Voluntary password systems should guide users to never reveal their password to other users and to change their password on a regular basis, a practice that can be enforced by the system. (The NCSC's *Password Management Guideline* (U.S. DOD, 1985a) represents such a guideline.)

Some form of access control must be provided to prevent unauthorized persons from gaining access to a password list and reading or modifying the list. One way to protect passwords in internal storage is by a one-way hash. The passwords of each user are stored as ciphertext. If the passwords were encrypted, per se, the key would be present and an attacker who gained access to the password file could decrypt them. When a user signs on and enters his password, the password is processed by the algorithm to produce the corresponding ciphertext. The plaintext password is immediately deleted, and the ciphertext version of the password is compared with the one stored in memory. The advantage of this technique is that passwords cannot be stolen from the computer (absent a lucky guess). However, a person obtaining unauthorized access could delete or change the ciphertext passwords and effectively deny service. The file of encrypted passwords should be protected against unauthorized reading, to further foil attempts to guess passwords.

The longer a password is used, the more opportunities exist for exposing it. The probability of compromise of a password increases during its lifetime. This probability is considered acceptably low for an initial time period; after a longer time period it becomes unacceptably high. There should be a maximum lifetime for all passwords. It is recommended that the maximum lifetime of a password be no greater than one year (U.S. DOD, 1985a).

## NETWORKS AND DISTRIBUTED SYSTEMS

### Security Perimeters

Security is only as strong as its weakest link. The methods described above can in principle provide a very high level of security even in a very large system that is accessible to many malicious principals. But implementing these methods throughout the system is sure to be difficult and time consuming. Ensuring that they are used correctly is likely to be even more difficult. The principle of "divide and conquer" suggests that it may be wiser to divide a large system into smaller parts and to restrict severely the ways in which these parts can interact with each other.

The idea is to establish a security perimeter around part of a system and to disallow fully general communication across the perimeter. Instead, there are gates in the perimeter that are carefully managed and audited and that allow only certain limited kinds of traffic (e.g., electronic mail, but not file transfers or general network "datagrams"). A gate may also restrict the pairs of source and destination systems that can communicate through it.

It is important to understand that a security perimeter is not foolproof. If it passes electronic mail, then users can encode arbitrary programs or data in the mail and get them across the perimeter. But this is less likely to happen by mistake, and it is more difficult to do things inside the perimeter using only electronic mail than to do things using terminal connections or arbitrary network datagrams. Furthermore, if, for example, a mail-only perimeter is an important part of system security, users and managers will come to understand that it is dangerous and harmful to implement automated services that accept electronic mail requests.

As with any security measure, a price is paid in convenience and flexibility for a security perimeter: it is harder to do things across the perimeter. Users and managers must decide on the proper balance between security and convenience.

## Viruses

A computer virus is a program that

- is hidden in another program (called its host) so that it runs whenever the host program runs, and
- can make a copy of itself.

When a virus runs, it can do a great deal of damage. In fact, it can do anything that its host can do: delete files, corrupt data, send a message with a user's secrets to another machine, disrupt the operation of a host, waste machine resources, and so on. There are many places to hide a virus: the operating system, an executable program, a shell command file, or a macro in a spreadsheet or word processing program are only a few of the possibilities. In this respect a virus is just like a Trojan horse. And like a Trojan horse, a virus can attack any kind of computer system, from a personal computer to a mainframe. (Many of the problems and solutions discussed in this section apply equally well in a discussion of Trojan horses.)

A virus can also make a copy of itself, into another program or even another machine that can be reached from the current host over a network, or by the transfer of a floppy disk or other removable medium. Like a living creature, a virus can spread quickly. If it copies itself just once a day, then after a week there will be more than 50 copies (because each copy copies itself), and after a month about a billion. If it reproduces once a minute (still slow for a computer), it takes only half an hour to make a billion copies. Their ability to spread quickly makes viruses especially dangerous.

There are only two reliable methods for keeping a virus from doing harm:

- Make sure that every program is uninfected before it runs.
- Prevent an infected program from doing damage.

### Keeping a Virus Out

Since a virus can potentially infect any program, the only sure way to keep it from running on a system is to ensure that every program run comes from a reliable source. In principle this can be done by administrative and physical means, ensuring that every program arrives on a disk in an unbroken wrapper from a trusted supplier. In practice it is very difficult to enforce such procedures, because they rule out any kind of informal copying of software, including shareware, public domain programs, and spreadsheets written by a colleague. Moreover, there have been numerous instances of virus-infected software arriving on a disk freshly shrink-wrapped from a vendor. For this reason, vendors and at least one trade association (ADAPSO) are exploring ways to prevent contamination at the source. A more practical method uses digital signatures.

Informally, a digital signature system is a procedure that one can run on a computer and that should be believed when it says, "This input data came from this source" (a more precise definition is given below). With a trusted source that is believed when it says that a program image is uninfected, one can make sure that every program is uninfected before it runs by refusing to run it unless

- a certificate says, "The following program is uninfected," followed by the text of the program, and
- the digital signature system says that the certificate came from the trusted source.

Each place where this protection is applied adds to security. To make the protection complete, it should be applied by any agent that can run a program. The program image loader is not the only such agent; others include the shell, a spreadsheet program loading a spreadsheet with macros, or a word processing program loading a macro, since shell scripts, macros, and so on are all programs that can host viruses. Even the program that boots the machine should apply this protection when it loads the operating system. An important issue is distribution of the public key for verifying signatures (see "Digital Signatures," above).

### Preventing Damage

Because there are so many kinds of programs, it may be hard to live with the restriction that every program must be certified as uninfected. This means, for example, that a spreadsheet cannot be freely copied into a system if it contains macros. Because it might be infected, an uncertified program that is run must be prevented from doing damage— leaking secrets, changing data, or consuming excessive resources.

Access control can do this if the usual mechanisms are extended to specify programs, or a set of programs, as well as users. For example, the form of an access control rule could be "user A running program B can read" or "set of users C running set of programs D can read and write." Then a set of uninfected programs can be defined, namely the ones that are certified as uninfected, and the default access control rule can be "user running uninfected" instead of "user running anything." This ensures that by default an uncertified program will not be able to read or write anything. A user can then relax this protection selectively if necessary, to allow the program access to certain files or directories.

Note that strong protection on current personal computers is ultimately impossible, since they lack memory protection and hence cannot ultimately enforce access control. Yet most of the damage from viruses has involved personal computers, and protection has frequently been sought from so-called vaccine programs.

### Providing and Using Vaccines

It is well understood how to implement the complete protection against viruses just described, but it requires changes in many places: operating systems, command shells, spreadsheet programs, programmable editors, and any other kinds of programs, as well as procedures for distributing software. These changes ought to be implemented. In the meantime, however, various stopgap measures can help somewhat. Generally known as vaccines, they are widely available for personal computers.

The idea behind a vaccine is to look for traces of viruses in programs, usually by searching the program images for recognizable strings. The strings may be either parts of known viruses that have infected other systems, or sequences of instructions or operating system calls that are considered suspicious. This idea is easy to implement, and it works well against known threats (e.g., specific virus programs), but an attacker can circumvent it with only a little effort. For example, many viruses now produce pseudo-random instances of themselves using encryption. Vaccines can help, but they do not provide any security that can be relied on. They are ultimately out of date as soon as a new virus or a strain of a virus emerges.

## Application Gateways

### What a Gateway Is

The term "gateway" has been used to describe a wide range of devices in the computer communication environment. Most devices described as gateways can be categorized as one of two major types, although some devices are difficult to characterize in this fashion.

- The term "application gateway" usually refers to devices that convert between different protocol suites, often including application functionality, for example, conversion between DECNET and SNA protocols for file transfer or virtual terminal applications.
- The term "router" is usually applied to devices that relay and route packets between networks, typically operating at layer 2 (LAN bridges) or layer 3 (internetwork gateways). These devices do not convert between protocols at higher layers (e.g, layer 4 and above).

Mail gateways, devices that route and relay electronic mail (a layer-7 application) may fall into either category. If the device converts between two different mail protocols, for example, X.400 and SMTP, then it is an application gateway as described above. In many circumstances an X.400 message transfer agent (MTA) will act strictly as a router, but it may also convert X.400 electronic mail to facsimile and thus operate as an application gateway. The multifaceted nature of some devices illustrates the difficulty of characterizing gateways in simple terms.

*Gateways as Access Control Devices*

Gateways are often employed to connect a network under the control of one organization (an internal network) to a network controlled by another organization (an external network such as a public network). Thus gateways are natural points at which to enforce access control policies; that is, the gateways provide an obvious security perimeter. The access control policy enforced by a gateway can be used in two basic ways:

1. Traffic from external networks can be controlled to prevent unauthorized access to internal networks or the computer systems attached to them. This means of controlling access by outside users to internal resources can help protect weak internal systems from attack.

2. Traffic from computers on the internal networks can be controlled to prevent unauthorized access to external networks or computer systems. This access control facility can help mitigate Trojan horse concerns by constraining the telecommunication paths by which data can be transmitted outside an organization, as well as supporting concepts such as release authority, that is, a designated individual authorized to communicate on behalf of an organization in an official capacity.

Both application gateways and routers can be used to enforce access control policies at network boundaries, but each has its own advantages and disadvantages, as described below.

*Application Gateways as PAC Devices*

Because an application gateway performs protocol translation at layer 7, it does not pass through packets at lower protocol layers. Thus, in normal operation, such a device provides a natural barrier to traffic transiting it; that is, the gateway must engage in significant explicit processing in order to convert from one protocol suite to another in the course of data transiting the device. Different applications require different protocol-conversion processing. Hence a gateway of this type can easily permit traffic for some applications to transit the gateway while preventing the transit of other traffic, simply by not providing the software necessary to perform the conversion. Thus, at the coarse granularity of different applications, such gateways can provide protection of the sort described above.

For example, an organization could elect to permit electronic mail (e-mail) to pass bidirectionally by putting in place a mail gateway while preventing interactive log-in sessions and file transfers (by not passing any traffic other than e-mail). This access control policy could be refined also to permit restricted interactive log-in, for example, that initiated by an internal user to access a remote computer system, by installing software to support the translation of the virtual terminal protocol in only one direction (outbound).

An application gateway often provides a natural point at which to require individual user identification and authentication information for finer-granularity access control. This is because many such gateways require human intervention to select services in translating from one protocol suite to another, or because the application being supported intrinsically involves human intervention, for example, virtual terminal or interactive database query. In such circumstances it is straightforward for the gateway to enforce access control on an individual user basis as a byproduct of establishing a "session" between the two protocol suites.

Not all applications lend themselves to such authorization checks, however. For example, a file transfer application may be invoked automatically by a process during off hours, and thus no human user may be present to participate in an authentication exchange. Batch database queries or updates are similarly noninteractive and might be performed when no "users" are present. In such circumstances there is a temptation to employ passwords for user identification and authentication, as though a human being were present during the activity, and the result is that these passwords are stored in files at the initiating computer system, making them vulnerable to disclosure (see "Authentication" in Chapter 3). Thus there are limitations on the use of application gateways for individual access control.

As noted elsewhere in this report, the use of cryptography to protect user data from source to destination (end-to-end encryption) is a powerful tool for providing network security. This form of encryption is typically applied at the top of the network layer (layer 3) or the bottom of the transport layer (layer 4). End-to-end encryption cannot be employed (to maximum effectiveness) if application gateways are used along the path between communicating entities. The reason is that these gateways must, by definition, be able to access protocols at the application layer, above the layer at which the encryption is employed. Hence the user data must be decrypted for processing at the application gateway and then re-encrypted for transmission to the destination (or to another application gateway). In such an event the encryption being performed is not really end-to-end.

If an application-layer gateway is part of the path for (end-to-end) encrypted user traffic, then one will, at a minimum, want the gateway to be trusted (since it will have access to the user data in clear text form). Note, however, that use of a trusted computing base (TCB) for a gateway does not necessarily result in as much security as if (uninterrupted) encryption were in force from source to destination. The physical, procedural, and emanations security of the gateway must also be taken into account as breaches of any of these security facets could subject a user's data to unauthorized disclosure or modification. Thus it may be especially difficult, if not impossible, to achieve as high a level of security for a user's data if an application gateway is traversed as the level obtainable using end-to-end encryption in the absence of such gateways.

In the context of electronic mail the conflict between end-to-end encryption and application gateways is a bit more complex. The secure messaging facilities defined in X.400 (CCITT, 1989a) allow for encrypted e-mail to transit MTAs without decryption, but only when the MTAs are operating as routers rather than as application gateways, for example, when they are not performing "content conversion" or similar invasive services. The privacy-enhanced mail facilities developed for the TCP/IP Internet (Linn, 1989) incorporate encryption facilities that can transcend e-mail protocols, but only if the recipients are prepared to process the decrypted mail in a fashion that suggests protocol-layering violation. Thus, in the context of e-mail, only those devices that are more akin to routers than to application gateways can be used without degrading the security offered by true end-to-end encryption.

## Routers as PAC Devices

Since routers can provide higher performance and greater robustness and are less intrusive than application gateways, access control facilities that can be provided by routers are especially attractive in many circumstances. Also, user data protected by end-to-end encryption technology can pass through routers without having to be decrypted, thus preserving the security imparted by the encryption. Hence there is substantial incentive to explore access-control facilities that can be provided by routers.

One way a router at layer 3 (and to a lesser extent at layer 2) can effect access control is through the use of "packet filtering" mechanisms. A router performs packet filtering by examining protocol control information (PCI) in specified fields in packets at layer 3 (and perhaps at layer 4). The router accepts or rejects (discards) a packet based on the values in the fields as compared to a profile maintained in an access-control database. For example, source and destination computer system addresses are contained in layer-3 PCI, and thus an administrator could authorize or deny the flow of data between a pair of computer systems based on examination of these address fields.

If one "peeks" into layer-4 PCI, an eminently feasible violation of protocol layering for many layer-3 routers, one can effect somewhat finer-grained access control in some protocol suites. For example, in the TCP/IP suite one can distinguish among electronic mail, virtual terminal, and several other types of common applications through examination of certain fields in the TCP header. However, one cannot ascertain which specific application is being accessed via a virtual terminal connection, and so the granularity of such access control may be more limited than in the context of application gateways. Several vendors of layer-3 routers already provide facilities of this sort for the TCP/IP community, so that this is largely an existing access-control technology.

As noted above, there are limitations to the granularity of access control achievable with packet filtering. There is also a concern as to the assurance provided by this mechanism. Packet filtering relies on the accuracy of certain protocol control information in packets. The underlying assumption is that if this header information is incorrect, then packets will probably not be correctly routed or processed, but this assumption may not be valid in all cases. For example, consider an access-control policy that authorizes specified computers on an internal network to communicate with specified computers on an external network. If one computer system on the internal network can masquerade as another authorized internal system (by constructing layer-3 PCI with incorrect network addresses), then this access-control policy could be subverted. Alternatively, if a computer system on an external network generates packets with false addresses, it too can subvert the policy.

Other schemes have been developed to provide more sophisticated access-control facilities with higher assurance, while still retaining most of the advantages of router-enforced access control. For example, the VISA system (Estrin and Tsudik, 1987) requires a computer system to interact with a router as part of an explicit authorization process for sessions across organizational boundaries. This scheme also employs a cryptographic checksum applied to each packet (at layer 3) to enable the router to validate that the packet is authorized to transit the router. Because of performance concerns, it has been suggested that this checksum be computed only over the layer-3 PCI, instead of the whole packet. This would allow information surreptitiously tacked onto an authorized packet PCI to transit the router. Thus even this more sophisticated approach to packet filtering at routers has security shortcomings.

### Conclusions About Gateways

Both application gateways and routers can be used to enforce access control at the interfaces between networks administered by different organizations. Application gateways, by their nature, tend to exhibit reduced performance and robustness, and are less transparent than routers, but they are essential in the heterogeneous protocol environments in which much of the world operates today. As national and international protocol standards become more widespread, there will be less need for such gateways. Thus, in the long term, it would be disadvantageous to adopt security architectures that require that interorganizational access control (across network boundaries) be enforced through the use of such gateways. The incompatibility between true end-to-end encryption and application gateways further argues against such access-control mechanisms for the long term.

However, in the short term, especially in circumstances where application gateways are required due to the use of incompatible protocols, it is appropriate to exploit the opportunity to implement perimeter access controls in such gateways. Over the long term, more widespread use of trusted computer systems is anticipated, and thus the need for gateway-enforced perimeter access control to protect these computer systems from unauthorized external access will diminish. It is also anticipated that increased use of end-to-end encryption mechanisms and associated access control facilities will provide security for end-user data traffic. Nonetheless, centrally managed access control for interorganizational traffic is a facility that may best be accomplished through the use of gateway-based access control. If further research can provide higher-assurance packet-filtering facilities in routers, the resulting system, in combination with trusted computing systems for end users and end-to-end encryption, would yield significantly improved security capabilities in the long term.

## NOTES

1. See TCSEC Section 3.2.3.1.1 (U.S. DOD, 1985d).

2. To appreciate cryptography, note that we do not always understand what "information" is. Information, in the sense of semantic content, is always in the mind of the beholder and is a combination of ordinary symbols (e.g., "East Wind, Rain") or extraordinary ones (e.g., Wehrmacht beer orders) and some richer context. To differentiate, "data" is an encoding, and "information" is the (always to some degree unknowable) meaning that the encoding may or may not convey to a human observer. With regard to automata, "information" refers to data that alters the behavior of the robots.

For example, the string RDAQN QRHIH FECCA DRSWV KIKSS HSPAX CUBS conveys 34 characters of data to everyone who has "read" access to this transaction but conveys a significant amount of information only to those who know the richer context of cryptosystem and key. Readers are invited to determine the key from the substantial hint that the plaintext is THERE ARE MORE THINGS IN HEAVEN AND EARTH; solutions may be verified by transforming RCVQD ALCFV CLLLL DLSCK KRVKT BRVAO AVUA from data to information.

3. The security of RSA is not known to be provably equivalent to the problem of factoring the modulus, although that seems to be the best way to attack it.

# Appendix C

# Emergency Response Teams

In the aftermath of the Internet worm incident has come a flurry of attempts to anticipate the next occurrences of a virus, propagating Trojan horse, or other widespread attack. As a result, several emergency response teams offering 24-hour service have been established, including the following:

- *The Computer Emergency Response Team (CERT):* Formed by the Defense Advanced Research Projects Agency and centered at the Software Engineering Institute at Carnegie Mellon University, CERT provides access to technical experts around the country. CERT is intended to provide both incident-prevention and incident-response services. It was an outgrowth of the November 1988 Internet worm incident, which was managed and resolved by an informal network of Internet users and administrators. CERT was established to provide the capability for a more systematic and structured response; in particular, it is intended to facilitate communication during system emergencies. Another role that has evolved is communication with vendors about software weaknesses or vulnerabilities that have emerged through practical experience with attacks on systems. CERT draws on the computer system user and development communities, and it also coordinates with the National Institute of Standards and Technology and the National Security Agency. It sponsors workshops to involve its constituents in defining its role and to share information about perceived problems and issues (Scherlis et al., 1990).
- *The Defense Data Network (DDN) Security Coordination Center (SSC):* Created by the Defense Communications Agency at SRI International to serve the (unclassified) DDN community as a clearinghouse for host and user security problems and fixes, the SSC expands on the

functions provided by SRI through the Network Information Center (NIC) that has served Milnet users but was not set up to address security problems. Interestingly, the SSC was launched after DARPA's CERT in recognition of the fact that there was no central clearinghouse to coordinate and disseminate security-related fixes to Milnet users (DCA, 1989).

• *The Computer Incident Advisory Capability (CIAC):* This capability was established by Lawrence Livermore National Laboratory to provide CERT-type services for classified and unclassified computing within the Department of Energy (DOE). The scale of DOE computer operations and attendant risks provided a strong motivation for an agency-specific mechanism; the DOE community has over 100,000 computers located at over 70 classified and unclassified sites. Like the Defense Communications Agency, DOE saw that a "central capability for analyzing events, coordinating technical solutions, ensuring that necessary information is conveyed to those who need such information, and training others to deal with computer security incidents is essential." DOE was able to draw on an established research capability in the computer security arena, at Lawrence Livermore National Laboratory (Schultz, 1990).

Because of the rapidity with which computer pest programs can spread both within the United States and worldwide, it is vital that such efforts be well informed, coordinated with one another, and ready to mobilize rapidly in emergencies. Note that none of these systems has yet been tested with a full-scale emergency on the scale of the Internet worm.

# Appendix D

# Models for GSSP

This section discusses three areas in which technical standards are set by the kind of private sector-public sector interaction that this committee is recommending for Generally Accepted System Security Principles (GSSP): the building codes, the Underwriters Laboratories, Inc., and the Financial Accounting Standards Board. The latter organization is responsible for what have been called Generally Accepted Accounting Principles (GAAP), a set of standards that provides a model for the GSSP proposal.

## SETTING STANDARDS—PRECEDENTS

### Building Codes

Building codes endeavor to establish standards for safe construction. The field is marked by extreme decentralization, with codes mandated and enforced by local municipalities. The quality of code enforcement depends on the particular code enforcement officials (Falk, 1975). The codes themselves are based on so-called model codes that are produced by a small number of competing organizations. These code-writing organizations are associations of enforcement officers and therefore can be thought of as representing the government sector exclusively. There is, however, significant private sector input into the process from the various materials suppliers and their trade associations.

Building codes contain both performance and specification standards. A pure performance standard would stipulate something like, "Walls of residences must resist the spread of fire to the degree necessary to allow occupants to escape." Such standards, because they are so difficult to evaluate (the only true test of failure would be in an actual fire) are generally recast in a testable form, such as, "Materials used in residence walls must resist an $x$ degree fire for $y$ minutes." Upholding even this standard requires the existence of testing capabilities that may be beyond the resources of an enforcement activity, and so the pressure from the evaluation community is for specification standards, such as, "Residence walls must be covered with a double layer of 3/4-inch sheetrock."

Performance standards are viewed as being fairer and as providing greater room for innovation, but they impose a much greater burden on the evaluators.

Building codes have been widely criticized as inhibiting innovation and raising construction costs by mandating outdated materials and labor practices. In part, this is a natural byproduct of the specification approach, which militates against new technologies that deviate from the required specifications. In some cases the problem reflects local failures to adopt the latest revisions to model codes (Falk, 1975).

## Underwriters Laboratories, Inc.

Underwriters Laboratories, Inc. (UL) was established essentially by an entrepreneurial process because insurance companies could not rate the hazards resulting from new technology, in this case, electric lighting. It began as a purely private sector activity and then, because of the quality of its work, became recognized by the government. It operates as both a standard-setting and an evaluation organization, issuing its famous "Seal of Approval" to equipment and components that meet its standards (Underwriters Laboratories, Inc., 1989, 1990b). As described by one journalist,

> The UL Mark . . . means that the equipment has been checked for potential hazards, using objective tests laid out in detailed handbooks called Standards. No federal law mandates such testing. But UL's clients, manufacturers who pay to have their products tortured and then listed by the lab, know that the Mark is an important selling point. (Williams, 1988, p. 79)

Underwriters Laboratories, Inc., has developed a preliminary draft of a software safety standard, scheduled to be completed in 1990 (Underwriters Laboratories, Inc., 1990a). It is forming an Industry Advisory Committee, open to interested parties, to assist it in drafting a formal UL standard. Burglary protection systems, motor control mechanisms (e.g., for temperature, speed), industrial computers (i.e., programmable machines), "smart" appliances, and medical devices have been identified by UL as having software that affects safety and thus should be evaluated. Note, however, that UL is a public safety organization. It does not necessarily deal with certification, verification, and so on, unless a device affects safety.

## Financial Accounting Standards Board

The history of the Financial Accouting Standards Board (FASB) dates to the stock market crash of 1929 and the entry of the government into the capital markets through the establishment of the Securities and Exchange Commission (SEC). In the late 1930s, when SEC activism was at a peak, the American Institute of Certified Public Accountants formed a part-time and volunteer Accounting Practices Board to set accounting standards. The clear aim of this activity was to forestall government-mandated standards; this aim persists in FASB's own description of what causes a standard to be promulgated, where potential SEC or congressional action is explicitly mentioned as a criterion in deciding whether a new standard is needed. Overwhelmed by the changes in the financial markets in the 1960s, the Accounting Practices Board instituted a study in the early 1970s that led to the establishment of a full-time independent institute, the Financial Accounting Foundation (FAF), to oversee the FASB and the production of what have been referred to as Generally Accepted Accounting Principles (GAAP) and other standards of financial accounting and reporting for private sector organizations. Similar standards are established by a newer sister unit of the FASB for the public sector, the Government Accounting Standards Board (GASB). According to its own literature,

> The mission of the Financial Accounting Standards Board is to establish and improve standards of financial accounting and reporting for the guidance and education of the public, including issuers, auditors, and users of financial information. . . .
> The FASB develops broad accounting concepts as well as standards for financial reporting. It also provides guidance on implementation of standards. . . .
> The Board's work on both concepts and standards is based on research conducted by the FASB staff and by others. (FASB, 1990)

The Financial Accounting Foundation, FASB, and GASB serve to maintain the independence of the accounting profession by providing an effective alternative to government regulation. The effectiveness of the alternative rests on the use of standards to maintain what is called the "decision usefulness" of accounting information. In simplified form, accounting information has decision usefulness if the standards under which it was generated permit meaningful comparison of financial data from different companies that are competing for capital (e.g., from potential purchasers of common stock). Accounting standards differ from engineering standards in that they are not subject to verification by experiment (e.g., failure of a beam under loading) and their wording balances the concerns of buyers and sellers in the capital markets.

In order to achieve this balance, the FASB has established an elaborate due process for the establishment of standards. The process appears to work reasonably well; the primary criticisms levied against the FASB are those of "standards overload," in which the establishment of a full-time standards-setting body has had the not surprising outcome that a large number of standards have been established. This prolificness combined with the large number of practicing accountants may be one reason why the FAF has earned some $10 million in revenue from sales of publications (FAF, 1990). Also, the FASB and GASB are independent of relevant professional organizations.

At the end of its first decade the FASB received approximately 40 percent of its financial support from the accounting profession and 60 percent from outside sources such as financial institutions and banks. More recently, the FASB has run deficits, in part because it "has always had the delicate problem of having to seek contributions from the very companies it sometimes alienates" (Cowan, 1990). The FAF considers contributions as essential to its viability (FAF, 1990).

The FASB and the GAAP can be viewed as a modified or hybrid form of professional self-regulation, in which a professional community, under constant threat of government intervention, prevents that intervention by satisfactorily handling the various problems themselves. The GAAP have force of law in that their use is required for financial reporting by companies that raise capital in the regulated markets. They are recognized as authoritative by the SEC (Sprouse, 1987). The SEC and the General Accounting Office maintain liaison with both the FASB and GASB.

## LESSONS RELEVANT TO ESTABLISHING GSSP

Each of the undertakings discussed in this appendix offers lessons that are relevant to the concept of GSSP and the manner in which GSSP may be defined and enforced.

The experience with building codes indicates clearly that having competing standards and decentralized evaluation and enforcement is counterproductive; these factors inhibit technological progress. It is also clear that any set of standards will always have some mix of performance and specification requirements. It appears to be a fundamental principle of standards and evaluation that performance standards permit more rapid evolution than do specification standards, but at the cost of difficulty of evaluation. Note that in both building code and computer security experience, major innovations have taken some ten years to go from concept to general acceptance.

The UL experience shows that an evaluation process can be initiated in the private sector and then accepted by government, and that it is not necessary to begin such an activity with a legal or administrative mandate. The FASB is also an example of a private effort that achieved government recognition.

The FASB's history shows quite clearly that a forcing function is needed both initially and in the long term. In the case of the FASB it is the threat of government regulation of a particular profession. The experience with the FASB, and to a lesser extent the building codes, shows the importance of determining, by consensus, standards that balance the interests of all involved parties, and of setting up those standards according to a due process. The FASB's history also illustrates the importance of institutional independence in balancing pressures and criticisms from interested parties.

Those concerned with setting standards for computer security should nevertheless be cautious in drawing too close an analogy to the FASB. Computer security does not involve an organized, recognized profession whose prerogatives are threatened. Much less money is involved (at least directly), and a clear forcing function, either in the form of an initiating incident or ongoing threat of government action, is not present, although a liability crisis for system vendors, were it to develop, could serve that purpose.

# Appendix E

# High-grade Threats

It is impossible to build systems that are guaranteed to be invulnerable to a high-grade threat, that is, a dedicated and resourceful adversary capable of and motivated to organize an attack as an industrial rather than an individual or small-group enterprise. Such activities have historically been conducted by the intelligence-gathering activities of governments and have generally posed a threat to the confidentiality of information. The rapidly decreasing cost of computer resources, the rapid spread of computer technology, and the increased value of information-based assets make it likely that high-grade threats will be encountered from other sources and with aims other than traditional espionage. A high-grade threat is distinguished from the common "hacker" or criminal by the following characteristics:

• The threat has extensive resources in money, personnel, and technology. In particular, the threat is able to construct or acquire, by legitimate or clandestine means, a duplicate of the system under attack. The attack team can then conduct extensive analysis and experimentation without the risk that their activities will alert the administrators of the target system. The attacker may also have more powerful computer resources.

• The threat is patient and motivated. The attack resembles an entrepreneurial enterprise in that the equivalent to risk capital is raised in advance and invested in anticipation of a major future reward. The attack is conducted as a full-time, organized effort with a multidisciplinary staff, each of whom is eager to "break" the system.

• The threat is capable of exploiting a successful attack for maximum long-term gain. In particular, the attacking team is able to take extraordinary measures to keep the existence of a successful attack secret from the target.

• The threat is adept in circumventing physical and procedural safeguards and has access to clandestine technology.

• The threat will deliberately seek the most obscure vulnerability hidden in the darkest corner of the system—on the grounds that this is the one that will permit the maximum long-term exploitation.[1]

The designers, implementors, and administrators of high-grade countermeasures must begin with the requirement that their system be safe from hacker or criminal attacks and then work to counter the specialized threat of large-scale, long-term, highly covert assaults. Hacker and criminal attacks must be prevented to preclude the high-grade attacker from obtaining "inside information" about the target system from cheap (if short-lived) penetrations and to ensure that the operation of the system is as stable as possible.

The functionality of system elements engineered to high-grade security standards must be even more modest than the functionality that is affordable for elements engineered to withstand hacker and criminal attacks. High-grade countermeasure engineering has traditionally been associated with communications security devices and subsystems; the committee anticipates that it will, in the future, be applied to selected computer security functions such as reference monitors. In particular, this committee does not foresee that it will ever be feasible to apply high-grade countermeasures to a multitude of system elements, since technical advances that benefit the designer of countermeasures often benefit the attacker even more.[2] This circumstance has important implications for the system-wide trade-offs that have to be made when a high-grade threat is considered.

The inevitability of "tunneling" attacks has to be taken into account and the analysis and control carried down to the lowest possible layer of abstraction. A tunneling attack attempts to exploit a weakness in a system that exists at a level of abstraction lower than that used by the developer to design and/or test the system. For example, an attacker might discover a way to modify the microcode of a processor that is used when encrypting some data, rather than attempting to break the system's encryption scheme. The requirement that tunneling attacks be anticipated can substantially increase the cost of high-grade countermeasures, because it can preclude the use of offshore components (in the case of national security systems) or components made by commercial rivals (in the case of industrial systems.)

A higher emphasis on reliability is required, because a high-grade threat must be assumed to have the ability to monitor system behavior and take advantage of component failures. This raises cost and lengthens the schedule in several ways; for example, adding redundancy increases both hardware and software costs.

Finally, the knowledge that a high-grade threat is waiting to attack a system or component leads developers of high-grade countermeasures to surround their system development with the most extreme forms of secrecy, so as to deny the attacker lead time in analyzing the design and developing attacks.

Because of the extreme cost, short "security life," and difficult tradeoffs associated with high-grade countermeasures, operations that assess a high-grade threat as possible but not likely should seriously consider strategies that focus on recovery from, rather than prevention of, attack.

## NOTES

1. Designers of countermeasures who anticipate hacker or common criminal attacks can ignore large classes of vulnerabilities on the grounds that there are easier ways to attack a system, because the low-grade threat will look for the easiest way in.

2. For example, as high-speed digital encryption system chips become more readily available, they may be used to encrypt specific data channels within a computer system. However, they may also be used by attackers to build special-purpose machines capable of breaking the encryption algorithm itself.

# Appendix F

# Glossary

**Access**

A subject's right to use an object. Examples include read and write access for data objects, execute access for programs, or create and delete access for directory objects.

**Access control**

The granting or denying to a subject (principal) of certain permissions to access an object, usually done according to a particular security model.

**Access control list**

A list of the subjects that are permitted to access an object, and the access rights of each subject.

**Access label**

See *Label*.

**Access level**

A level associated with a subject (e.g., a clearance level) or with an object (e.g., a classification level).

**Accountability**

The concept that individual subjects can be held responsible for actions that occur within a system.

**Accreditation**

1. The administrative act of approving a computer system for use in a particular application. See *Certification*. 2. The act of approving an organization as, for example, an evaluation facility.

**Administratively directed access control (ADAC)**
Access control in which administrators control who can access which objects. Contrast with user-directed access control (UDAC). See *Mandatory access control.*

**Assurance**
Confidence that a system design meets its requirements, or that its implementation meets its specification, or that some specific property is satisfied.

**Auditing**
The process of making and keeping the records necessary to support accountability. See *Audit trail analysis.*

**Audit trail**
The results of monitoring each operation of subjects on objects; for example, an audit trail might be a record of all actions taken on a particularly sensitive file.

**Audit trail analysis**
Examination of an audit trail, either manually or automatically, possibly in real time (Lunt, 1988).

**Authentication**
Providing assurance regarding the identity of a subject or object, for example, ensuring that a particular user is who he claims to be.

**Authentication sequence**
A sequence used to authenticate the identity of a subject or object.

**Authorization**
Determining whether a subject (a user or system) is trusted to act for a given purpose, for example, allowed to read a particular file.

**Availability**
The property that a given resource will be usable during a given time period.

**Bell and La Padula model**
An information-flow security model couched in terms of subjects and objects and based on the concept that information shall not flow to an object of lesser or noncomparable classification (Bell and La Padula, 1976).

**Beta testing**
Use of a product by selected users before formal release.

**Biba model**
An integrity model in which no subject may depend on a less trusted object (including another subject) (Biba, 1975).

**Capability**
An authenticating entity acceptable as evidence of the right to perform some operation on some object.

**Certification**
The administrative act of approving a computer system for use in a particular application. See *Accreditation.*

**CESG**
The Communications-Electronics Security Group of the U.K. Government Communications Headquarters (GCHQ).

**Challenge-response**
An authentication procedure that requires calculating a correct response to an unpredictable challenge.

**Checksum**
Digits or bits summed according to arbitrary rules and used to verify the integrity of data.

**Ciphertext**
The result of transforming plaintext with an encryption algorithm. Also known as cryptotext.

**Claims language**
In the ITSEC, the language that describes the desired security features of a "target of evaluation" (a product or system), and against which the product or system can be evaluated.

**Clark-Wilson integrity model**
An approach to providing data integrity for common commercial activities, including software engineering concepts of abstract data types, separation of privilege, allocation of least privilege, and nondiscretionary access control (Clark and Wilson, 1987).

**Classification level**
The security level of an object. See *Sensitivity label*.

**Cleanroom approach**
A software development process designed to reduce errors and increase productivity (Poore and Mills, 1989).

**Clear text**
Unencrypted text. Also known as plaintext. Contrast with ciphertext, cryptotext.

**Clearance level**
The security level of a subject.

**CLEF**
In the ITSEC, a Commercial Licensed Evaluation Facility.

**CoCom**
Coordinating Committee for Multilateral Export Controls, which began operations in 1950 to control export of strategic materials and technology to communist countries; participants include Australia, Belgium, Canada, Denmark, France, Germany, Greece, Italy, Japan, Luxembourg, the Netherlands, Norway, Portugal, Spain, Turkey, the United Kingdom, and the United States.

**COMPUSEC**
Computer security.

**COMSEC**
Communications security.

**Confidentiality**
Ensuring that data is disclosed only to authorized subjects.

**Correctness**
1. The property of being consistent with a correctness criterion, such as a program being correct with respect to its system specification, or a specification being consistent with its requirements.
2. In ITSEC, a component of assurance (together with effectiveness).

**Countermeasure**
A mechanism that reduces the vulnerability of a threat.

**Covert channel**
A communications channel that allows two cooperating processes to transfer information in a manner that violates a security policy, but without violating the access control.

**Criteria**
Definitions of properties and constraints to be met by system functionality and assurance. See *TCSEC, ITSEC.*

**Criticality**
The condition in which nonsatisfaction of a critical requirement can result in serious consequences, such as damage to national security or loss of life. A system is critical if any of its requirements are critical.

**Crypto-key**
An input to an encryption device that results in cryptotext.

**Cryptotext**
See *Ciphertext.*

**Data**
A sequence of symbols to which meaning may be assigned. Uninterpreted information. Data can be interpreted as representing numerical bits, literal characters, programs, and so on. (The term is used often throughout this report as a collective, singular noun.) See *Information.*

**Data Encryption Standard (DES)**
A popular secret-key encryption algorithm originally released in 1977 by the National Bureau of Standards.

**Delegate**
To authorize one subject to exercise some of the authority of another.

**Denial of service**
Reducing the availability of an object below the level needed to support critical processing or communication, as can happen, for example, in a system crash.

**Dependability**
The facet of reliability that relates to the degree of certainty that a system will operate correctly.

**Dependence**
The existence of a relationship in which the subject may not work properly unless the object (possibly another subject) behaves properly. One system may depend on another system.

**Digital signature**
Data that can be generated only by an agent that knows some secret, and hence is evidence that such an agent must have generated it.

**Discretionary access control (DAC)**
An access-control mechanism that permits subjects to specify the access controls, subject to constraints such as changes permitted to the owner of an object. (DAC is usually equivalent to IBAC and UDAC, although hybrid DAC policies might be IBAC and ADAC.)

**DTI**
Department of Trade and Industry, U.K.

**Dual-use system**
A system with both military and civilian applications.

**Effectiveness**
1. The extent to which a system satisfies its criteria. 2. In ITSEC, a component of assurance (together with correctness).

**Emanation**
A signal emitted by a system that is not explicitly allowed by its specification.

**Evaluation**
1. The process of examining a computer product or system with respect to certain criteria. 2. The results of that process.

**Feature**
1. An advantage attributed to a system. 2. A euphemism for a fundamental flaw that cannot or will not be fixed.

**Firmware**
The programmable information used to control the low-level operations of hardware. Firmware is commonly stored in Read-Only Memorys (ROMs), which are initially installed in the factory and may be replaced in the field to fix mistakes or to improve system capabilities.

**Formal**
Having a rigorous respect for form, that is, a mathematical or logical basis.

**FTLS**
Formal top-level specification. (See "Security Characteristics" in Chapter 5.)

**Functionality**
As distinct from assurance, the functional behavior of a system. Functionality requirements include, for example, confidentiality, integrity, availability, authentication, and safety.

**Gateway**
A system connected to different computer networks that mediates transfer of information between them.

**GCHQ**
Government Communications Headquarters, U.K.

**Group**
A set of subjects.

**Identity-based access control (IBAC)**
An access control mechanism based only on the identity of the subject and object. Contrast with rule-based access control. See *Discretionary access control.*

**Implementation**
The mechanism that (supposedly) realizes a specified design.

**Information**
Data to which meaning is assigned, according to context and assumed conventions.

**Information-flow control**
Access control based on restricting the flow of information into an object. See, for example, *Bell and La Padula model.*

**INFOSEC**
Information security. See also *COMPUSEC* and *COMSEC.*

**Integrity**
The property that an object is changed only in a specified and authorized manner. Data integrity, program integrity, system integrity, and network integrity are all relevant to consideration of computer and system security.

**Integrity level**
A level of trustworthiness associated with a subject or object.

**Integrity policy**
See *Policy*.

**ITAR**
International Traffic in Arms Regulations (Office of the Federal Register, 1990).

**ITSEC**
The *Information Technology Security Evaluation Criteria*, the harmonized criteria of France, Germany, the Netherlands, and the United Kingdom (Federal Republic of Germany, 1990).

**Kernel**
A most trusted portion of a system that enforces a fundamental property, and on which the other portions of the system depend.

**Key**
An input that controls the transformation of data by an encryption algorithm.

**Label**
A level associated with a subject or object and defining its clearance or classification, respectively. In TCSEC usage, the security label consists of a hierarchical security level and a nonhierarchical security category. An integrity label may also exist, consisting of a hierarchical integrity level and a nonhierarchical integrity category (Biba, 1975).

**Letter bomb**
A logic bomb, contained in electronic mail, that is triggered when the mail is read.

**Level**
1. The combination of hierarchical and nonhierarchical components (TCSEC usage). See *Security level, Integrity level.* 2. The hierarchical component of a label, more precisely referred to as "hierarchical level" to avoid confusion. In the absence of nonhierarchical categories, the two definitions are identical.

**Logic bomb**
A Trojan horse set to trigger upon the occurrence of a particular logical event.

**Mandatory access control (MAC)**
1. Access controls that cannot be made more permissive by users or subjects (general usage, roughly ADAC). 2. Access controls based on information sensitivity represented, for example, by security labels for clearance and classification (TCSEC usage, roughly RBAC and ADAC). Often based on information flow rules.

**Model**
An expression of a policy in a form that a system can enforce, or that analysis can use for reasoning about the policy and its enforcement.

**Monitoring**
Recording of relevant information about each operation by a subject on an object, maintained in an audit trail for subsequent analysis.

**Mutual authentication**
Providing mutual assurance regarding the identity of subjects and/ or objects. For example, a system needs to authenticate a user, and the user needs to authenticate that the system is genuine.

**NCSC**
The National Computer Security Center, part of the National Security Agency, which is part of the Department of Defense.

**Node**
A computer system that is connected to a communications network and participates in the routing of messages within that network. Networks are usually described as a collection of nodes that are connected by communications links.

## Nondiscretionary
Equivalent to mandatory in TCSEC usage, otherwise equivalent to administratively directed access controls.

## Nonrepudiation
An authentication that with high assurance can be asserted to be genuine, and that cannot subsequently be refuted.

## Object
Something to which access is controlled. An object may be, for example, a system, subsystem, resource, or another subject.

## Operating system
A collection of software programs intended to directly control the hardware of a computer (e.g., input/output requests, resource allocation, data management), and on which all the other programs running on the computer generally depend. UNIX, VAX/VMS, and DOS are all examples of operating systems.

## Orange Book
Common name for the Department of Defense document that is the basic definition of the TCSEC, derived from the color of its cover (U.S. DOD, 1985d). The Orange Book provides criteria for the evaluation of different classes of trusted systems and is supplemented by many documents relating to its extension and interpretation. See *Red Book, Yellow Book*.

## OSI
Open Systems Interconnection. A seven-layer networking model.

## Outsourcing
The practice of procuring from external sources rather than producing within an organization.

## Password
A sequence that a subject presents to a system for purposes of authentication.

## Patch
A section of software code that is inserted into a program to correct mistakes or to alter the program.

**Perimeter**

A boundary within which security controls are applied to protect assets.  A security perimeter typically includes a security kernel, some trusted-code facilities, hardware, and possibly some communications channels.

**PIN**

Personal identification number.  Typically used in connection with automated teller machines to authenticate a user.

**Plaintext**

See *Clear text*.

**Policy**

An informal, generally natural-language description of desired system behavior.  Policies may be defined for particular requirements, such as security, integrity, and availability.

**Principal**

A person or system that can be authorized to access objects or can make statements affecting access control decisions.  See the equivalent, *Subject*.

**Private Key**

See *Secret key*.

**Protected subsystem**

A program or subsystem that can act as a subject.

**Public key**

A key that is made available without concern for secrecy.  Contrast with private key, secret key.

**Public-key encryption**

An encryption algorithm that uses a public key to encrypt data and a corresponding secret key to decrypt data.

**RAMP**

Rating Maintenance Phase.  Part of the National Computer Security Center's product evaluation process.

**Receivers**

Subjects reading from a communication channel.

## Red Book

The *Trusted Network Interpretation of the Trusted Computer System Evaluation Criteria*, or TNI (U.S. DOD, 1987).

## Reference monitor

A system component that enforces access controls on an object.

## Requirement

A statement of the system behavior needed to enforce a given policy. Requirements are used to derive the technical specification of a system.

## Risk

The likelihood that a vulnerability may be exploited, or that a threat may become harmful.

## RSA

The Rivest-Shamir-Adelman public key encryption algorithm (Rivest et al., 1978).

## Rule-based access control (RBAC)

Access control based on specific rules relating to the nature of the subject and object, beyond just their identities—such as security labels. Contrast with identity-based access control. See *Mandatory access control*.

## Safety

The property that a system will satisfy certain criteria related to the preservation of personal and collective safety.

## Secrecy

See *Confidentiality*.

## Secret

Known at most to an authorized set of subjects. (A real secret is possible only when the size of the set is one or less.)

## Secret key

A key that is kept secret. Also known as a private key.

## Secret-key encryption

An encryption algorithm that uses only secret keys. Also known as private-key encryption.

**Secure channel**

An information path in which the set of all possible senders can be known to the receivers, or the set of all possible receivers can be known to the senders, or both.

**Security**

1. Freedom from danger; safety.  2. Computer security is protection of data in a system against disclosure, modification, or destruction. Protection of computer systems themselves. Safeguards can be both technical and administrative.  3. The property that a particular security policy is enforced, with some degree of assurance. 4. Often used in a restricted sense to signify confidentiality, particularly in the case of multilevel security.

**Security level**

A clearance level associated with a subject, or a classification level (or sensitivity label) associated with an object.

**Security policy**

See *Policy*.

**Sender**

A subject writing to a channel.

**Sensitivity label**

A security level (i.e., a classification level) associated with an object.

**Separation of duty**

A principle of design that separates functions with differing requirements for security or integrity into separate protection domains. Separation of duty is sometimes implemented as an authorization rule specifying that two or more subjects are required to authorize an operation.

**Shareware**

Software offered publicly and shared rather than sold.

**Signature**

See *Digital signature*.

**Simple security property**

An information-flow rule stating that a subject at a given security level can read only from an object with a security label that is the same or lower (Bell and La Padula, 1976).

### Smart card

A small computer in the shape of a credit card. Typically used to identify and authenticate its bearer, although it may have other computational functions.

### Source code

The textual form in which a program is entered into a computer (e.g., FORTRAN).

### Specification

A technical description of the desired behavior of a system, as derived from its requirements. A specification is used to develop and test an implementation of a system.

### Spoofing

Assuming the characteristics of another computer system or user, for purposes of deception.

### State

An abstraction of the total history of a system, usually in terms of state variables. The representation can be explicit or implicit.

### State machine

In the classical model of a state machine, the outputs and the next state of the machine are functionally dependent on the inputs and the present state. This model is the basis for all computer systems.

### STU-III

A secure telephone system using end-to-end private-key encryption.

### Stub

An artifact, usually software, that can be used to simulate the behavior of parts of a system. It is usually used in testing software that relies on those parts of the system simulated by the stub. Stubs make it possible to test a system before all parts of it have been completed.

### Subject

An active entity—e.g., a process or device acting on behalf of a user, or in some cases the actual user—that can make a request to perform an operation on an object. See the equivalent, *Principal*.

**System**
1. A state machine, that is, a device that, given the current state and inputs, yields a set of outputs and a new state (see *State machine*). 2. An interdependent collection of components that can be considered as a unified whole, for example, a networked collection of computer systems, a distributed system, a compiler or editor, a memory unit, and so on.

**TCB**
See *Trusted computing base.*

**TCSEC**
The Department of Defense *Trusted Computer System Evaluation Criteria* (U.S. DOD, 1985d). See *Orange Book.*

**Tempest**
U.S. government rules for limiting compromising signals (emanations) from electrical equipment.

**Threat**
The potential for exploitation of a vulnerability.

**Time bomb**
A Trojan horse set to trigger at a particular time.

**Token**
When used in the context of authentication, a physical device necessary for user identification.

**Token authenticator**
A pocket-sized computer that can participate in a challenge-response authentication scheme. The authentication sequences are called tokens.

**Trapdoor**
A hidden flaw in a system mechanism that can be triggered to circumvent the system's security.

**Trojan horse**
A computer program whose execution would result in undesired side effects, generally unanticipated by the user. A Trojan horse program may otherwise give the appearance of providing normal functionality.

## Trust
Belief that a system meets its specifications.

## Trusted computing base (TCB)
A portion of a system that enforces a particular policy. The TCB must be resistant to tampering and circumvention. Under the TCSEC, it must also be small enough to be analyzed systematically. A TCB for security is part of the security perimeter.

## Trusted system
A system believed to enforce a given set of attributes to a stated degree of assurance (confidence).

## Trustworthiness
Assurance that a system deserves to be trusted.

## Tunneling attack
An attack that attempts to exploit a weakness in a system at a low level of abstraction.

## User authentication
Assuring the identity of a user. See *Authorization.*

## User-directed access control (UDAC)
Access control in which users (or subjects generally) may alter the access rights. Such alterations may, for example, be restricted to certain individuals by the access controls, for example, limited to the owner of an object. Contrast with administratively directed access control. See *Discretionary access control.*

## Vaccine
A program that attempts to detect and disable viruses.

## Virus
A program, typically hidden, that attaches itself to other programs and has the ability to replicate. In personal computers, "viruses" are generally Trojan horse programs that are replicated by inadvertent human action. In general computer usage, viruses are more likely to be self-replicating Trojan horses.

## Vulnerability
A weakness in a system that can be exploited to violate the system's intended behavior. There may be security, integrity, availability, and other vulnerabilities. The act of exploiting a vulnerability represents a threat, which has an associated risk of being exploited.

**Worm attack**

A worm is a program that distributes itself in multiple copies within a system or across a distributed system. A worm attack is a worm that may act beyond normally permitted behavior, perhaps exploiting security vulnerabilities or causing denial of service.

**Yellow Book**

The Department of Defense *Technical Rationale Behind CSC-STD-003-85* (U.S. DOD, 1985b). Guidance for applying the TCSEC to specific environments.

**ZSI**

Zentralstelle für Sicherheit in der Informationstechnik. The German Information Security Agency (GISA).